THE WAYWARD LIBERAL

THOMAS E. VADNEY

THE
Wayward
LIBERAL

A POLITICAL BIOGRAPHY OF
DONALD RICHBERG

THE UNIVERSITY PRESS
OF KENTUCKY

Standard Book Number 8131–1243–5
Library of Congress Catalog Card Number 75–132832

COPYRIGHT © 1970 BY THE UNIVERSITY PRESS OF KENTUCKY

A statewide cooperative scholarly publishing agency serving Berea College, Centre College of Kentucky, Eastern Kentucky University, Kentucky State College, Morehead State University, Murray State University, University of Kentucky, University of Louisville, and Western Kentucky University.

Editorial and Sales Offices: Lexington, Kentucky 40506

To

C. H. V.

and

O. L. V.

Contents

Preface

The title of this study is somewhat paradoxical. "Wayward Liberal" conjures up images of the agnostic, whereas Donald Richberg's story is that of a persistent faithfulness to outdated concepts of liberalism rather than a turning away to something new. True, the usual stereotype of Richberg is that of the old Progressive turned conservative, of the "traitor" to organized labor who defected to big business. Yet the real paradox is to be found in the ever-changing meaning of liberalism itself. The problem was that after the New Deal of Franklin Roosevelt liberalism came to mean something different than it had in the days of the Progressives of 1912, but Richberg refused to trade the old liberalism for the new. Even in his later reputedly conservative years, he privately felt that his views were essentially consistent with his youthful identification with the Progressives, and in many respects he was correct. Though after the 1930s Richberg superficially gave the appearance of having changed, the reality was that he had not. The words *liberal* and *progressive* no longer described what Richberg stood for because they had taken on a new meaning.

Attempting to locate Donald Richberg in the American reform tradition raises a difficult problem of definition. For much of this study, I shall speak of Richberg's ideological and political position in terms of specific ideas and programs. But it will at times be necessary to use such overworked categories as "liberal," "progressive," and "conservative." Such generalizations, of course, are imprecise, yet language would be unduly cumbersome without them. The problem can be partly resolved by agreeing at the outset on how these terms will be used, even though these definitions may be arbitrary to some degree.

The term *progressive* will be used interchangeably with *liberal*. Both will denote sympathy for reform movements regardless of political party, and generally will indicate a receptivity to increased government activity and regulation of economic life within the confines of the capitalist system. Both terms require the addition of a time dimension, for the emphasis on government intervention which they denote increased markedly after the New Deal, culminating in an idealization of the welfare state. The term *Progressive*, capitalized, will refer to the formal political party created in 1912 by Theodore Roosevelt, or to the 1924 movement which nominated Wisconsin Senator Robert M. La Follette, Sr., for president. *Conservative* will denote an identification with the business community and especially with the interests of its larger units, the corporations. It will carry with it such connotations as opposition to government regulation and to increased government activity, reluctance to acknowledge organized labor as a factor in economic policymaking, and a general preference for the status quo.

The problem of definition can never be completely solved, for the ideas and movements which terms represent are not static, so that they can only be understood relative to the context in which they are used. A constant awareness of the setting in which ideas emerge and evolve is thus necessary for an accurate interpretation of their meaning.

Many people contributed to the successful conclusion of this project. In particular, I wish to thank David C. Mearns and the staff of the Manuscripts Division of the Library of Congress; Miss Elizabeth Drewry, director of the Franklin D. Roosevelt Library, and her assistants, librarian Joseph Marshall and archivists Jerome Deyo and Robert Parks; Archie Motley, manuscripts librarian of the Chicago Historical Society; Miss Ruth Davis of the State Historical Society of Wisconsin; and the many archivists and librarians at the National Archives in Washington, D. C.; the Federal Records

Center in Suitland, Md.; the Oral History Research Office of Columbia University; the Social Welfare History Archives of the University of Minnesota; and the University of Chicago Library. David A. Shannon of the University of Virginia, Robert Berkhofer, Jr., of the University of Wisconsin, Ralph F. de Bedts of Old Dominion University, and my former colleagues at the University of Minnesota, George Green and Clarke Chambers, provided me with the benefit of their critical comments. I owe a special debt of gratitude to E. David Cronon of the University of Wisconsin, under whose direction this study was initiated.

THE WAYWARD LIBERAL

CHAPTER I

The Making
of a Progressive

In his prime, Donald Richberg was once described as resembling "an amiable woodchuck"—tall and a bit chubby, yet surprisingly loose and agile, with an ever-ready smile and a glad hand.[1] But beneath the easygoing exterior there was a studiously intense individual, one given to theorizing and moralizing about social and economic problems, about matters of law and the Constitution, and about the ultimate questions of life itself. A man of soaring ambition, Richberg immersed himself in the world of big business, organized labor, and national politics. His work was his life, and his need for personal recognition and success prodded him on to higher and higher levels of achievement.

In historical perspective, what draws attention to the political career of Donald Richberg is his reputation as an old progressive turned conservative. Gerald Johnson, reviewing Richberg's autobiography in 1954, classified him as a "played-out liberal" of a type known to Americans ever since Tom Paine and John Randolph. Others have reiterated this conclusion time and again.[2]

Although historians have instinctively hit upon this puzzle as the most relevant question to ask about Richberg, their pet image of the "tired liberal" is not really a very illuminating answer. And so far, historians have said little about why Richberg became a liberal or progressive in the first place. Yet it is essential to determine the nature and content of his early progressivism before deciding whether or how he moved away from it. The thesis presented here is that Richberg remained relatively immobile in ideology, at the level of abstract political theory, though not in his active life in the world of law and politics, where his fortunes were affected by his career-situation, his friendships and personal connections, and his deep-seated need for personal recognition.

On the surface, Richberg's public political loyalties appear very unstable. By stages he was a Theodore Roosevelt Progressive, a labor lawyer representing the cautious ambitions of the railway unions in the 1920s, a New Dealer promoting the corporate-state ideals of the National Recovery Administration, and finally a propagandist against organized labor and civil rights in the 1940s and 1950s. The apparent change in Richberg was made all the more dramatic by the way in which he lost his old friends in the progressive camp and took up with new friends in the business world.

Yet compared to his wavering loyalties in the world of active politics, Richberg's intellectual life was characterized by remarkable consistency—even inflexibility. This reveals a great deal about the kinship between the progressives of 1912 and the conservatives of the 1950s, and partly explains Richberg's new associations in his later career. Richberg continued to invoke the values of his youth even as the world around him moved on to a new concept of liberalism, a concept most simply equated with the welfare state and an extension of government activities far beyond anything foreseen in 1912. His apparent migration from left to right politically —using the scale of the 1950s—was due not only to factors peculiar to himself, but more importantly to a metamorphosis in the meaning of liberalism over a fifty-year period. Liberalism at midcentury did not mean the same thing as at the beginning of the century. For example, the welfare state goals of Harry Truman's Fair Deal, though largely unrealized, were practically beyond the imagi-

¹ Jonathan Mitchell, "Grand Vizier: Donald R. Richberg," *New Republic* 82 (April 24, 1935): 301.

² Reviews of *My Hero: The Indiscreet Memoirs of an Eventful but Unheroic Life*, by Donald Richberg: Gerald Johnson, New York *Herald Tribune*, Nov. 28, 1954; George Mowry, *Saturday Review* 37 (Nov. 6, 1954): 21, 43; Arthur Schlesinger, Jr., New York *Times*, Oct. 31, 1954.

nation of even the New Nationalists of Theodore Roosevelt with their belief in vigorous government and nationally defined purpose. The New Nationalist program appeared to assign a large role to government action only by the standards of the early 1900s, not by those of the post-New Deal world. The values of the progressives were closer to the nineteenth century than they were to the welfare state. Richberg's pilgrimage from the progressivism of his youth to the conservatism of his later years must be set against the whole background of developments in the meaning of liberalism generally; then, in a strictly intellectual sense, his movement may be interpreted as having been more apparent than real. After the 1920s, liberalism evolved at a much quicker pace and in different directions than Donald Richberg.

The fact remains, however, that Richberg's public activities—if not his ideology—did change dramatically in character over the years. Besides the evolution in the meaning of liberalism and Richberg's own intellectual immobility, the personality factor must be accorded an important place in explaining his alignment with the conservatives of the 1940s and 1950s. It strongly influenced his life in active politics as distinguished from his theoretical political beliefs, though one reinforced the other. Outstanding among Richberg's characteristics was an intense yearning for attention and support. Easily hurt by criticism and susceptible to flattery, he possessed great personal ambition and was frequently bothered by anxiety. He could be sly. Yet his friends and associates considered him a man of considerable charm; often he was the life of the party, and he genuinely enjoyed the part.

All these traits made Richberg vulnerable to the influence of the people around him and made it difficult for him to hold out against their disapproval. This compelling need for acceptance gave other people a very real power over Donald Richberg, so that it made a difference who his friends were. As progressives and labor leaders became alienated by his failure to keep pace with the evolution of liberalism, their place was taken by leaders in the business community, who reinforced Richberg's ideological immobility. This process culminated in the New Deal. It was the New Deal and the growth of big government that eventually made apparent the differences between the old liberalism and the new liberalism. Richberg served President Franklin Roosevelt as general counsel and later head of the National Recovery Administration, an agency dominated and staffed largely by the business community. Surrounded by associates hostile to his liberal reputation, he felt compelled to justify his prior connections with organized labor by leaning over backwards to be fair to the business community. In the process, he created new friends in the business world while eroding the loyalty of the liberal camp, which by then was rapidly redefining its programs and methods far beyond those of 1912 or of the 1920s. Throughout, the personal factor reinforced the ideological, for as Richberg's notion of liberalism failed to advance, the character of his supporters changed. The trend became so pronounced that when Richberg returned to the private practice of law in 1935, he no longer could rely on a labor clientele but instead eventually joined one of Washington's leading firms dealing principally in corporation law.

The New Deal, then, brought out the limitations inherent in Donald Richberg's understanding of liberalism and helped crystallize his position. Until the administration of Franklin Roosevelt, the evolution of liberalism generally had not proceeded at such a pace as to move ahead of Richberg. In fact, his limitations were those of the old progressives of the early 1900s as a whole. The commitment of many of them to reform, however fervent it might have been, hardly was so radical as to envision the welfare state and the immense federal bureaucracy that would be required to administer it. Ideological factions appear in every political movement, of course, but for most progressives, the assumptions of the competitive system were accepted as given, so that the use of political power, even among those reformers who emphasized government planning and intervention, had as its objective simply the more efficient and humane functioning of a system regarded as fundamentally desirable. Reform was a way of making capitalist values more viable by increasing—not displacing—opportunity, individualism, and competition. For many progressives, social welfare was to be a by-product of these virtues, and not the direct objective of the liberal program. The middle-class background of so many of the nation's political leaders, regardless of party, undoubtedly permitted them to take such values for granted, and this class characteristic affected progressive leaders as much as those of a more conservative identification.

Richberg himself emerged from just such a middle-class background, one that would have prepared him to have been a regular Republican or Democrat as easily as a Progressive. Though early in his career he decided to identify with the reform camp, this identification had about it all the moral fervor and earnestness of Victorian America and contained no serious challenge to the competitive values that had placed his family in the comfortable circumstances which it enjoyed. Such a background had important consequences for how Richberg marked out the boundaries of liberalism. Given those influences, it is not surprising that his early idea of reform was as much moral as it was political, and directed more against evil men than against a defective economic system.

Grandfather Louis Richberg had immigrated to America from Germany in 1851. Of middle-class Lutheran stock, he established himself as a merchant in New York City and remained there until 1854, when he moved his family to Chicago and set up a meatpacking business. Richberg's father, John C. Richberg, attended Knox College in Galesburg, Illinois, and the United States Naval Academy during the Civil War. He read law in St. Louis and eventually entered into legal practice in Chicago. When he came into his inheritance in the early 1880s, he moved the family to East Clinton, Tennessee, and spent two years trying to make a success of a zinc mining and smelting venture. The failure of this enterprise forced him to return to Chicago, where he eventually built a successful law practice representing individuals, corporations, and the Chicago City Treasurer and Board of Assessors. During the 1870s, John Richberg served as a member and as president of the Chicago Board of Education and oversaw a reform program that included equal pay for men and women teachers and discontinuance of Bible reading in the classroom. Later in his career he was interested in legal reform, especially divorce legislation (he himself had been divorced before marrying Richberg's mother), and in a movement to do away with local and state diversity in laws dealing with common problems. Governor John Peter Altgeld of Illinois appointed him to a commission to promote uniformity of legislation among the several states.

The Richberg maternal heritage included a number of strong-willed women who were not afraid to challenge accepted social and religious mores. Richberg's grandmother and mother were Vermonters and had family roots that went back to the Revolutionary War. Both women studied and practiced medicine, and each cultivated an interest in spiritualism. A militant suffragist, grandmother Marenda Briggs Randall was divorced by her husband on grounds of desertion in 1857. Richberg's mother, Eloise Randall Richberg, met his father while principal of the Clark School in Chicago. After her children were grown, she undertook the study of homeopathy. When her husband objected to her practicing medicine upon the completion of her program of studies, they separated and were reunited only when John C. Richberg suffered a stroke in 1909.[3]

Neither of Donald Richberg's parents subscribed to an organized religion, and his own religious education was eclectic; they sent him to a number of different Sunday schools as a child. The result was that Richberg likewise never identified with a particular church, though his characteristic behavior was very much that of a moralizer. Depending on circumstances, Richberg could be exceedingly self-righteous. In place of a formal religion, he developed an

[3] Richberg, *My Hero: The Indiscreet Memoirs of an Eventful but Unheroic Life* (New York, 1954), 8–14, 29–31; Richberg, *Tents of the Mighty* (New York, 1930), 14–15, 18, 26; Richberg, "Memories for My Grandchildren," 2–4, and other memorabilia in the possession of Mrs. John H. Small III (formerly Mrs. Donald Richberg), Charlottesville, Va.; interview by the author with Mrs. John H. Small III, Charlottesville, Va., Jan. 11–12, 1967; "Commission for the Promotion of Uniformity of Legislation in the United States," *Chicago Legal News* 26 (May 26, 1894): 312; Mary Grace Canfield, "Dr. Marenda Briggs Randall," *The Vermont Standard* (Woodstock, Vt.), Aug. 15, 1935; Eloise O. Richberg, horoscope for Richberg, June 1902, Donald Richberg Papers, Library of Congress, Box 51; obituary, Dr. Eloise Richberg, Hyde Park, Ill., *Herald*, Oct. 10, 1924; Richberg to John S. Lord, Nov. 23, 1943, in the possession of John S. Lord, Chicago.

ethical philosophy and a highly abstract concept of the spiritual world and, as he described it, viewed the "Guiding Power of the Universe" as "inchoate" and as having "no sense of personality about it." His mother's ideas about spiritualism fascinated him, so that he maintained a lifetime interest in the subject. Although Richberg shunned any loyalty to organized religion, he shared many of its ideals, but saw a more rational approach as the way to realize them. For Richberg, the social sciences would provide the key to improving man's lot, not formal religion. Yet the rational content of his ethical system did not eliminate the moralizing style of thought and action of a man who, after all, was born and raised in the Victorian Age. Despite his analytical approach to ethics, Richberg's values were shaped by his background perhaps more than he realized.[4]

There was little, however, in Richberg's early growth to indicate the depth of his future commitment to reform rather than some other brand of politics. Writing his memoirs years later, Richberg recalled that he was young for his age in school and therefore often felt himself an outsider. In time, he compensated for this feeling of inferiority by a concerted involvement in extracurricular activities, an involvement which by the time of college was so total that it almost cost him his bachelor's degree from the University of Chicago. Richberg allocated his limited academic energies mainly to courses in English, history and anthropology. He frankly admitted that his objective was to study only what interested him and to take courses that would not require much work or interfere with his outside activities. He never did any formal course work in political science, economics, or other subjects that later would be the substance of his mature intellectual interests. As Richberg recalled his undergraduate days at Chicago, "We are not exactly molly-

[4] Interview with Mrs. John H. Small III, Jan. 11–12, 1967; Richberg, "I have a faith. . . ," ca. 1915, and "If there is in your heart an abounding faith. . . ," n.d., Richberg Papers, L.C., Boxes 5 and 8; Richberg, *Tents,* 222–32. In addition, see Richberg, *A Man of Purpose* (New York, 1922), 9–10, 239, for an autobiographical sketch of his religious upbringing as represented by the main character of the novel, Rodney Merrill, and for an exact copy of Richberg's early statement of religious beliefs as cited here.

coddles and no professor ever called us 'grinds.' " He barely grad-
uated with his class in 1901, doing so only by the grace of the fac-
ulty, which waived a special requirement imposed on students such
as Richberg who had cut chapel services and lectures too many
times.[5]

In accordance with his father's wishes, Richberg entered Harvard Law School in the fall of 1901, but his years at Harvard
proved to be a repeat performance of his undergraduate days. Richberg did not look forward to the practice of law, especially in
partnership with a domineering father, as was the family's expectation. He never developed any enthusiasm for his studies nor applied himself scholastically beyond what he later described as
"something less than average."[6]

What Richberg was really dreaming about throughout his undergraduate and law school days was a literary career. He spent a large
part of his time working on plays, short stories, poetry, and essays,
but his efforts failed to attract any attention from outside college
circles at the time. These interests brought Richberg together with
his first wife, Elizabeth Herrick; she was the sister of Robert Herrick, author and professor at the University of Chicago. They were
married in December 1903, during Richberg's final year of law
school. Both had literary ambitions, and Richberg was tempted to
abandon his law studies and take a full-time position as a reporter
for a New York newspaper. But marriage made such dreams unrealistic, for as the head of a household Richberg required a more
substantial income than journalism or the theater offered. Consequently, he was forced to rescue his flagging law studies by a massive cramming session in May 1904 and once again barely suc-

[5] Richberg, *My Hero*, 16–19; Richberg, *Tents*, 12; Richberg, "Memories
for My Grandchildren," 5–9; H. P. Judson to William Rainey Harper
[May–June 1901]; Harper to James H. Tufts, May 21, 1901; Tufts to
Harper, June 7, 1901, The Presidents' Papers, ca. 1889–1925, University
of Chicago Library, Donald Richberg folder.

[6] Richberg, *My Hero*, 19–20; Richberg, "Memories for My Grandchildren," 8–9. See also Harvard Law School, Annual Examinations, June
1903, Record of D. R. Richberg," Richberg Papers, l.c., Box 51; Richberg's
average grade for his second year of law was a C.

ceeded in saving his degree. In July 1904 a reluctant Donald Richberg entered into partnership with his father in Chicago.[7]

The first years of law practice proved to be all that Richberg had dreaded. Faced with the routine tasks assigned to fledgling lawyers, he found little that appealed to him in what he later recalled as long days of studying, wrangling, and worrying over "a thousand petty questions of no real importance." For Richberg, these were "meaningless years of groping," lost in the "fog of an uncertain purpose." Four months after joining his father's firm, he confessed to William Rainey Harper, president of the University of Chicago, "Law is . . . my livelihood and not my ambition."[8]

A number of factors were of special importance in drawing Richberg out of this miasma and sparking his interest in reform politics. Among the more important were his perception of what the practice of law was really like and what it implied for his self-respect, and the contrast between his business life and his social life. Of course, given Richberg's outgoing personality and the involvement of his father's firm in corporation law and city politics, it was likely that he would have been caught up in Chicago political life anyway, but there were other factors that helped determine the nature of his involvement. They help explain why he identified with the reformers rather than with the regular party politicians.

Richberg's initial response to the practice of law was unfavorable. The seamy side of business and politics was starkly apparent after life in Cambridge. The Richberg firm's representation of the Chicago City Treasurer and Board of Assessors gave him an inside view of municipal politics, but he was not attracted by what he saw. Equally repugnant was the idea of serving some of the firm's business clients.

Richberg's social life added to his frustrations. He and his wife Elizabeth lived in the vicinity of the University of Chicago. Rich-

---

[7] Richberg, *My Hero*, 20, 207–10; Richberg, "Memories for My Grandchildren," 11–12; Richberg, Miscellaneous plays, articles, songs, and poetry, Richberg Papers, L.C., Boxes 5, 28–30, 32.

[8] Richberg, *Tents*, 20–21; [Richberg] to Harper, Oct. 20, 1904, Richberg Papers, L.C., Box 1.

berg was a member of the Quadrangle Club and the University Club and moved easily in university social circles. Often he played tennis with Nobel Prize winners Robert Millikan and Albert Michelson, or went partying with such literary luminaries as Robert Herrick, his wife's brother, or Robert Morss Lovett and William Vaughn Moody.

What might have been a stimulating intellectual atmosphere proved at the social level quite irritating to Richberg. Later he remembered his university friends as intelligent, highly motivated people, but described their social life as "a superficial sort of existence." It was merely relaxation. Both Richberg, with his longstanding passion for writing and his insider's view of city politics, and his wife, with her love of literature and the theater, fitted in well enough. But Richberg felt that his friends were moving ahead in their professions while he was not. For them, socializing was a brief respite from a steady advance in more important pursuits. Years later Richberg would recall how "after the relaxation of a hilarious evening, I went back to a dusty office full of dusty problems in which I had little interest beyond a natural desire to do a good job and earn a decent fee."

Richberg's wife was of little help in his search for direction and purpose. Having decided that she had no talent for acting and having given up a possible career as a newspaperwoman, she sought refuge in the very entertainments that exacerbated Richberg's sense of frustration. Her continual demands for partying and theater-going made him all the more aware of the aimlessness of these early years of law practice. The resulting antagonism would lead to divorce in 1915. For now, Richberg only wanted to use his spare time for more serious pursuits than what he would later remember as nights of "smoking and drinking and dancing and eating and singing and wasting time in all sorts of pleasant ways." What Richberg wanted from his wife was moral support for his own ambitions, not demands for attention on her part.

It was the very starkness of the contrast between his business life and his social life which finally mobilized Richberg and led him into reform politics. What he saw happening in the downtown offices of lawyers and businessmen seemed unimportant compared with what was going on in Professor Michelson's physics laboratory or in Charles E. Merriam's political science classes. His work seemed sordid beside that of his university friends. Not surprisingly, Richberg's first avenue of escape was in writing. But what began as escape ended in reform politics.[9]

Writing provided Richberg with an outlet for his indignation against the alleged evils he confronted in the day-to-day practice of law. It helped him clarify his ideas about law as a profession and his place in it. Throughout his life, Richberg turned to his own experiences as sources of literary inspiration. His serious efforts, whether they were treatises destined only for the eyes of other members of the legal guild or whether they were articles for popular consumption, always reflected his current interests in law or politics. Even in his lighter writing, he usually made his novels and stories serve a more serious purpose than simple entertainment. Richberg's writing usually taught a lesson or contained a moral, even at the cost of interfering with the plot. Sometimes he would slip into the essay form in the middle of a story; characters frequently gave orations on love, law, economics, or conventional moralities. Writing for Richberg was a way of blowing off steam generated either in his work or in his personal life.

As a consequence, Richberg's discontent with his profession manifested itself in explicit terms. In the October 1909 issue of *The Atlantic Monthly*, for example, he published a critique of the legal guild which clearly articulated his sense of personal frustration with being—as he saw it—the paid hireling of clients looking for someone to invent "legal sophistries . . . to justify any sort of conduct." Instead, he argued that the lawyer could not leave ethical considerations to his clients, relying on them to pursue good over evil and merely effecting their objectives like a blameless, amoral robot. The lawyer was not simply a lowly employee but a member of a profession and an officer of the court. As such, he had the duty to exercise independent judgment in the interest of the general welfare. The lawyer was not "a mere business man." Richberg

[9] Richberg, *My Hero*, 29–31, 210–11; Richberg, *Tents*, 13–25, 214–19; interview with Mrs. John H. Small III, Jan. 11–12, 1967. The quotations are from *Tents*, 20–21, and *My Hero*, 211.

would accept no lesser status for the profession and, by implication, for himself.[10]

Richberg's views were hardly notable for their originality, and this lack of newness characterized most of his writing for the rest of his life. His literary talent lay in his ability to articulate and synthesize much of what people around him were thinking. He was a skilled popularizer and propagandist. His critique of the trust problem, for example, was typical muckraking. Dozens of essays, short stories, and even novels such as *The Shadow Men* published in 1911 and *In the Dark* published in 1912 became the vehicles of his moral indignation and of his proposals for institutional reform. Yet like many muckrakers, his assessment of the corporation and its alleged evils represented no challenge to the essential characteristics of the economic system which he criticized. In fact, he described the corporate form of business organization as "part and parcel of a splendid and tremendous commercial development." Far from proposing any radical changes in American business institutions, Richberg's purpose in publicizing corporate evils and proposing reform was to protect, not destroy, the corporations by insuring that "their activities will not arouse the popular condemnation under which they are at present laboring."[11]

Not all Richberg's literary efforts were polemics. He was capable of engaging in writing simply for its own sake. On balance, though, a strong moralizing tone dominated most of his fiction and drama as well as his essays. He wrote because he enjoyed it, but the tensions of his business and personal life demanded an outlet, and proselytizing almost invariably crept into his work.

Consequently, writing itself became an important catalyst in activating Richberg's interest in reform politics. In later years, he saw

[10] Richberg, "The Lawyer's Function," *The Atlantic Monthly* 104 (Oct. 1909): 489–92; Richberg, *Tents*, 22–23.

[11] Richberg, *The Shadow Men* (Chicago, 1911); Richberg, *In the Dark* (Chicago, 1912); Richberg, Miscellaneous articles, mss. of novels, and short stories, Richberg Papers, L.C., Boxes 5, 9, 32; Richberg, "Why Should Not Corporations Be Imprisoned?" and "The Imprisonment of Criminal Corporations," both in *The Imprisonment of Criminal Corporations*, Aug. 1907, 3–9, 20–32, pamphlet in Richberg Papers, L.C., Box 5. The quotations are from "The Imprisonment of Criminal Corporations," 32.

The Shadow Men, one of his novels indicting contemporary business practices, as having had a specific role in developing his bud-
ding progressivism: "To begin with, I had to give up my games
and parties and lots of good times in order to write. This helps one
develop a martyr complex, which every reformer should have in
some degree." More important was his observation that "writing
down an incoherent revolt tends to strengthen it and make it real—
if it is soundly based."[12]

A number of factors, then, all came together in Donald Richberg to create a blend of moral concern, personal anger, and self-
righteousness which provided some of the motive power behind his
progressivism: his middle-class background and Victorian morality; the shock of returning from Harvard to the practice of law in
Chicago and the apparent end of his dreams of a literary career;
the state of the legal profession; the contrast between his business
life and his social life; the apparent professional success of his university friends; his wife's demands for attention and her failure
to provide moral support; and his tendency to nurse all these grievances in the privacy of his own literary world. This is not to suggest that Richberg's reformism was a delusion or that there were
no evils in twentieth-century America that needed changing, but
simply to say that his assessment of his personal and professional
situation provided him with a heightened receptivity to progressivism. The tensions that Richberg encountered, it is true, could
have been dealt with in several different ways besides becoming
a progressive. The results might have been very different—perhaps a Babbitt or an introvert instead of a crusading reformer. Furthermore, such tensions are present in all men to some degree. And
despite Richberg's preoccupation with the status of his profession,
it is a truism that a sense of individual worth is essential to the
normal personality.

Richberg's response to the seeming pointlessness of his social life
and the apparent evils he found in the world of law and business
was appropriate from both a psychological and an objective historical standpoint. Psychologically, reform was to prove a way for
Richberg to give greater meaning to his existence and to end the

[12] Richberg, *Tents,* 24–25.

aimlessness of his early career. Objectively, the evils that he saw were real enough and it would take a mature personality to be moved to do something about them rather than simply to shrink from becoming involved. The easier resolution of Richberg's problem would have been to go along with the status quo, but he did not choose to do so. Since personality has both an emotional and a rational dimension, a satisfactory explanation of Richberg's identification with reform can only be achieved by somehow encompassing both. Reform did serve a personal need for Richberg, but it was likewise a logical response to objective conditions as he perceived them in his professional life. It was this coincidence between the rational and the emotional which created a commitment to public service in Richberg which was to endure throughout his career.

CHAPTER II

The Anxious Reformer

Richberg's first taste of political activity came within a year after he joined his father's law firm—in the 1905 Chicago mayoralty campaign. In this and succeeding contests, he consistently lined up with the city's independents on such issues as traction franchises, utility rate regulation, municipal ownership of public utilities, corruption in city administration, and the other perennial problems of American municipal government at the turn of the century. Richberg was one of the younger members of a group of future Progressive party leaders which included Harold Ickes, Jane Addams, Raymond Robins, Charles E. Merriam, and Medill McCormick.[1]

It was not until the end of the first decade of the twentieth century, however, that it became clear that the progressive spirit was crystallizing into a national political movement. Men such as former President Theodore Roosevelt and Senator Robert Marion La Follette of Wisconsin encouraged the trend. In their attempts to take over leadership of the movement, they helped bring a certain degree of coherence to the diversity of independent political organizations, like Chicago's, which had been evolving at the city and state levels since the late nineteenth century. Concrete evidence that the movement had attained national proportions came in the 1910 congressional elections. Progressive and independent candidates made sufficient inroads into the two major political parties to throw control of the House of Representatives to the Democrats for the first time in sixteen years; in the Senate, progressive Republicans held the balance of power, and the Old Guard leadership had to rely on them to maintain a Republican majority.

Chicago was swept along by these currents, so that 1911 found its independent political elements fielding a mayoral candidate based on the progressive sentiment that had been growing in the city since the turn of the century. The independents coalesced behind Charles E. Merriam, professor of political science at the University of Chicago. In a short time on the city council, Merriam had built a reputation as a vigorous opponent of machine politics and corruption in government. His campaign was managed by Harold L. Ickes, one of Chicago's leading independents and a future secretary of the interior under President Franklin Roosevelt. The reformers planned to challenge the incumbent mayor, Fred A. Busse, a machine politician, in the Republican primaries. Chicago independents were still operating within the framework of the two-party system, though by the end of the campaign some such as Richberg were to have reservations about this strategy. For Chicago, the 1911 mayoralty contest was to be the catalyst of the city's organized Progressive party.

Much to the surprise of the regular party organization, Merriam won the Republican nomination over two other candidates after Busse withdrew from the race. As leader of the Merriam anti-machine campaign in the primaries, however, Ickes found it difficult to work with the regular party organization after his candidate had won the nomination, so that winning the election proved to be another matter. Merriam narrowly missed a victory over Carter H. Harrison, Jr., a popular Democrat who had been mayor four times prior to 1905. The independents were convinced that the regular Republicans had worked against Merriam as a way of destroying the progressive wing of the party, even though he was their official mayoral candidate. As Richberg told Merriam, "Your defeat was to be laid to your supposed political allies and not to your supposed opponents." He urged that "one of two things must be done by the men in this town who believe it is worth while to

[1] Donald Richberg, *My Hero: The Indiscreet Memoirs of an Eventful but Unheroic Life* (New York, 1954), 26–29; Harold L. Ickes, *The Autobiography of a Curmudgeon* (New York, 1943), 89–114; Chicago *Examiner*, April 1, 1907.

fight for better government; either clean up one of the political parties or form a new party." After the apparent betrayal of the mayoralty contest, Richberg was among those prepared to take the latter course. For the time being, though, Chicago's independents under the guidance of Harold Ickes set up a small executive committee, incorporated as the Progressive-Republican League of Illinois, to keep their ranks intact until the next round.[2]

In 1912, before the presidential campaign, the backers of the Progressive-Republican League made yet another attempt to penetrate the regular Republican party machinery by running candidates in the April state and county primaries. Richberg agreed to seek the nomination for state's attorney, the office of prosecutor for Cook County; he had not previously considered running for office, but yielded to a draft in order to support the progressive effort. But once again, the reformers found the regular party organization unresponsive; the progressive slate went down to defeat and Richberg ran sixth in a field of nine.[3]

Yet later in the spring as the preconvention presidential campaign drew nearer, many Chicago progressives forgot the setbacks suffered in the local and state primaries and turned to a new drive to win the Republican nomination for Theodore Roosevelt. They were soon caught up in a successful campaign to pass a presidential primary law in their state, a move that eventually led to Roosevelt's winning the Illinois delegation to the Republican national convention.[4] William Howard Taft's grip on the Republican party, however, was too strong for even Roosevelt to break, so that when the president won renomination, Roosevelt bolted the Republican

[2] Richberg, *My Hero*, 36–37; Richberg, *Tents of the Mighty* (New York, 1930), 25–26; Ickes, *Curmudgeon*, 117–44, 148; Charles E. Merriam, *Chicago: A More Intimate View of Urban Politics* (New York, 1929), 281–87; Richberg to Merriam, April 5, 1911, Charles E. Merriam Papers, University of Chicago Library, Box 21; Ickes to William Draper Lewis, Jan. 27, 1919, Harold L. Ickes Papers, Library of Congress, Box 8.

[3] Ickes, *Curmudgeon*, 148–51; Richberg, *My Hero*, 38–39; Richberg, *Tents*, 25–27; Chicago *Tribune*, Feb. 8, 16, 17, 19, 21, March 4, 13, 17, 26, 29, April 7, 10, 11, 1912.

[4] Ickes, *Curmudgeon*, 158–60; Ickes to Lewis, Jan. 27, 1919, Ickes Papers, Box 8.

convention and created the new Progressive party to back his candidacy. At last, the diverse groups of reformers and independents in Chicago and around the country had a national political organization.

Like many Illinois Progressives, Richberg was swept along by the enthusiasm for Roosevelt. The commitment of his friends undoubtedly strengthened his own involvement in the campaign, especially since Richberg initially had no liking for Roosevelt personally, though he supported his program. But in a short time, the excitement of the campaign made Richberg into a dedicated follower with a total commitment—to the man as well as his platform.[5]

Richberg's part in the Progressive campaign, once the party had decided to run not only a national but a state and county ticket in the fall general elections in Illinois, typified what was to become his characteristic role in various future reform movements. With one other lawyer, Edward B. Burling, Richberg was placed in charge of all Progressive party litigation involved in securing a place for the party's candidates on the Illinois ballot.[6]

This was the beginning of Richberg's role as one of the leading technicians in the service of reform for the next several decades. Owing to personal embarrassments—his two divorces in 1915 and 1924—Richberg considered himself ineligible on practical grounds to aspire to an elective office; he had sought the Republican nomination for state's attorney in 1912 and would seek election to the Cook County Circuit Court in 1915, but thereafter felt that his private difficulties rendered any future effort futile.[7] Yet identifying with reform causes fulfilled keenly felt psychic and intellectual needs for Richberg; he could not simply ignore their demand for an outlet. Reform provided him with a chance to employ his talents as a lawyer in a way that would safeguard his self-respect. It offered an opportunity to restore the legal profession to what he

[5] Richberg, *My Hero*, 44–46; Richberg, *Tents*, 31–34.
[6] Richberg, *My Hero*, 46–47; Richberg, *Tents*, 36–37; Richberg to Theodore Roosevelt, Nov. 19, 1912, Theodore Roosevelt Papers, Library of Congress, Series 1, Box 231.
[7] Richberg, *My Hero*, 38–39, 70, 137–38, 207–14, 218–19.

regarded as its rightful place as arbiter of the public good and brought an excitement to the practice of law that he never felt in the service of private clients. Though he considered himself unacceptable as a candidate for elective office, Richberg found the role of the behind-the-scenes technician equally satisfying; he could provide essential services to the Progressive party and to future liberal causes, while at the same time finding personal fulfillment in service of a quasi-public nature. As a lawyer, he had the expertise needed for writing political platforms and for translating the ideas of the party leadership into workable proposals. The very profession that he had once despised was to provide Richberg with a way to participate in the kind of undertaking which he found personally and intellectually satisfying.[8]

Despite their work on the Progressive party's legal problems, Richberg and Burling were not sanguine about the party's chances at the polls, especially in view of the nomination of Woodrow Wilson by the Democrats.[9] The Republicans were divided and the Democrats were running a candidate chosen from their own progressive wing. Yet Wilson's victory was not enough to put an end to the new movement or to Richberg's hopes for its eventual success —at least for the moment. Many like Richberg regarded the Progressive party as the true guardian of liberalism. They believed that the Democratic party, presumably dominated by urban bosses and Southern conservatives, could not possibly sustain a reform image, however earnest Wilson's intentions; its victory was to be attributed simply to the Republican-Progressive split. The inevitable Democratic failure would clear the way for the triumph of the Progressive party.

In Richberg's case, such hopes were the function of personal

[8] See Richberg, "Memories for My Grandchildren," 17, unpublished manuscript in the possession of Mrs. John H. Small III (formerly Mrs. Donald R. Richberg), Charlottesville, Va.; Richberg, "Legislative Reference Bureaus for Political Parties," *Proceedings of the American Political Science Association at Its Tenth Annual Meeting, Supplement to the American Political Science Review* 8 (Feb. 1914): 222–33; Richberg, "The Lawyer's Function," *The Atlantic Monthly* 104 (Oct. 1909): 489–92.

[9] Richberg, *My Hero*, 47–49.

need as well as of an assessment of the political realities. What reform activity had done for him personally was to transform the practice of law from a petty service for private interests into a service enhanced by the public interest. The law had thus taken on greater meaning, a meaning which overcame his early disillusion with political morality and which had definite implications for his future career. For his own psychic security and in light of his evaluation of the state of the legal profession, Richberg found it congenial to believe in the future of the Progressive party and his place in it.

In fact, 1913 saw Richberg turn full time to the work of the Progressive party. He joined the newly created Progressive National Service in New York City as director of its Legislative Reference Bureau, a post which he held until the virtual demise of the Service in the spring of 1914. The Service had been authorized in December 1912 by a conference of Progressive leaders meeting in Chicago for a postmortem on the presidential election. The idea behind the project was to create an organization separate from the office-seeking political machinery to serve as the party's educational arm and legislative reference bureau. As such, the Service represented an attempt to put Progressive ideals into action and was well suited to rationalizing Richberg's commitment to the legal profession. Its principal work would be to prepare model legislation for Progressive congressmen and state legislators and propaganda for popular consumption. Hopefully, it would bring impartial scientific knowledge rather than self-interest to bear on policymaking and took as its model Charles McCarthy's Legislative Reference Library in the State of Wisconsin.[10]

George Perkins, chairman of the Progressive party's National

[10] Richberg, "Legislative Reference Bureaus for Political Parties," 222–33; Frances A. Kellor, The Progressive Service of the National Progressive Party ([New York], Jan. 25, 1913), pamphlet in Donald Richberg Papers, Library of Congress, Box 41; S. J. Duncan-Clark, The Progressive Movement (Boston, 1913), 302–16; Richberg, My Hero, 50–55; Richberg, Tents, 40–48; Edward A. Fitzpatrick, McCarthy of Wisconsin (New York, 1944), 67–69; Progressive Party, National Committee, Minutes, Dec. 11, 1912, Theodore Roosevelt Papers, Series 13d.

Executive Committee, and William Draper Lewis, dean of the University of Pennsylvania Law School and chairman of the Legislative Reference Committee charged with setting up the Bureau, initially hoped to engage McCarthy himself. McCarthy, however, felt that he had built too large a stake in Wisconsin to risk leaving it unprotected. A deteriorating money situation further impeded the Legislative Reference Committee's search, and the Bureau existed solely on a makeshift basis until March 1913, when Richberg was hired. The decision to turn to Richberg came after a long and unsuccessful search to find someone of greater experience in legislative reference work, but with McCarthy out of the running, that proved impossible. Although Richberg had given yeoman service in the 1912 campaign, he had had no experience in the tasks assigned to the Legislative Reference Bureau. Yet by March he was the most acceptable lawyer the Progressives could obtain.[11]

Richberg's personal situation made him eager to participate in the experiment, but his New York experiences proved to be less than a vindication of the lawyer's role in policymaking. Though occasionally receiving advice and suggestions from Lewis's Legislative Reference Committee, Richberg was limited in what he could do, for he and one assistant were all that constituted the entire Legislative Reference Bureau. Like many Progressive party ventures, the Bureau was more impressive on paper than in action. Richberg's principal achievement was to prepare ten bills for the Progressive delegation in Congress; none were original proposals but embodied longstanding ideals common to reformers of many different political affiliations, and most of them were drafted with the help of members of the Legislative Reference Committee. In the face of the Wilson administration's program, none of the Progressive party proposals had a chance. Otherwise, most of Richberg's

[11] Charles McCarthy to George Perkins, Dec. 9, 1912, cited in Fitzpatrick, *McCarthy*, 68–69; William Draper Lewis to McCarthy, Jan. 11, 1913; Bernard S. Van Rensselear to McCarthy, Feb. 8, 1913; McCarthy to Richberg, April 21, 1913, Charles McCarthy Papers, State Historical Society of Wisconsin, Box 10; Richberg to McCarthy, May 3, 1913; McCarthy Papers, Box 11; Lewis to Richberg, March 18, 1913; Richberg to Lewis, April 1, 1913, Richberg Papers, L.C., Box 1.

time was spent in preparing propaganda for the party and advertising its hopes for more concrete achievements in the future. Nothing came to fruition in the way of preparing model legislation for
the use of Progressive leaders in the states.[12]

The National Progressive Service as a whole realized equally
negative results. It never really solved the problem of its own internal organization nor clearly defined its objectives and procedures
of operation. Such questions occupied the attention of Frances
Kellor, chief of the Service, to the very end of its existence. In addition, budgetary and personnel problems plagued the Service, and
Kellor herself became the center of constant disputes of a personal
nature among Service employees. With his own high-strung personality, it was not surprising that Richberg found himself repeatedly at odds with Kellor. Problems concerning the Legislative Reference Bureau's budget and the relationship between the National
Service and the local party organizations in the states created icy
relations between the two. Exacerbating their disagreements over
specific policy questions were the different ways in which each
perceived the other's proper role and authority in the Service. Richberg considered himself primarily responsible to Lewis's Legislative Reference Committee, which had hired him in the first place,
whereas Kellor as chief of the Service considered him subject to
her administrative directives. Kellor's dismissal of Paxton Hibben
as director of the Educational Bureau precipitated open hostilities
between the two; Hibben had been a classmate of Richberg's at
Harvard, and he came to the defense of his old friend. Lacking
firsthand knowledge of conditions in the Service, party leaders resolved the dispute in favor of Kellor, though providing for additional supervision over her work. But the decision left Richberg
and other members of the Service thoroughly demoralized.[13]

<hr />

[12] "Special Report of the Progressive National Service, to the Progressive
National Executive Committee. For the Period of the Second Quarter
April 1st–May 15th, 1913," n.d., Raymond Robins Papers, State Historical
Society of Wisconsin, Box 5; Richberg to Lewis, Dec. 1, 1913, Richberg
Papers, l.c., Box 1; Progressive Party, National Legislative Reference Com-
mittee, *Progressive Congressional Program* (New York, 1914).

[13] [Richberg], "The Service has suffered . . . ," memorandum, n.d.;

Yet the days of the National Progressive Service were numbered anyway. Largely because of a shortage of available funds, the party's National Executive Committee decided that in 1914 the Service would have to be cut back drastically so as to give priority to the vote-getting political machinery. Nineteen fourteen was an election year for Progressive congressmen and state officials, and the need to give attention to the practical matter of winning public office was becoming more and more apparent. The time for idealistic experiments was over, and the supporters of the Progressive Service had failed to make the most of it. When funds ran out for the directorship of the Legislative Reference Bureau in March, Richberg returned to Chicago to resume law practice in his father's office once again.[14]

The same factors that initially had drawn Richberg to the Progressive National Service kept him loyal to the party, despite his less-than-happy experiences in New York. His desire to justify his work in terms of the public welfare did not disappear with the breakup of the Service. Even as it crumbled around him, he persisted in his favorable evaluation of its potentialities, if not its accomplishments. In a paper prepared for the American Political Science Association during the last days of the Service, he gave an account of his continuing faith in its possibilities. Richberg saw the Progressive National Service not only as a mechanism for developing a liberal legislative program but also as a vehicle for transforming the legal profession from a gang of parasites living off the troubles of mankind into an agency for the betterment of the general welfare: "There is in the work that combination of law and politics and social science which is rapidly creating a new profes-

Paxton Hibben to Executive Committee of the National Committee of the Progressive Party, Nov. 18, 1913; Hibben, Dec. 7, 1913, with attached letter, Kellor to Hibben, n.d., Richberg Papers, L.C., Box 41; [Richberg] to Herbert Knox Smith, Dec. 6, 1913; George Perkins to Donald Richberg, Dec. 18, 1913; Smith to Richberg, Dec. 9, 1913, Richberg Papers, L.C., Box 1; [Robins] to H. Edward Dreier, Dec. 29, 1913, Robins Papers, Box 6.
[14] Progressive Party, Executive Committee, Minutes, Jan. 24, 1914, Theodore Roosevelt Papers, Series 13d; Lewis to Richberg, Jan. 29, 1914, Richberg Papers, L.C., Box 1.

sion, which might be termed that of social counselor. It may be regarded as one of the large divisions into which the profession of law is separating."

The Progressive Service, and especially Richberg's Legislative Reference Bureau, were to be an integral part of this transformation—in fact, its primary catalyst: "During the transition period between the almost purely parasite lawyer of today and the social counselor of tomorrow legislative reference bureaus may serve as postgraduate schools in which young lawyers may be brought in touch with the needs of their generation in the way of jurisprudence." By setting up national and state bureaus, political parties could serve as the channels conveying the people's need for up-to-date concepts of social justice to members of the bar, so that in every community there might develop "groups of earnest young men devoted to the idea of helping the law to keep pace with the great strides of social and industrial needs." An apprenticeship in such a bureau would give the young lawyer some sense of the general welfare which might counteract the forces of private privilege.[15]

The persistence of Richberg's vision in the face of the reality can be understood in terms of his personal situation and his interpretation of the state of political morality. Implementing the Service idea had proved far more difficult than its sponsors had anticipated, and the bulk of its troubles had come from within, not from without. But for someone such as Richberg, who had long justified his career in terms of the status of his profession, the tendency to perceive the Service in terms of ideals and hopes rather than realities comes as no surprise. Richberg's New York adventure thus paradoxically became part of a larger complex of experiences that reinforced rather than eroded his identification with reform.

Consequently, Richberg's return to Chicago meant no slackening in his dedication to the Progressive party, though as the 1914 elections approached, its future was more and more clouded. Harold Ickes had joined the Richberg law firm in 1913, and his presence reinforced Richberg's commitment to reform politics. Within a few months, Richberg was at work promoting the candidacy of Raymond Robins for election to the United States Senate on the Pro-

[15] Richberg, "Legislative Reference Bureaus for Political Parties," 229–30.

gressive ticket. Once again, he operated behind the scenes preparing propaganda against the Republicans and Democrats and overseeing the litigation necessary to nominate candidates under Illinois law. But once again, the Progressives' efforts were unavailing, and Robins came in a poor third, defeated by the Republican machine candidate, Lawrence Sherman. Even Richberg began to feel discouraged about the future of the party.[16]

Although Richberg fought to preserve the Progressive party as an independent political force until 1916, he realized that the results of the 1914 campaign gave inescapable proof that its strength had rapidly dissipated. In Illinois, only Medill McCormick and H. S. Hickes of Rockford won state offices and were returned to the House of Representatives in Springfield. No Progressive candidate for Congress or the state senate won. What happened in Illinois was repeated all across the country. Nineteen fifteen was no better for Chicago Progressives, and their attempt to take over the Republican primaries in the mayoralty contest failed. Furthermore, of four Progressives included on a compromise judicial slate made up by a coalition of Progressives and regular Republicans, all but one were defeated, and Richberg was among those who failed to win office. As an organization, the Illinois Progressive party was in a shambles by the spring of 1915.[17]

Yet Richberg needed the Progressive party as much as it needed him. Regardless of the ill-fortunes of its organizational life, he repeatedly encouraged Theodore Roosevelt to run again as the party's presidential candidate in 1916, arguing that whatever political power the Progressives had was the product of the personal popularity of the Bull Moose himself, and that unless Roosevelt ran, the

[16] Richberg, *My Hero*, 58–59, 61; Richberg, *Tents*, 52–53; Richberg, "Opinion with Reference to the Right of the Senatorial Committees of the Progressive Party (for Social Justice) to Determine the Number of Candidates to be Nominated by Their Party for Representative at the Primary of Sept. 9, 1914," Robins Papers, Box 7; Robins to Richberg, Nov. 7, 1914, in the possession of Mrs. John H. Small III (recently deposited in Richberg Papers, L.C.).

[17] Richberg, *My Hero*, 70; Richberg, *Tents*, 53–54; Ickes, *Curmudgeon*, 170–76; Chicago *Daily News*, Jan. 25, 1915; Ickes to Robins, Dec. 17, 1914; Ickes to Robins, Jan. 6, 1915, Robins Papers, Box 8.

party would be finished. This was starkly apparent after the results of 1914–1915.[18] But throughout, Roosevelt's position remained ambiguous, while he toyed with doubts about whether the Progressive party itself was an adequate vehicle of reform, whether a new bid for the presidential nomination would be best sought through it or through the Republican party, and whether his stand on military preparedness would affect these other calculations.

In addition to the role that reform work played in Richberg's view of the political situation, the war in Europe and American preparedness likewise became factors in his thinking about Roosevelt's chances for election in 1916. The war issue reinforced what was already a deep commitment to the Roosevelt candidacy on Richberg's part. Though of a German background himself, and hence suspect in the eyes of many anglophiles in the United States, Richberg was as vehemently in favor of military preparedness as Roosevelt himself. His extremely sensitive nature was likely to make him respond to any reflection upon his Americanism. Hence, he viewed Roosevelt's strong preparedness position in highly positive terms—terms that undoubtedly reflected his own personal needs but may not have accurately reflected the objective division of public opinion as he tried to report it to Roosevelt. Over and over again, Richberg professed to see an "evidently increasing Roosevelt sentiment here in Illinois at least, after a period of what was plainly a decline." Again, Richberg's outlook was as much the product of his own hopes as of the political realities.[19]

By the time of the 1916 Progressive nominating convention, Richberg joined a small band of party leaders in nominating Roose-

[18] Richberg to Roosevelt, Sept. 22, 1913, Theodore Roosevelt Papers, Series 1, Box 259; Richberg to Roosevelt, Nov. 5, 1915, Theodore Roosevelt Papers, Series 1, Box 290; Richberg, *Who Wins in November? The "Inside Politics" That Will Decide the Presidency in 1916* (Chicago, 1916), 60.

[19] Richberg to Roosevelt, Sept. 1, 1915, Theodore Roosevelt Papers, Series 1, Box 288; Richberg to Roosevelt, Nov. 5, 1915, Theodore Roosevelt Papers, Series 1, Box 290; Richberg to Roosevelt, Aug. 25, 1916, and Richberg to Roosevelt, Sept. 8, 1916, both in Theodore Roosevelt Papers, Series 1, Box 311; interview with Mrs. John H. Small III, Charlottesville, Va., Jan. 11–12, 1967.

velt over his protest and that of his strategy planners, headed by George W. Perkins, who wished to amalgamate with the Republican party. If the Republicans nominated an acceptable candidate, Roosevelt and Perkins were prepared to support him. To Roosevelt, the most important objective in 1916 was the defeat of Woodrow Wilson; he therefore wished to avoid splitting the Progressives and the Republicans as in 1912.

In the eyes of people such as Donald Richberg and Harold Ickes, Perkins was seriously underestimating Roosevelt's strength in the country and the possibility of maintaining an independent political party if the Republicans failed to respond to Progressive overtures with favorable terms. Richberg believed—or perhaps hoped—that Roosevelt's popularity had increased spectacularly in the period from January to June 1916, after hitting a low point sometime in 1915. He therefore considered the Perkins strategy out of step with a constantly changing situation; the Progressives need not wield their power negatively. Richberg and Ickes were afraid that Perkins was bent more on returning to the Republican party at any price than on promoting either the development of a controlling Progressive element within the Republican party or, alternatively, the preservation of a separate Progressive party.[20]

Consequently, at the Progressive nominating convention, Ickes headed up a group of Roosevelt backers which went to elaborate lengths to insure his nomination. Privy to the Ickes strategy were Richberg and a group of important party leaders including Raymond Robins, Gifford Pinchot, Chester H. Rowell, Matthew Hale, William Allen White, Henry Allen, Victor Murdock, Bainbridge Colby, Hiram Johnson, and John M. Parker. But given the overwhelming pro-Roosevelt sentiment of the delegates themselves, elaborate planning was not as necessary as Ickes and Richberg seemed to have imagined, so that the Bull Moose was asked to head up the ticket again despite his own feelings about the question.

[20] Ickes, "Who Killed the Progressive Party?" *American Historical Review* 46 (Jan. 1941): 308–22; George F. Mowry, *Theodore Roosevelt and the Progressive Movement* ("American Century Series"; New York, 1960), 323–44; Richberg to Roosevelt, Nov. 5, 1915, Theodore Roosevelt Papers, Series 1, Box 290; Richberg, *Who Wins in November?* 59–64.

When the Republicans nominated Supreme Court Justice Charles Evans Hughes and he immediately accepted, Roosevelt's decision whether to accept the Progressive nomination was a foregone conclusion. He had repeatedly asserted his belief that President Wilson had to be defeated at all costs because of his vacillating foreign policy; a Progressive-Republican coalition presumably could do this. Most important, it was known that Hughes was an acceptable candidate to Roosevelt. He therefore declined the Bull Moose nomination; the choice for the Progressives then was either to follow Roosevelt back into the Republican fold, or make an independent campaign in the face of desertion by the one leader who had a chance of winning. The new Progressive National Committee voted thirty-two to six, with nine abstentions, to follow Roosevelt.[21]

The Ickes Progressives in Chicago generally went over to the Hughes camp, though the management of the campaign was in the hands of Republicans who had no sympathy for those whom they regarded as renegades. But with Roosevelt's defection, there was little choice. Richberg perhaps found it easier than many other Progressives to transfer his loyalties to the Republican party. His adulation of Roosevelt went far to rationalize any inconsistencies in his course of action. What Roosevelt had decided was best. The Progressives had known Roosevelt's feeling about the nomination when they had called him to be their standard bearer. They had placed the fate of the party in his hands, knowing the risk. Richberg felt that they must now abide by his decision. Although Hughes appointed a number of Progressives, including Harold Ickes, to his campaign committee in a conciliatory gesture, most Old Guard Republican leaders remained resentful toward them, so that people such as Ickes and Richberg had little to say about running the 1916 campaign.[22]

[21] Ickes, "Who Killed the Progressive Party?" 322–33; Richberg, *Who Wins in November?* 64–68; Richberg, *My Hero,* 64, 86–88.

[22] Ickes, "Who Killed the Progressive Party?" 334–37; Richberg, *Who Wins in November?* 67–82; Richberg, *My Hero,* 88–91; Richberg, *Tents,* 74–78; Richberg to Roosevelt, Sept. 8, 1916, Theodore Roosevelt Papers, Series 1, Box 311; Richberg to Roosevelt, Nov. 21, 1916, Theodore Roosevelt Papers, Series 1, Box 314.

With the Republican's defeat by President Wilson, Richberg found himself with the problem of finding a new outlet for his reform energies. Roosevelt's support of Hughes was the coup de grace that finished the Progressive party as an independent political force. But Richberg's career problem for the present was complicated not only by the demise of the Progressive party but also by his family situation; his political activities and the recently growing needs of his dependents placed him in desperate need of money. For a time, he would have to be concerned with the more practical side of life.

Richberg's personal life reached a turning point in 1915. Until then he had been free from any extraordinary family obligations. But in March of that year, his father suffered a stroke for the second time. The first occasion had been in 1909, but within a few months he had recovered and resumed his law practice. Now he was rendered completely helpless and lingered in that state until his death in February 1918. Richberg thus found himself at the head of a household with numerous financial obligations. Besides his mother and father, he acquired several other dependents. Over the next several years, his brother Windsor and his sister Leda, as well as his two half-sisters Elsinore and Fanelia, required either partial or complete support.

Richberg was burdened with these obligations for the greater part of his life. But the impact was especially severe in 1915, for his absence in New York in 1913–1914, his recent devotion of much time and energy to nonremunerative political work, and his father's 1909 illness had left the Richberg law firm in a poor financial condition. Although Harold Ickes was also a partner in the firm, he too had dedicated a large part of his energy to politics rather than law. Furthermore, Richberg's campaign in 1915 for circuit court judge necessitated an outlay of $2,500 from personal funds for campaign expenses. And when John C. Richberg finally died, he left not an inheritance but what his son considered a heavy burden of debt, which took several years to pay off. Richberg's brothers and sisters were of no assistance in lightening this burden.

Added to Richberg's anxieties in 1915 was his separation from his first wife. Their relationship had long been deteriorating, and

Richberg took the onus of leaving her. He provided separate maintenance until 1917, when she sued for divorce on grounds of desertion. Alimony payments then followed for several years, until she voluntarily relieved him of this obligation. Nevertheless, Richberg was burdened with alimony until 1952, for in 1918 he had remarried, only to be disappointed again. As in his first marriage, Richberg found that his new wife failed to give him the kind of moral support that he required. She pursued her own interests instead of sharing his, and retained old associations which made him jealous. In 1924, they were divorced, but in December of that same year, Richberg married for a third time. His new venture was to prove highly successful; at last he had found a woman who could subordinate her ambitions to his.

Events in 1915 thus conspired to make Richberg acutely aware of his financial status. The experience was one that he later viewed as marking for him "the end of youth," and it left a lifetime impression which made Richberg solicitous about the financial arrangements of his future career commitments. He had been careless about such matters for too long. Yet there lingered in Richberg a desire to feel that his work had a public service dimension as well. His immediate personal problem was to find a way of combining practicality and politics, so that he might earn an adequate living while still serving reform.[23]

As a partial solution to the dilemma, Richberg and Ickes decided to take two more partners into the firm, John S. Lord and Morgan Davies, both of whom brought additional clients and were more interested in practicing law than dabbling in politics. But fortunately for him, Richberg did not have to dedicate his energies entirely to private clients. He soon found a new outlet for his reform proclivities to take the place of the defunct Progressive party, one that at the same time provided him with additional income. Richberg became Special Counsel for the City of Chicago in Gas Matters.[24]

Richberg's appointment came about as the result of lobbying on the part of his old friend, Alderman Charles E. Merriam. The new

[23] Richberg, "Memories for My Grandchildren," chapt. D; Richberg, My Hero, 71–72, 210–14; Richberg, Tents, 54–56.

[24] Richberg, My Hero, 61.

mayor of Chicago, William Hale Thompson, had created a Select Committee on Gas Litigation in the Chicago City Council to redeem his campaign promise to investigate rising gas rates. Neither Merriam nor Richberg had supported the Thompson brand of reform in the 1915 elections, but Merriam—by then one of the city's most outspoken reformers—was appointed to the special committee anyway, perhaps to mollify critics of alleged political connections between the mayor and the Peoples Gas Light and Coke Company, which was the public utility under fire. The committee's first task was to engage counsel to carry on an investigation and to prosecute long-pending litigation against the company. Merriam proposed Richberg for the job, while the chairman of the Select Committee, Alderman James H. Lawley, backed another candidate, Glenn E. Plumb. After the First World War, Plumb was to become well known as the promoter of the Plumb Plan for the public management of the nation's railway network. As a result of a political deal after a long deadlock on the Select Committee, Richberg was engaged as counsel with Plumb as his assistant.[25]

From 1915 until the mid-1920s, Richberg was involved in three principal stratagems against the gas company. He pressed litigation already initiated by the City Corporation Counsel for recovering alleged overcharges, negotiated a new agreement between the city and the company controlling future rates, and managed the city's interest in valuation proceedings against Peoples Gas as the basis for regulating future profits and rates. In each instance, Richberg enjoyed temporary successes during the course of litigation or negotiation, thereby encouraging the city council's hopes for a clean sweep. He ultimately failed, however, in his efforts to recover excess charges and to reach a permanent *modus vivendi* with the company over rates. The valuation proceedings did result in a lower rate base than the company had hoped for at various times, but it was not as low as Richberg had wanted.

Although engaged by a committee appointed by Mayor Thompson, Richberg was constantly at odds with him over the handling of the proceedings. This only confirmed Richberg's suspicions that the mayor was using the rate controversy as a smokescreen for a do-

[25] Ibid., 72–73.

nothing policy. Furthermore, Samuel Insull was chairman of the gas company's board of directors, and thus provided Richberg with the very kind of symbol that epitomized the evils he saw in the world of business. To Richberg's mind, Insull was the sort of figure who would make a likely character in one of his muckracking novels. Actually, Insull's desire to raise gas rates was the product of a more complex situation than a simple grasping for profits. Increasing labor and supply costs had placed the Peoples Gas Company in a precarious financial situation. Furthermore, expenses to be undertaken for plant and equipment modernization designed to ease the problem in the long run would exacerbate it in the short run. Though Richberg's negotiations with the company over future rates revealed some awareness of its problems and the consequences of a financial breakdown, his conduct of the gas proceedings at times exhibited the overriding moral fervor of the deeply committed reformer. Someone like Insull, concerned primarily with the survival of a company with very shaky financial resources, was mystified by Richberg's tendency to turn the problem into an ethical rather than a practical question. In that respect, the Chicago gas fight was tailormade for satisfying Richberg's desire to remain in reform work. The gas proceedings were completed by 1925, after the entire fight, including engineering as well as legal expenses, had cost Chicago approximately $400,000. Richberg resigned as special counsel in 1927, when Mayor Thompson returned to office after having been out of power for one term. Thompson considered the expense of the Richberg campaign out of proportion to the results.[26]

The Chicago gas fight thus bridged the gap between the demise of the Progressive party and Richberg's work in labor law during

[26] Ibid., 74, 102–11; Richberg, *Tents,* 109–21; Forrest McDonald, *Insull* (Chicago, 1962), 158–61, 177–82, 205–13; *Journal of the Proceedings of the City Council of the City of Chicago* (Chicago, 1916–1928), 1915–1916, 4–5, 2060, 2483–85; 1916–1917, 387–89, 1297–1304, 4325–33; 1917–1918, 353–54, 731–38, 1073, 1242–43, 1902–1908, 2025–26, 2380; 1918–1919, 92–93, 112, 222, 230–31, 267–72, 290–91, 302, 743–52, 1168–69, 1221–24, 1371–74; 1920–1921, 628–32, 1569–70; 1924–1925, 3647–49, 4405–4406; 1926–1927, 3913–14; 1927–1928, 161–62, 1288.

the 1920s. His experiences as special counsel had reconfirmed his identification with the role of the behind-the-scenes technician, the man with the know-how to protect the public interest. Equally important, they strengthened his interest in public utility regulation and industrial organization, so that Richberg's thinking about such questions continued to mature throughout these years.

The First World War likewise stimulated Richberg's theorizing about industrial relations. His family situation and his involvement in the city's dispute with Peoples Gas discouraged him from seeking a commission in the armed forces, but he volunteered as a patriotic speaker for the Illinois Council of Defense.[27] Richberg quickly became disillusioned, however, by the contrast between the democratic idealism which he preached from the platform and the reality of coercive practices on the homefront, especially in labor relations. Furthermore, Richberg came to believe that the war effort itself was endangering the very object of battle—democracy. The "forced competition of war" was changing the character of the Allied governments; the necessity for a rapid and efficient reorganization of industry to meet the challenge of foreign aggression made once democratic regimes turn to authoritarian methods to marshal the needed effort and resources for self-defense. Richberg feared that "governments so reorganized" would not easily return to democracy once the exigencies of battle had passed.

In Richberg's mind, this wartime trend arose from a longer-range difficulty, namely, the oligarchic organization of industry itself. The majority of those interested in a given enterprise, the workers, had no part in decisions which intimately affected their lives; instead, capital interests imposed decisions on workers through a hierarchical system of authority. Nowhere was it recognized that labor and capital had a common interest in the success of an enterprise and that one way to insure the enthusiastic support of both was by granting each a voice in determining policy. But the war effort threatened to strengthen the inherent authoritarian features of industrial organization.[28]

[27] Richberg, *My Hero*, 91–93; Richberg, *Tents*, 80.
[28] Richberg, "Democratization of Industry," *The New Republic* 11 (May 12, 1917): 49–51.

Richberg's thinking moved in the direction of a modified corporate state ideal, with each major interest group organized to carry out a specific role in a larger undertaking defined on a companywide or even an industrywide basis. His argument for giving greater recognition to organized labor and encouraging unionization revolved around the idea that the "principal job" of the nation's industrial leadership was "to attract and organize men into a cooperating machinery of production wherein their self-interest will lie in the efficiency and profitableness of the business." Only secondarily was it necessary "to obtain the capital . . . to provide the physical machinery to be operated by the organized labor power." To Richberg, the conclusion seemed inescapable that "capital cannot live without men; but men can manage to exist without capital. Therefore, although capital and labor are somewhat interdependent, capital is more dependent upon labor than labor is upon capital." The reason for labor strife was that contemporary industrial leadership persisted in organizing the interests of capital only. Unionization was the inevitable response of the workers. Richberg believed that "labor organizers have merely done the work which the industrial leadership should have done; that is, they have organized productive labor power."

Richberg's solution developed over time, becoming by degrees more and more explicit. The general answer could be easily formulated: "A steady flow of capital into industrial enterprises has been obtained by providing for a board of directors elected by capital contributors and charged with the responsibility of protecting their interests. A steady flow of labor could also be obtained by so organizing corporations that representatives chosen by the labor contributors would participate jointly with representatives of capital contributors in the direction of the enterprise." Richberg maintained that his plan was not a form of socialism, because "it leaves the control of a business in the hands of those who actually carry on that business." His proposal did not make industry subject to "a political control whereby it is regulated by those who do not participate in furnishing either labor or capital," nor did it "contemplate the elimination of capital or of the rights of owners of capital." Instead, "it merely aims at eliminating the autocratic domination of capital contributors in an institution whose success or failure depends upon obtaining the voluntary and wholehearted support of labor contributors."[29]

The more detailed solution proposed by Richberg grew out of the hypothesis that the relations of employer and employee were "relations arising out of the corporate form of organization." The corporation was nothing more than the modern method of organizing capital and labor in a common project. Therefore, the most effective way to attack abuses in industrial relations was "by changing the form of corporate organization." Such a change could be easily accomplished because incorporation was a privilege granted by the state through the issuance of a charter; by redefining the terms of incorporation to provide for the representation of labor as well as capital interests, a democratic state could bring about a reformation in industrial institutions, making them more consistent with the character of the state itself. The democratizing of industry would eradicate a remnant of feudalism in the United States and would prevent the war effort from becoming a sham and a fraud.

Beyond the recognition of labor's right to organize into unions, Richberg proposed a new concept of stockholding: the creation of two kinds of stocks, labor shares and capital shares. The number of capital shares would depend upon the amount of capital investment required in an enterprise; the number of labor shares would be calculated according to the investment required to yield dividends equivalent to the salaries paid to employees. These dividends would in effect become the workers' salaries. Dividends on capital investment would be paid after salaries had been met. Equally important, the system of shareholding would provide an equitable method of measuring the relative voice of labor and capital interests in determining company policy. Although Richberg felt that a trial period would be necessary in which capital would have the dominant control, he believed that once the plan was fully implemented, both capital and labor would become aware of their common interest in the success of the enterprise, so that neither would seek to dominate the other.

[29] Richberg, "Industrial Failure and a Remedy," 1920, mss. in Richberg Papers, L.C., Box 5.

Richberg envisioned the end result as "the reestablishment of competition between industrial units and the establishment of cooperation inside industrial units," which would "eliminate the present antisocial class organization of industries whereby the representatives of capital in different units combine, and the representatives of labor in different units combine, and each group wages war on the other with the resultant loss of industrial efficiency." Class war would end. "The present demand for collective bargaining . . . would disappear in its present form," and labor would find a formal place within the corporate structure itself.[30]

Of course, Richberg's ideas were lost in the labor strife that followed the First World War and which seemed to bear out his fear that the war itself would exacerbate the contradiction between America's industrial organization and its governmental organization—between autocracy and democracy. For now, his ideas could only be expressed in magazine articles and in correspondence with such people as Herbert Hoover, vice-chairman of an industrial conference held in 1920 under the auspices of the Wilson administration.[31] But the time was soon coming when his ideas on labor relations would count for more than mere echoes of the Progressives' faith in the rationality and harmony of human relationships.

Since his early days as an independent in Chicago politics, Richberg's career situation thus had evolved in a direction which assured him of the psychic security and ideals necessary to resolve his doubts about law as a profession. Though the old Progressive organization of 1912 had fallen apart by 1916, Richberg found new outlets for his need to feel that he was serving the public good. Furthermore, the Chicago gas fight and the war crusade helped mature his interest in industrial organization. They helped him de-

[30] Richberg to Herbert Hoover, Jan. 28, 1920; Richberg to Ed D. Kneass, April 6, 1920, Donald Richberg Papers, Chicago Historical Society, Box 1; Richberg, "Outline of Suggested Industrial Program," [1920] Richberg Papers, L.C., Box 5.

[31] Richberg to Hoover, Jan. 21, 1920; Hoover to Richberg, Jan. 23, 1920, Richberg Papers, C.H.S., Box 1; Hoover, The Memoirs of Herbert Hoover, Vol. 2: The Cabinet and the Presidency, 1920–1933 (New York, 1952), 30–31; Richberg, "Democratization of Industry," 49–51.

velop clear notions about the place of labor and capital in industry. Consequently, when an opportunity came at the right moment, Richberg was prepared psychologically and intellectually to give himself to another task which was consistent with his past work as a reformer—that of labor lawyer.

CHAPTER III

Labor Lawyer

Donald Richberg's eminence as a labor advocate in the 1920s testified to his competence as a lawyer and to his deep commitment to causes which he identified with the public interest. His initial involvement with organized labor, however, was somewhat the product of chance. Prior to 1920, Richberg had had no labor clients in his private practice, nor had he been involved in any court battles with unions. His only contact with Chicago labor leaders had been in the form of casual acquaintances made during the course of political campaigning for the city's various reform groups or for the Progressives. Given Richberg's preoccupation with political organization during the heyday of the Progressive party and with public utility law during the Chicago gas fight, his failure to become actively involved in trade union circles comes as no surprise. This was simply one of many issues which were beyond his capacity as far as active participation was concerned; another was race relations. In this respect, Richberg was like many other Progressives, in that certain kinds of issues—such as the trust problem, child labor, corruption in government, and institutional reform—engaged their attention while others went practically unnoticed. Richberg's battles with Samuel Insull and the social consequences of the First World War had broadened his horizons, but thus far had resulted only in a heightened concern for industrial and labor problems; his active energies were wholly absorbed by politics and by city work.

It was the Chicago gas fight that brought Richberg into the labor camp in an active way. His assistant in the city work, Glenn

Plumb, had long been deeply involved in labor advocacy and currently was representing the railway labor unions in proceedings before the Interstate Commerce Commission (ICC) to support Senator Robert La Follette's program for the valuation of railroad properties as a basis for ratemaking. Over the years, Plumb had become one of the more important lawyers working for railway labor. At the end of the First World War he formulated the Plumb Plan for public management of the nation's railway system. As interest in the plan became widespread, Plumb found himself more and more involved in speechmaking and other promotional activities, and consequently recommended to his clients that Richberg take over the contest before the ICC. The railway unions proved agreeable, and Richberg thus entered upon one of the most important phases of his career. By the time of Plumb's death in the summer of 1922, Richberg had been sufficiently groomed in the work of the railway unions so that he appeared to be a logical successor to his former associate. Though Richberg had no standing as a labor lawyer prior to 1920, events at the beginning of the decade quickly brought him to a strategic position within the labor movement.[1]

Richberg's active involvement in labor representation, however much the product of chance, was congenial both from the personal and from the intellectual standpoint. His self-conscious articulation of the role of the lawyer as a semi-public official bound to guard the public good was a key factor in his psychic security. This was an abiding concern, one that continually provided a coherent rationale for his legal advocacy. This was true even in his later years when Richberg dedicated his legal talents to the service of what were then known as conservative causes. Yet the justification was the same. Always Richberg had to conceive his role as being in the public service. Someday he would view the growing power of labor unions, a power that he helped to create, as a threat to freedom of choice and individual initiative; he was thus able to rationalize his later affiliations with the business world in terms of defending the businessman's freedom of action against the collective, coercive

[1] Donald Richberg, *Tents of the Mighty* (New York, 1930), 123–24; Richberg, *My Hero: The Indiscreet Memoirs of an Eventful but Unheroic Life* (New York, 1954), 112–14.

power of organized labor armed with one-sided federal legislation. In the 1920s, however, Richberg saw the balance of power between labor and capital in a different light; it was the employing classes that wielded coercive power over the laboring classes. This was the rationale for his work as a labor lawyer for more than ten years.[2]

Richberg's new identification thus reinforced the trends that had been developing in his thinking about industrial relations. As the decade of the 1920s opened, his speeches and writings continued to emphasize coercion as the main internal contradiction within the American democratic system—especially economic coercion. He condemned the use of force by either labor or capital, though as the representative of the railway workers most of his energies were concentrated against management abuses. Political or economic democracy could work only where compulsion was absent, and where each party had the right and—equally important—the ability to carry out its role in the system. Richberg's battles for railway labor were not directed so much at forcing capital to do something for labor, as simply at procuring and safeguarding the right of labor to do things for itself—mainly to organize unions independent of employer influence and to bargain over wages and working conditions with management. Paternalism, or the "welfare capitalism" which some employers felt would pacify the labor front in the 1920s, was no part of Richberg's ideal, as it was merely another form of capital coercion. Yet socialism was not his answer either, for the same reason that it meant the use of coercive power by one class, the proletariat, against the rest of society.

If the businessmen of the 1920s had understood Richberg's theory of labor relations, they might not have branded him a radical. Though the idea of dealing with employees on a basis of equality annoyed many large employers, at heart Richberg's theory emphasized the traditional American values of individualism and free enterprise. His solution was not really labor dominance of the industrial world but simply its recognition as having a place in the economic system equally important as that of capital. The fundamental principles of free enterprise—private ownership and mini-

[2] Richberg to David B. Robertson and Bert M. Jewell, Feb. 25, 1949, Donald Richberg Papers, Library of Congress, Box 2.

mal state regulation—were left undisturbed. Nevertheless, anyone who served labor in that era ran the risk of being stereotyped as a socialist or worse. In Richberg's case, such a charge was absurdly wide of the mark.

In the evolution of democracy in economics, Richberg believed that the lawyer had a crucial role. He viewed history as advancing in terms of the wider and wider diffusion of liberty, and seemed to harbor the hope that there was something inevitable in this progression, so that history was on his side. But the greatest obstacle to this inevitable advance, as he saw it, was the failure of the law to keep abreast of social change or the "ever changing ethics of the human will." The most remarkable breakdown had occurred in the law of industrial relations, which was suited to an earlier primitive or frontier society of self-sufficient individuals and which was increasingly irrelevant to a contemporary society whose defining characteristic was the interdependence of producers. What modern jurisprudence had failed to comprehend was that this opened up a new area for legal action; modern men were "dependent for the absolute necessities of life upon the continuous service of large groups of other workers, usually remote from them and not subject to their influence in any fixed way except through the processes of government." Instead of acknowledging this interdependence, "the natural resistance of law" and "the natural density of the legal mind" had combined with the result that lawyers too often served the purposes of only one segment of modern society. The outcome was the development of "a class-conscious, paternalistic state, through which the ruling class coerces its subjects to live, to work, to pursue happiness, even if possible to think, as the ruling class in its superior wisdom deems desirable." Perhaps as a labor lawyer, Richberg might compensate for the "resistance to change inherent in the institutions for creating and enforcing the law."[3]

In many ways, the 1920s were an auspicious time for a man such

[3] Richberg, "The Fight against Ignorance," *Life and Labor* 8 (Feb. 1918): 32–34; Richberg, "The Key of Knowledge," A Paper Read before the Law Club of Chicago, Feb. 25, 1921, copy in Richberg Papers, L.C., Box 5; Richberg, "Developing Ethics and Resistant Law," *Yale Law Journal* 32 (Dec. 1922): 109–22.

as Donald Richberg, who dreamed of a business-labor common-wealth of cooperation. Unionism in the 1920s hit a low point, making labor leaders as a group more amenable to cooperating with businessmen rather than fighting them. Overall membership in the American Federation of Labor (AFL) declined, and several industries that might have been likely targets for unionization remained untouched by AFL organizers. As the decade progressed, the deteriorating position of labor was evident in the less frequent use of the strike as a bargaining weapon. There were several reasons for this: division within the ranks of a heterogeneous labor force; the prevalence of a social climate that viewed business approvingly; the expansion of new and as yet unorganized industries with antiunion managements; the growing obsolescence of craft unionism in the face of technological progress; company unions; welfare capitalism; and relative if uneven prosperity.

Yet the lack of militancy among many labor leaders was not simply the result of negative forces, but also grew out of a positive identification with the values of the business community itself. As the Republican party's slogan of the "New Era" permeated American society, so too it reached into the ranks of labor. For many historians, William Green, Samuel Gompers's successor as president of the AFL, was to become the symbol of the new respectability of the labor movement. As one student of the New Era described it, "With business supreme, the A. F. of L. sought to sell itself as a necessary auxiliary of business."[4] The time was ripe for Richberg's theories.

Richberg's opportunity was not long in coming. The railway shopmen's strike of 1922, which labor historian Irving Bernstein has called "the greatest strike of the decade," helped make Rich-

---

[4] Irving Bernstein, *The Lean Years: A History of the American Worker,* 1920–1933 (Boston, 1960), 83–108. For a sampling of Richberg's understanding of the desire of union leaders to cooperate with the business community, see Richberg to Henry J. Allen, June 15, 1922, Donald Richberg Papers, Chicago Historical Society, Box 1. Here Richberg expressed the opinion that "trade unionism, with its present limitations, is a passing phase," one to be superseded by an era of "co-operative and more democratic organization of industry."

berg one of the leading advocates of the labor movement in the United States.[5]

The shopmen's strike grew out of the railway labor unions' dissatisfaction with the rulings of the Railroad Labor Board, an agency of the federal government set up under the Transportation Act of 1920. The Transportation Act had returned the railroads to private management after the First World War, when as part of the war effort they had been taken over and operated by the United States Railroad Administration, headed by Secretary of the Treasury William Gibbs McAdoo. Because the government had been concerned with maintaining continuity of service to keep the flow of war material moving, the railway unions were able to win concessions over representation and bargaining rights on most of the nation's railroads. But the establishment of the Railroad Labor Board after the war inaugurated a series of rulings on wages and working conditions which the unions felt would reverse this favorable trend.

The Board's first decision, in July of 1920, resulted in wage increases for the shop employees (machinists, blacksmiths, boilermakers, sheet metal workers, electrical workers, and carmen), but soon the period of rapid inflation that followed the war turned into a short depression. The railroads began to dismiss shop and maintenance workers. Further, they applied to the Railroad Labor Board for a reduction in the wage scale. This was allowed in June of 1921, and in August the Board permitted the roads to change work rules governing overtime and special jobs, resulting in further wage cuts.

In addition, the shop crafts had another grievance—the railroads' practice of farming out repair work on their equipment to outside shops not governed by the Railroad Labor Board. In this way, the roads circumvented the standards established by the Board and further jeopardized the position of the railway unions. In December 1921 the shop crafts complained to the Railroad Labor Board; it ruled in their favor in May 1922, but the roads simply ignored the Board's decision. To the railway employees, the Board appeared to be a highly unsatisfactory instrument for maintaining peaceful in-

[5] Bernstein, *The Lean Years*, 211.

dustrial relations, one subservient to the demands of the roads but lackadaisical in effectuating the demands of labor.[6]

The last straw came in the spring of 1922. The roads applied for and were granted another wage reduction. The lowest paid and most poorly organized workers, the maintenance-of-way men and the shop crafts, suffered cuts, while the better-established transportation brotherhoods (such as engineers, firemen, conductors, trainmen, and switchmen) were spared any loss in earnings. The Railway Employees' Department, an organization of the shop crafts affiliated with the AFL (unlike the transportation brotherhoods, which were unaffiliated), appealed to the Railroad Labor Board for an immediate hearing. Instead, the Board scheduled a hearing for only four days before the effective date of the wage cuts. Thereupon, the Railway Employees' Department took a strike vote, and 400,000 members of the shop crafts walked out on July 1. The maintenance-of-way men, through the efforts of their president, secured a special hearing and a separate settlement, and so did not strike. The transportation brotherhoods also remained at work.[7]

Glenn Plumb's death in the summer of 1922 assured that Richberg would be a dominant figure in developments; his work representing the railway unions in valuation proceedings before the Interstate Commerce Commission was extended to a general representation of the shop crafts and the brotherhoods. Richberg worked closely with Bert Jewell, head of the Railway Employees' Department of the AFL, and other members of counsel for the shop crafts, Frank L. Mulholland and James S. Easby-Smith.[8]

Throughout July Benjamin Hooper, chairman of the Railroad Labor Board, and President Warren Harding attempted to get the strikers to return to work as the first step in negotiating a settlement, but the employees were adamant. To the strikers, the Railroad Labor Board still appeared to be management's agent, as when

[6] John R. Commons, ed., *History of Labor in the United States, 1896–1932*, Vol. 4: *Labor Movements*, by Selig Perlman and Philip Taft (New York, 1935), 515–18; Philip Taft, *The A. F. of L. in the Time of Gompers* (New York, 1957), 471–72.

[7] Commons, *History of Labor*, 4: 518–19; Richberg, *My Hero*, 115–16; Richberg, *Tents*, 125.

[8] Richberg, *Tents*, 130.

it demanded that they resume work by July 10 or suffer the loss of seniority rights. At the end of July, after threats had failed, Harding suggested a return to work while all issues were submitted to the Railroad Labor Board without prejudice to either side. The strikers were willing, but the railroad presidents demanded the cancellation of employees' seniority rights as the price of negotiations. Thenceforth, the strike issue ceased to be wages and instead became seniority; the original question had been superceded by one generated by the strike itself.[9]

In August, Harding renewed his efforts to convince the roads that they should relent, but they remained adamant on the seniority question. They felt that they had mastered the strike and need not compromise. The dispute entered a new phase, however, when United States Attorney General Harry Daugherty applied for a temporary restraining order on September 1 in the Chicago District Court of Judge James Wilkerson, a Harding appointee. His complaint charged that the shop craft strike was a criminal conspiracy in restraint of interstate commerce because the employees had no "legal right" to refuse to abide by the decisions of the Railroad Labor Board and because the strike evidenced "contempt for the United States and the government thereof." The very right of railway labor to strike was at stake.[10]

Though probably intended as the death sentence for what the managements regarded as a broken strike, the injunction evoked an immediate response from the shop unions. Richberg, prevented by the restraining order from communicating with his clients, moved to challenge the court, arguing that the strike was legal, that the attorney general obtained the order through fraud, and that a criminal trial was required in a criminal prosecution.[11]

[9] Commons, *History of Labor*, 4: 520–21; *The Case of the Railway Shopmen: A Brief Statement of Facts concerning the Controversies Which Precipitated the Strike* ([Washington, D. C.], 1922), 7–8.

[10] Commons, *History of Labor*, 4: 521–22; Jewell, J. F. McGrath, John Scott, W. H. Johnston, E. C. Davison, J. W. Kline, J. A. Franklin, J. J. Hynes, J. P. Noonan, M. F. Ryan to Richberg, Frank L. Mulholland, and James S. Easby-Smith, April 30, 1923, Richberg Papers, L.C., Box 41.

[11] Commons, *History of Labor*, 4: 521–22; Richberg, *My Hero*, 117; Richberg, *Tents*, 127; Taft, *A. F. of L. in the Time of Gompers*, 404–406.

Richberg was appalled at the government move. He felt that negotiations which had recently started with Daniel Willard of the Baltimore and Ohio and thirteen railroads were beginning to make headway. The injunction coming when it did could only mean that it was not intended to end the strike but to destroy organized labor on the roads. It immobilized the use of union funds, prohibited picketing and persuasion by any legitimate means, and closed off ordinary channels of communication through "letters, printed or other circulars, telegrams, telephones, word of mouth, oral persuasion, or suggestion, or through interviews to be published in newspapers or otherwise in any manner whatsoever."[12]

While incidents of violence had occurred throughout the strike and had provided the attorney general with an excuse for action, Richberg was keenly aware of the futility of contesting court orders against alleged criminal acts. He had convinced the union executives to urge their followers to avoid violence, as the unions were not prepared to defend every case of lawbreaking in support of the strike. Otherwise, union resources would be taxed beyond endurance. At one time, over three hundred suits were outstanding against the shop craft unions. Frank Mulholland and government attorneys had taken depositions on the various charges of violence against the unions throughout the country, and Richberg decided that there was sufficient evidence to sustain the government's case that unlawful action had been resorted to by many strikers. Arguing against injunctions to prevent violence was pointless, so Richberg convinced his clients not to contest the Daugherty injunction on such grounds. They would surely lose and the result would be a condemnatory opinion on the record, an opinion that might make trouble in the future.[13]

Developments in another case, *Pennsylvania Railroad Company v. United States Railroad Labor Board et al.* in early 1923 also rein-

[12] Richberg, *Tents*, 126–28; Richberg, *My Hero*, 117; Felix Frankfurter and Nathan Green, *The Labor Injunction* (New York, 1930), 62–63, 253–63.
[13] Richberg, *My Hero*, 116–19; Jewell, McGrath, Scott, Johnston, Davison, Kline, Franklin, Hynes, Noonan, Ryan to Richberg, Mulholland, and Easby-Smith, April 30, 1923, Richberg Papers, L.C., Box 41.

forced Richberg's argument that the unions should not carry the fight against the Daugherty injunction to a conclusion. The case involved a Board ruling that the Pennsylvania had violated the Transportation Act by establishing a company union and refusing to deal with the independent railway unions. The Supreme Court decision destroyed whatever power the Railroad Labor Board may have had for enforcing its rulings: "The jurisdiction of the [Railroad Labor] Board to direct the parties to do what it deems they should do is not to be limited by their constitutional or legal right to refuse to do it. Under the Act there is no constraint upon them to do what the Board decides they should do except the moral constraint . . . of publication of its decisions."[14]

While the Pennsylvania case terminated the Board's enforcing power, it also relieved the labor unions from obeying its rulings. The 1922 strike was consequently legal, and the attorney general could not obtain an injunction on the grounds that the unions had no legal right to refuse to obey the Board. The right to strike was secure. Since Richberg refused to question the right of the government to enjoin acts of violence, the virtual settling of the right to strike by the Pennsylvania suit left no further issues that the union leaders wanted tested in court. To the disappointment of the government attorneys, Richberg, Mulholland, and Easby-Smith all withdrew from the Daugherty injunction case in May 1923.[15]

The settlement that eventually emerged from the strike underlined the need for effective legislation governing labor relations on the railroads. Though the shopmen had inaugurated the walkout by demanding wage increases and an end to farming out, seniority rights subsequently became the main issue. The final settlement was concluded on a road-by-road basis, so that all strikers did not fare alike. About 225,000 returned to work with their seniority safe and their right to maintain independent unions intact. The other

[14] 261 U. S. 72 (1923). See Eliot Jones and Homer B. Vanderblue, *Railroads: Cases and Selections* (New York, 1925), 720–30.

[15] Jewell, McGrath, Scott, Johnston, Davison, Kline, Franklin, Hynes, Noonan, Ryan, to Richberg, Mulholland, and Easby-Smith, April 30, 1923, Richberg Papers, L.C., Box 41; Richberg, *My Hero*, 118; Taft, *A. F. of L. in the Time of Gompers*, 474.

175,000 were not so fortunate and for the most part found themselves herded into company unions.[16]

Incidental to the 1922 strike was a criminal contempt case which, in Richberg's words, "resulted in a landmark decision by the Supreme Court." A man by the name of Michaelson had been held in contempt of court for having violated an injunction issued during the shopmen's strike. Michaelson demanded trial by jury, but was refused despite the provision of the Clayton Antitrust Act that a man accused of violating an injunction by a criminal act committed outside the court was entitled to a jury trial. Unlike a civil contempt, the judge alone could not try such a case. Although the railway union executives had decided not to contest every case that arose from the numerous injunctions issued during the shopmen's strike, Richberg and his clients decided that the Michaelson case, involving trial by jury and the constitutionality of a federal law guaranteeing that right, was too important to let go by default. Richberg took the case to the Supreme Court, which sustained his distinction between a civil contempt, primarily remedial in nature and intended to bring about compliance with a court order, and a criminal contempt, primarily a punishment for crime and hence a subject for trial by jury. Being a criminal act, the offense required criminal proceedings, separate from the original case that gave rise to the contempt.[17]

There was a curious parallel between the shopmen's strike and a novel which Richberg had completed a year or so before the walkout began—A Man of Purpose. Here Richberg painted a romantic picture of the role of the lawyer in defending what were portrayed as the downtrodden laboring masses, voiceless without a spokesman like Richberg. The story revolved around the search of a young lawyer for some kind of meaning in life, for an answer to the question of whether the great reward lay in service to one's self or to the people generally. The climax came when Rodney Merrill, the hero, stood up in court to denounce an injunction issued by the judge, a man seeped in prejudice against the working

[16] Commons, History of Labor, 4: 522–23; Taft, A. F. of L. in the Time of Gompers, 474.

[17] 266 U. S. 42 (1924); Richberg, My Hero, 124–25.

classes—in this instance, striking miners. Merrill was held in contempt of court, but not before he had delivered a damning blow against judge-made law to become a martyr for justice.[18]

That Richberg identified with Rodney Merrill is clear from a more than coincidental conformity between the events of his own life and that of his leading character. Reviewers commonly saw this concurrence. Though Richberg denied it publicly, it was there, and he would admit it privately.[19] As he confided to Paxton Hibben, his old friend from Progressive Service days, "In some ways I am my principal character, and in some ways I am not." Richberg's design for *A Man of Purpose* was "to write the life of a man whose progress toward disillusionment had been sufficiently like mine so that I could be sure of the essential realism of the story and yet show his faith triumphant."[20]

A Man of Purpose represented an attempt by Richberg to formulate a consciously felt need to believe that he was serving the public welfare and that his work for the railway labor unions had an ethical value in its own right. A man with such a moralizing frame of mind as Richberg required this kind of justification. And the often melodramatic quality of the story reflected his romanticizing of this need.

For Richberg and the railway unions, the 1922 strike terminated the already questionable usefulness of the Railroad Labor Board. Some substitute arrangement for dealing with labor problems in the industry would have to be worked out. Richberg and his clients seized on this as an opportunity to shape the future conditions under which labor might work. For now, the right to strike was safe. The next step would be to safeguard the right of railway employees to form labor organizations of their own choos-

[18] Richberg, *A Man of Purpose* (New York, 1922), 295–304, 318.

[19] Morris Fishbein, Review of *A Man of Purpose*, by Richberg, *Chicago News*, Aug. 19, 1922; Review of *A Man of Purpose*, Richmond, Va., *Evening Dispatch*, April 22, 1922; Review of *A Man of Purpose*, Philadelphia *Record*, April 9, 1922; Richberg, *A Man of Purpose*, 328–29; Richberg to Thomas Y. Crowell Co., Feb. 4, 1922, and Richberg to Boetius H. Sullivan, April 11, 1922, Richberg Papers, c.h.s., Box 1.

[20] Richberg to Paxton Hibben, Jan. 17, 1922, Richberg Papers, c.h.s., Box 1.

ing, without interference from employers, and to secure the right to bargain collectively with management. This effort led to the Railway Labor Act of 1926, in which Richberg was to play a major part.

Work on what was to evolve into the Railway Labor Act began as soon as the outcome of the 1922 strike became clear in the fall. Richberg was convinced that the most practical way to fight the railroads was through legislation and not through the courts. In late 1923 Bert Jewell, president of the Railway Employees' Department of the AFL, sought Richberg's advice on instituting litigation against roads which set up company unions, but Richberg believed that such efforts would simply be a waste of time and money, neither of which the railway workers could afford to sacrifice. He foresaw little success in court action: "As the courts are at present constituted and influenced by outside opinion, they are the branch of Government most partisan in opposition to the claims of organized labor." The courts gave precedence to property rights over human rights. The wisest course was "political action in getting new laws made by the legislatures and obtaining executive support of such laws."[21]

After the 1922 strike broke up, a "Special Legislative Committee Representing the Recognized Railroad Labor Organizations" prepared a tentative outline of what railway labor wanted, and by February 7, 1923, its report was in the hands of Warren S. Stone, grand chief of the Brotherhood of Locomotive Engineers and a leading figure in advocating cooperation among the several rail unions. A meeting of union executives called by Stone considered the recommendations in June and then turned them over to Richberg and other railway union attorneys for revision. Samuel Gompers, president of the AFL, suggested action along lines similar to what the railway unions had in mind and encouraged their efforts to formulate a new law.[22]

[21] Richberg to Jewell, Dec. 9, 1923, cited in Jewell to Robertson, Dec. 11, 1923, Richberg Papers, C.H.S., Box 2.

[22] H. E. Wills, J. G. Luhrsen, J. J. Dermody, J. F. Anderson (Special Legislative Committee Representing the Recognized Railroad Labor Organizations) to Warren S. Stone, Feb. 7, 1923; Jewell to Richberg, June 18,

Richberg and David E. Lilienthal carried out most of the draft-ing of the railway unions' bill. Lilienthal was fresh out of Harvard Law School and had joined Richberg in August 1923. He came with the recommendation of Felix Frankfurter, law professor at Harvard and a future counselor of President Franklin Roosevelt. Richberg preferred to keep his office as small as possible; in fact, earlier in 1923 he had left his father's old firm to practice alone largely for this reason. But with Frankfurter's backing, Lilienthal was hired. At the beginning of his career, Lilienthal's principal in-terest was labor law, and after a thorough search of the oppor-tunities in the profession, he decided that working for Richberg would place him at the center of action.

Immediately recognizing Lilienthal's talents, Richberg put him to work researching and drafting the railway bill. He prepared material on industrial arbitration, mediation, and conciliation; on individual and collective employment contracts; and on court prece-dents and statute law dealing with labor organization.[23]

By late November, the Richberg revision was ready for submis-sion to the other attorneys of the railway unions, Oscar J. Horn, Frank L. Mulholland, Thomas M. Stevenson, and John M. Grimm. Though the draft represented the handiwork of Richberg and Lil-ienthal, Richberg was essentially following the wishes of the rail-way union executives themselves; as he reported, the draft was "in no sense the production of the attorneys, i.e., . . . they have not taken it upon themselves to revise the material submitted in any substantive way, but have merely sought to express the purposes

---

1923; Samuel Gompers to Richberg, Sept. 13, 1923, with draft of "Act Concerning the Granting of Injunctions" and "Act Concerning Labor Organizations"; Richberg to Gompers, Oct. 4, 1923, Richberg Papers, c.h.s., Box 2; Taft, *The A. F. of L. from the Death of Gompers to the Merger* (New York, 1959), 67–68.

[23] Richberg, *My Hero*, 126–28; Richberg to Donald H. Riddle, Feb. 3, 1949, Richberg Papers, l.c., Box 2; David E. Lilienthal, *The Journals of David E. Lilienthal*, Vol. 1: *The TVA Years, 1939–1945, Including a Selection of Journal Entries from the 1917–1939 Period* (New York, 1964), 14–16; Richberg to Robertson, Oct. 27, 1923; Lilienthal to John B. Andrews, Sept. 11, 1923; Lilienthal, "Material on Legislative Program," Nov. 13, 1923, Richberg Papers, c.h.s., Box 2.

of the executives in most apt form and manner and in such a way that the validity of the provisions proposed may be most effectively supported."[24]

The union executives and Richberg sought the active support of both management and the administration before bringing their proposal to the halls of Congress. Given the general labor situation in the 1920s, the railway unions could expect to accomplish little without the support of those outside its own ranks. The 1922 strike had proved that. Richberg consulted with Secretary of Commerce Herbert Hoover, both alone and in company with executives of the railway unions; he also was in contact with Samuel Gompers and AFL officials. The unions were most concerned about convincing Hoover that their proposal for national boards of adjustment was to be preferred to the roads' hope that regional boards would be established. Specifically, the unions hoped this would create uniform national rulings, thereby establishing national standards and spreading gains made by stronger unions to weaker ones. Additionally, national rather than regional boards would strengthen the standard railway unions as a whole in gaining general recognition as the representatives of the employees rather than localized company unions, due to the latter's restricted area of operation. The union executives would not yield to Hoover's proposals that the president be given special power to intervene in industrial disputes that threatened to create a national emergency in transportation. Consultations were also had with Secretary of Labor James J. Davis.

Perhaps the most important outcome of these consultations resulted when Secretary Hoover sought the cooperation of the railway presidents in working out some plan with the unions. But the railway presidents were adamant and refused to confer at all. The initiative thus remained with the railway labor executives assisted by Richberg, and there it stayed throughout the writing of the act. Despite Hoover's cooperativeness, the unions' bill did not gain administration support in Congress for another two years.[25]

[24] Richberg to Robertson, Nov. 28, 1923, Richberg Papers, C.H.S., Box 2.
[25] "Memorandum of Legal Services of Donald R. Richberg," Dec. 1923; Robertson to Richberg, Dec. 29, 1923; Richberg to Robertson, Jan. 17, 1924, Richberg Papers, C.H.S., Box 2; Bernstein, *The Lean Years*, 219–20;

Once the bill was ready, Richberg took it to Senator Robert La Follette of Wisconsin and others for counsel on legislative strategy. On the advice of La Follette, who had a longstanding interest in rail legislation, especially on matters of ratemaking and valuation, Richberg and the railway union executives, aided by Gompers and other AFL leaders, decided to ask Senator Robert Howell of Nebraska and Congressman Alben Barkley of Kentucky to introduce the bill into the first session of the Sixty-eighth Congress. Both Howell and Barkley promised the closest cooperation with the railway unions in fighting for the new legislation and introduced the bill in their respective chambers on February 28, 1924.[26]

Hearings in the Senate began promptly before the Committee on Interstate Commerce. Richberg and David B. Robertson, president of the Brotherhood of Locomotive Firemen and Enginemen and the successor to Warren Stone as the leader of cooperative ventures by the rail unions, presented the workers' case. Robertson concentrated on the practical questions involving working conditions on the roads; Richberg, as counsel for the brotherhoods and shopmen, outlined the legal aspects of proposed legislation.[27]

In brief, the draft bill provided machinery for settling disputes arising out of both the negotiation of new agreements and the application of old agreements. The disputants first would hold conferences among themselves; these failing, they might turn to a Mediation Board; if the Board failed, it might recommend voluntary arbitration. In addition, the unions sought nationwide Boards

---

"Progress of the Howell-Barkley Bill to Date: Report of Sub-Committee of Chief Executives of Railway Labor Organizations Supporting the Howell-Barkley Bill, Dated February 16, 1925, to be Submitted for Consideration of Meeting of Chief Executives in Chicago, Feb. 20, 1925," Richberg Papers, C.H.S., Box 4.

[26] Richberg, *My Hero*, 128; Robertson to Richberg, Feb. 26, 1924; Robertson to Richberg, Feb. 27, 1924; Robertson to Richberg, Feb. 28, 1924, Richberg Papers, C.H.S., Box 3; "Progress of the Howell-Barkley Bill to Date"; Taft, *A. F. of L. from the Death of Gompers*, 67–69.

[27] Richberg to Robertson, March 8, 1924, Richberg Papers, C.H.S., Box 3; U. S., Congress, Senate, 68th Cong., 1st sess., Committee on Interstate Commerce, *Arbitration between Carriers and Employees: Boards of Adjustment*, Hearings on S. 2646 (1924), 1–29.

of Adjustment especially to assist negotiations over grievances concerning the application of agreements; these Boards would include members nominated by the standard railway unions and would be invoked before such disputes went to the Mediation Board, which it was anticipated would devote most of its energies to new contract negotiations rather than disputes over the enforcement of established contracts.[28]

In defending the bill before the Senate committee, Richberg indicated that there was no ultimate weapon of enforcement "except general condemnation and public opposition" against a recalcitrant. While apparently unrealistic in its lack of an effective enforcing power, anything stronger would have stood no chance of winning the support of the roads.[29]

In fact, the unions were forced to compromise on the use of the strike as a weapon in order to win management support before the bill eventually passed. The final draft of 1926 contained a provision for an Emergency Board appointed by the president upon the recommendation of the Board of Mediation in cases where negotiations had broken down and where a substantial interruption of interstate commerce was threatened. The Board's function was simply to investigate the dispute and report back within thirty days. Most important, both employers and employees would be obliged not to change the conditions of work or resort to a lockout or strike during the investigation, or for thirty days after the Emergency Board's report. Irving Bernstein has picked out this provision as "the main price the unions paid for employer support of the statute." But the Wilkerson injunction in the 1922 shopmen's strike had shown that the unions could not stand alone in an industrial dispute without some way of marshaling support from either management or government; hopefully the draft bill would do this, so its passage was worth a high price.[30]

[28] David E. Lilienthal, "A Practical Plan for Railroad Peace" [March 1924], Richberg Papers, c.h.s., Box 3; Robertson to Richberg, Dec. 8, 1923, Richberg Papers, c.h.s., Box 2.

[29] Senate Committee on Interstate Commerce, *Arbitration between Carriers and Employees*, 1924, 20.

[30] Bernstein, *The Lean Years*, 218–19.

Richberg's congressional testimony emphasized that the proposed legislation represented no great departure from former collective bargaining procedures on the railways as developed up to the time of the Transportation Act of 1920. He pursued this argument even though the bill took the unusual step of empowering the standard railway unions to participate in nominating members of the Adjustment Boards, a provision which would have had important implications for union recognition had it not been eliminated from the final bill in 1926. Nevertheless, Richberg estimated "that approximately 90 percent of the contents of the bill is a transcription or adaptation of existing law and that the small portion which may be described as 'new' consists largely of improvements in detail, the desirability of which has been shown by experience under existing laws." The unions had based their proposals on earlier attempts to set up mediation or arbitration machinery as tried out in the Erdman Act of 1898 and the Newlands Act of 1913. Richberg often reiterated that the unions' bill represented no radical departure from past experience.

The weak bargaining position of railway labor and the faith of people such as Richberg in cooperation as the only way to mutually satisfactory and enduring labor agreements was reflected in the bill's provisions imposing a duty on both labor and management to "exert every reasonable effort to make and maintain agreements concerning rates of pay, rules, and working conditions, and to settle all disputes . . . arising out of the application of said agreements or otherwise." The burden of this obligation was to require parties subject to the bill to avail themselves of all the machinery provided for conference, mediation, and voluntary arbitration before resorting to lockouts or strikes. More concretely, thirty days notice was required before either party could seek changes in agreements, thus avoiding arbitrary and summary changes in working conditions, sudden discharge of workers, or a strike without warning. Negotiations hopefully would be under way before old agreements expired. This might obviate the one-sided power of employers to impose changes in wages and work conditions under threat of discharge, a situation that had repeatedly come to the attention of the Railroad Labor Board through complaints by the unions prior to the 1922 strike. Now at least employer and employee would talk things over first.

Fundamental to the unions' position, of course, were the bill's guarantees that workers would be free to organize their own unions without interference from employers. Both sides were to select their own representatives for bargaining purposes "without interference, influence, or coercion exercised by either party over the self-organization or designation of representatives by the other." Nevertheless, there was no denying the perilous health of the trade union movement in the 1920s, so that the goal of the rail workers was in fact of a limited nature; they did not seriously expect to make the standard rail unions the exclusive bargaining agent for workers on the roads. Though employers might not interfere with worker organization, Richberg explained during the congressional hearings that the bill "imposes no obligation upon a railroad to maintain what is called a 'closed shop'; it grants no special privileges to any particular labor organization; it leaves all railroad employees just as free as railroad managements to select their own representatives and to enter into agreements with full liberty of contract." Thus did the New Era define the upper limits of union power. By recognizing these limits, the union executives and Richberg hoped to gain the support of management and of the Republican administration, without which little could be expected in the way of legislation.

In sum, Richberg described the bill as "essentially a codification of industrial law for the railroads. It is not a radical or even a novel piece of legislation." But his assertion that "the act is drawn on the theory that nothing is accomplished in matters of this kind by attempting to swing a club, except the compulsion to live up to the agreement and to make agreements," was really an inadvertent confession that the railway labor unions were helpless unless management could be won over.[31]

For the time being management did not appear amicable. The railway presidents conducted a publicity campaign which misrep-

[31] Senate Committee on Interstate Commerce, *Arbitration between Carriers and Employees*, 1924, 17–21, 24–25. For the text of the act as passed in 1926, see U. S., *Statutes at Large* (1926), 44:577.

resented the proposed legislation and the motives of the unions in presenting it. They claimed that the bill had been prepared without public discussion or consultation with the presidents of the roads, a blatant distortion of Secretary Hoover's attempts to get them to confer with the union leaders. The notion was spread that the public was unrepresented in the new machinery for settling disputes, whereas in reality more rather than less public representation was provided for as compared with the railroad-supported Transportation Act of 1920. The chief executives of the railway unions regarded the roads' publicity campaign as of a "purely destructive obstructive character"; they accused the railroad presidents of offering "no constructive suggestions for improvement of the measure, although they presented no criticism of the fundamental principles actually underlying the bill."[32]

Although the Senate committee reported the bill favorably, no action was possible in the House, so that Barkley and Richberg decided not to press the matter at that session of Congress. It was hoped that the groundwork laid in the first session of the Sixty-eighth Congress would prepare the way for something more constructive in the second session.[33]

While the railway unions were waging battle in Congress on behalf of their legislative program, the Railroad Labor Board, still functioning under the authority of the Transportation Act, once again discredited itself as far as the employee organizations were concerned. In 1924, the railway engineers and firemen on forty-three western railroads sought separate conferences with the several managements to negotiate pay increases commensurate with those in effect on the eastern roads. Management suggested consolidating the negotiations and holding a joint conference between representatives of all the roads and of all the unions. But when the conference was held, the employees found that the management

[32] "Progress of the Howell-Barkley Bill to Date"; Lilienthal to Edward Keating, April 22, 1924; Robertson to Chief Executives, May 4, 1924; Richberg to Walter Lippmann, May 8, 1924; Richberg to Editor, New York *Sun*, May 8, 1924, Richberg Papers, C.H.S., Box 3; Richberg, "Railway Publicity Agents Poison Public Opinion," *Labor*, Dec. 13, 1924, 2, 4.

[33] "Progress of the Howell-Barkley Bill to Date"; Richberg, *My Hero*, 128–29.

representatives were not authorized to make binding agreements; they simply sought concessions and then planned to refer the workers back to the individual roads for separate negotiations. Though the management representatives had not negotiated in good faith in accordance with the Transportation Act, the Railroad Labor Board attempted to intervene to force a settlement. The employee organizations, represented by Richberg in test cases requiring the appearance of union officials before the Board, challenged the Board's action because it had the effect of "aiding the railroads in refusing to hold conferences as required by the Transportation Act." Furthermore, the Board's decision would not have been binding in any case, nor enforceable in the courts. Richberg's contentions were eventually upheld, though not before the Railroad Labor Board had once again made itself appear to be the partisan agent of the carriers and completely unacceptable to the workers' organizations.[34]

The second session of the Sixty-eighth Congress saw little progress for the employees' legislative program. Richberg prepared propaganda on behalf of the bill and worked to counteract unfavorable management publicity in the press. Between sessions, the Republican, Democratic, and Progressive party conventions had all endorsed revision of the Transportation Act along lines suggested by the railway unions. The president's message to Congress of December 3, 1924, backed efforts to obtain new legislation, although it did not specifically endorse the Howell-Barkley bill. Consequently, Richberg and the union officers took the opportunity for further consultation with the administration, and several conferences took place with Secretary of Commerce Hoover and Senator Albert B. Cummins, president pro tem of the Senate, in which

[34] "Summary of Statement Made to U. S. Railroad Labor Board of Position of Employes in Regard to Docket No. 4055—Hearing July 24, 1924"; "Outline of Argument for Respondents," *Railroad Labor Board* v. *D. B. Robertson*, and *Railroad Labor Board* v. *J. McGuire*, District Court of the United States, Northern District of Illinois, Eastern Division, all in Richberg Papers, c.h.s., Box 3; "Material for the Report of the Executive Committee of the American Federation of Labor on the Howell-Barkley Bill and Developments Concerning the Railroad Labor Board, 1924–1925," 2–6, Richberg Papers, c.h.s., Box 4; Lilienthal, *Journals*, 1:15.

the cooperation of the railroad presidents was sought—again without success. Indeed, on November 19, 1924, the Association of Railroad Executives had declared "that there is no condition existing today which calls for any urgent legislative action by Congress with respect to the railroads, either as to rates, labor relationship, or valuation."

There was no action on the bill in the Senate, though Senator Howell wanted to present it as an amendment to other legislation in February 1925. In the House, Congressman Barkley once again decided not to press the matter in view of additional attempts to obtain the cooperation of the railroad executives. Further, promoters of the bill thought it would be a tactical error to force consideration in view of the congested calendar and the shortness of the second session, which was to end March 4, 1925. Consequently, the union executives had to be content with the knowledge "that a general understanding of the uselessness and menacing qualities of the Railroad Labor Board now prevails at least in Congress, if not with the public at large."[35]

Although the labor organizations were not hopeful of obtaining negotiations with the railroads for several months after the Sixty-eighth Congress ended, events were moving toward just such a meeting. Throughout this period, Colonel Alfred P. Thom, general counsel of the railroad presidents, kept in touch with Richberg, Howell, and Barkley. He was persuaded that the atmosphere in Congress was favorable to doing away with the Transportation Act and substituting new legislation, and that the roads ought to cooperate in preparing a bill in their own self-interest. His point of view carried weight among the railroad presidents, and the Executive Committee of the Association of Railroad Executives finally appointed a committee on March 20, 1925, "for the purpose of taking up the whole labor situation." By the beginning of the summer, the executives through W. W. Atterbury, president of the

[35] "Progress of the Howell-Barkley Bill to Date"; "Memorandum of Howell-Barkley Bill Progress, Feb. 1–20, 1925"; "Memorandum of Suggestions for Program for Howell-Barkley Bill," Chicago, Nov. 5, 1924; Jewell and Richberg, press release, Washington, D. C., Dec. 5, 1924; Jewell to Richberg, Dec. 6, 1924, Richberg Papers, c.h.s., Box 4.

Pennsylvania Railroad and a member of the special committee, suggested to union leaders that conferences on the proposed legislation would be agreeable to management.

This was the opportunity that the chief executives of the employee organizations had been waiting for. Gathering in Washington on July 27–28, they authorized the conferences with management. The initial meeting on August 13 resulted in the formation of a subcommittee of employee and management representatives to draw up the outlines of a bill that both sides could support. The point of departure in these talks was the Howell-Barkley bill presented by the railway unions in the Sixty-eighth Congress. Neither Thom nor Richberg participated in person, though both were "invisibly present," as Richberg described it. The matters discussed contained broad policy implications, something that the men themselves had to decide. They did not want lawyers to solve their problems for them, but merely to implement their decisions. Meetings continued throughout the fall and winter, so that on December 3, the chief executives of the employee organizations met in Washington and approved the principles of the agreed-upon draft, and the railroad presidents followed suit on December 21. The labor executives approved the bill unanimously, and the railroad executives assented 199 votes (cast by 52 carriers) to 48 votes (cast by 20 carriers).[36]

Even before the railroad presidents gave their formal approval on December 21, the conferees decided to report to the White House the progress being made, so that President Calvin Coolidge could recommend the bill in his annual message to Congress. This he did, pointing out that the bill deserved support because it was the result of a joint effort and therefore offered a firm foundation for labor peace in the railroad industry.

The final touches were put on the bill in a conference between Colonel Thom, with representatives of the railroad presidents, and Richberg, with representatives of the employee organizations, held

[36] "Report of Sub-Committee on Passage of Railway Labor Act: Report to Chief Executives of Railway Labor Organizations for Consideration at Their Meeting in Washington, May 17, 1926," 1–3, Richberg Papers, c.h.s., Box 5; Jewell, "Memoranda," Chicago, Ill., Aug. 19, 1925, Richberg Papers, c.h.s., Box 4; Richberg, *My Hero,* 129.

January 5–6, 1926. James A. Emery, general counsel for the National Association of Manufacturers, was allowed to appear before the meeting and made a last-ditch effort to talk the roads out of supporting a compromise bill. He offered amendments which the employee representatives regarded as crippling, but the management representatives were not swayed by his efforts to prevent an agreement.[37]

The joint bill differed from the ideal desired by the employees and first set forth in the Howell-Barkley bill in that it provided for an Emergency Board to intervene in the event of a failure to agree and if in the opinion of the Board of Mediation the dispute threatened a substantial interruption of interstate commerce. This was the Board appointed by the president to investigate and report on unresolved disputes; during the investigation and for thirty days thereafter, management was not to change the conditions of work and labor was not to strike. The workers thus paid the price of restricting their right to strike in order to win the support of the carriers for new legislation. Further, Boards of Adjustment to handle grievances over the application of agreements were to "be created by agreement between any carrier or group of carriers, or the carriers as a whole, and its or their employees." While this left the way open for the formation of national Boards as the unions desired, it also provided a loophole whereby regional or system Boards might be established, as the railroads wanted. Simply by failing to agree, the railroads could prevent the formation of national Adjustment Boards; none were set up by the act itself. Further, the bill permitted disputants to create any *ad hoc* negotiating arrangements they desired; they were not forced to utilize the machinery provided in the act, but only to make a reasonable effort to negotiate in some manner. Irving Bernstein has called this last provision "the capstone of the carriers' victory." Otherwise, in essentials the bill conformed to that outlined in the measure presented by Senator Howell and Congressman Barkley in the Sixty-eighth Congress.[38]

In order to avoid any unnecessary antagonisms, Richberg and

[37] "Report of Sub-Committee on Passage of Railway Labor Act: Report to Chief Executives . . . May 17, 1926," 3–4; Richberg, *Tents,* 184–85.

[38] U. S., *Statutes at Large* (1926), 44:577; Lilienthal, "A Practical Plan for Railroad Peace"; Bernstein, *The Lean Years,* 218–20.

the union executives agreed that the new bill should be turned over to Senator James Watson and Congressman James S. Parker to be introduced in their respective chambers of Congress. Watson and Parker were the chairmen of the committees that would have to hold hearings and recommend the bill to the House and Senate. Turning the bill over to them would smooth the way for approval, as the railroads had vigorously fought Howell and Barkley on the earlier version.[39]

In the hope of clearing away the last remnants of opposition, Richberg and Colonel Thom met with President Coolidge to remove his lingering doubts about giving unreserved support to the compromise measure. Coolidge was impressed with the objections voiced by some holdout railroads and by the National Association of Manufacturers (NAM). He urged Richberg and Thom to accept the NAM's amendments. Thom was willing, but Richberg held out on the grounds that the draft bill was the joint product of the railroads and the workers. To change the bill now meant disturbing the understanding that had been achieved and giving the roads an excuse for not cooperating in its enforcement. Coolidge finally yielded to this argument, albeit reluctantly. With support from both management and labor, the bill passed through Congress expeditiously, the House approving 381 to 13 and the Senate 69 to 13, and Coolidge signed the Railway Labor Act into law on May 20.[40]

For Richberg, the Railway Labor Act of 1926 marked one of the high points of his entire career. Forever after he would take a benevolent, fatherly interest in its application and amendment, whether or not he was directly involved. Yet his role in both its

[39] "Report of Sub-Committee on Passage of Railway Labor Act: Report to Chief Executives . . . May 17, 1926," 4–5; Richberg, *My Hero*, 129–30.

[40] Richberg, *My Hero*, 130–32; Bernstein, *The Lean Years*, 216; "Report of Sub-Committee on Passage of Railway Labor Act: Report to Chief Executives . . . May 17, 1926," 1, 5–22; U. S., Congress, House, 69th Cong., 1st sess., Committee on Interstate and Foreign Commerce, *Railroad Labor Disputes*, Hearings on H. R. 7180 (1926); U. S., Congress, Senate, 69th Cong., 1st sess., Committee on Interstate Commerce, *Railway Labor Act* (1926), 2 vols.

passage and in the 1922 shopmen's strike, which had inspired the bill, was that of the behind-the-scenes technician, subordinate to the union executives. This was the role that Richberg had cultivated, for it offered him the opportunity to turn his technical competence in the law to the service of a cause he believed in. Although not directly possessing power himself, Richberg found that his work as general counsel of the railway labor executives enabled him to exercise it by proxy. He was their agent, but his ideas carried weight with the union executives as well.

The noncoercive character of the Railway Labor Act was indicative of the concurrence between Richberg's views and those of the labor executives. Richberg's opportunity came about because the weak condition of labor in the 1920s precluded a more forceful measure and because union leaders, caught up in the business ethic of the New Era, were receptive to cooperative ventures between management and labor. They were ready to listen to what Richberg had to say. As far as the Railway Labor Act was concerned, Richberg got what he wanted.

From the personal standpoint, and despite the discouragements of many long-drawn-out court and legislative battles, Donald Richberg's days as a labor lawyer were among the most satisfying of his entire career. Again he seemed to have found a way of harmonizing his career situation with his personal psychic and intellectual needs. Though he had his complaints, Richberg's contentment with his work seemed greater than at any other time of his life. He threw himself into his job, with its defeats as well as victories, and enjoyed every minute of it. It seemed to provide the right mixture of martyrdom and security, of struggle and triumph, to sustain his need to do battle for the public welfare. The struggle provided a test of his dedication; the triumph vindicated his rightness. These were years of hard work, but they also had their moments of glory, and both elements—for Richberg—were vital. For the next decade, he immersed himself in the work of the railway labor organizations so that the story of Donald Richberg in the 1920s is almost exclusively the story of his labor battles.

CHAPTER IV

Empire-Building

Just as the shopmen's strike had led to agitation for new railroad legislation to replace the Transportation Act of 1920, so too the Railway Labor Act of 1926 inspired a further development in the organization of railroad labor. By joining together, the shop crafts and the transportation brotherhoods had been able to destroy the Railroad Labor Board and secure passage of the Railway Labor Act —objectives that each union working separately could never have realized. The lesson was not lost on Richberg; the informal alliances that had carried out the shopmen's strike and worked for new legislation must be formalized in a more permanent organization consolidating the resources of all the rail unions. Making the Railway Labor Act work and defending it from the courts was an ongoing job that required continuous surveillance and resources beyond the capabilities of any one union. What once could be done through informal, single-issue alliances must now be done through permanent institutions.

Richberg's efforts, combined with the momentum created by the success of the rail unions' past joint ventures, culminated in the founding of the Railway Labor Executives' Association (RLEA) in August 1926. Though such a development was the logical outcome of the unions' recent cooperative activities, it nevertheless required someone like Richberg to cement the relationship. Despite the proved benefits of association, each union remained jealous of its own autonomy, but largely through Richberg's efforts, they "finally worked out the scheme of a council of executives who could work out uniform policies which they would then persuade their organizations to follow." As Richberg later told it, "The major factor that led to the creation of R.L.E.A. was my insistence on the necessity for uniform, or at least harmonious handling of disputes and litigation by the organizations under the Railway Labor Act."[1]

Prior to the founding of the RLEA as a permanent, multi-issue alliance, there had been a few attempts to create formal organizations of all the railway unions, but except for the Railway Employees' Department of the AFL, made up of only the shop crafts, these ventures were primarily single-issue or political projects. The AFL did try to bring the transportation brotherhoods into the Railway Employees' Department, but never succeeded in winning their loyalty. The AFL came closest to success in 1919, when the brotherhoods applied for affiliation, but shortly thereafter they withdrew their application on the grounds that they did not wish to surrender autonomy in railroad matters. Though resentful of the brotherhoods' aloofness, Samuel Gompers and the AFL acquiesced in this separatism and made no attempt to set up dual unions or otherwise challenge the brotherhoods' jurisdiction. Of the organizations created prior to the RLEA, the two most important that Richberg had something to do with were the National Conference on Valuation of American Railroads and the Conference for Progressive Political Action.[2]

Sponsored by Senator Robert La Follette, Sr., of Wisconsin and the railway unions, the National Conference on Valuation of American Railroads was founded May 26, 1923. Its purpose was to lobby for a valuation by the Interstate Commerce Commission of the capital investment in the nation's railroad system. The La Follette Valuation Act of 1913 and the Transportation Act of 1920, both amending the Interstate Commerce Act, had directed the ICC to determine the original investment and the cost of reproduction at current prices of all railroads and to use these findings as a base for regulating rates so as to allow a return on capital of approxi-

[1] Donald Richberg, "Memorandum for Mr. Levy," May 19, 1952, Donald Richberg Papers, Library of Congress, Box 44.

[2] Philip Taft, The A. F. of L. in the Time of Gompers (New York, 1957), 462–67.

mately 6 percent. While the Commission had produced the information on reproduction cost, it encountered difficulties in uncovering the original cost, owing to incomplete records, stock-watering, and obstruction by the roads, which hoped to see reproduction cost made the exclusive base for setting rates. When Richberg became involved in the work of the Valuation Conference, he estimated that if the railroads' view prevailed, they would be valued at least $10 billion more than the probable estimates of building them in the first place. According to his figures, this would mean an increase in passenger and freight rates totaling a minimum of $550 million each year.[3]

Actually, it was Glenn Plumb and not Richberg who had first interested the railway unions in working for lower rates and profits and supporting Senator La Follette's attempts to have the ICC carry out the valuation of the nation's railroads. After the First World War, when Plumb became involved in promoting his plan for public ownership of the railway system, Richberg had taken over the work of representing the unions before the ICC. After Plumb's death in 1922, he had emerged as the railway organizations' foremost attorney—especially after the shopmen's strike. Thus, when the unions along with Senator La Follette and other sponsors decided in 1923 to expand the base of support for their campaign by creating the Valuation Conference, Richberg was made general counsel of the new organization.[4]

Richberg's job was to go before the ICC on behalf of the Conference and work for full compliance with the Valuation Act. The ICC allowed Richberg to appear in a number of valuation proceedings and argue the position of the Valuation Conference. At the outset of his campaign, Richberg was optimistic that eventually a

---

[3] Donald Richberg, *My Hero: The Indiscreet Memoirs of an Eventful but Unheroic Life* (New York, 1954), 120–21; Richberg, *Tents of the Mighty* (New York, 1930), 146–47; Belle Case La Follette and Fola La Follette, *Robert M. La Follette, June 14, 1855–June 18, 1925* (New York, 1953), 2:1070; U. S., *Statutes at Large* (1913), 37:701, and (1920), 41:456, 488–91; Richberg, "Railroad Valuation and the Public," *The Locomotive Engineers Journal* 57 (June 1923): 455–57, 460.

[4] Richberg, *My Hero*, 112–15, 119–21; Richberg, *Tents*, 141–50, 153.

majority of the ICC would support the Conference position. Hence, his activities initially were restricted to participating in pending valuation proceedings before the ICC itself, rather than resorting immediately to court action. Eventually, however, Richberg's work did culminate in a landmark case in the United States Supreme Court—the St. Louis and O'Fallon Railroad case. But that was some years in the future. At the beginning, Richberg had good grounds for hoping that the ICC would be favorably disposed to his point of view, and so he proceeded cautiously.

More helpful than court action to compel the ICC to evaluate original cost, in Richberg's opinion, would have been additional legislation from Congress directing the Commission to undertake the project despite the obstacles set up by the roads. Richberg worked with La Follette on this problem, and the senator introduced a bill in 1924 to strengthen the valuation and ratemaking sections of the Interstate Commerce Act. In addition, Richberg undertook a publicity campaign designed to reach the general public on behalf of the original cost theory, and to counteract railroad propaganda in favor of reproduction cost. He felt that any possible legislation would have to depend on an informed public for support, and regarded the legislative and publicity aspects of his valuation work as intimately related. Nonetheless, in the end it was Richberg's legal endeavors that consumed most of his energy and proved to be most significant.[5]

The issue of reproduction cost versus original cost was squarely presented in the O'Fallon case. The ICC sued the St. Louis and

[5] Richberg, "Work of National Conference on Valuation of American Railroads from Its Organization May 26, 1923, to January 1, 1924," Report to Robert M. La Follette, Chairman, Executive Committee, National Conference on Valuation of American Railroads, Richberg Papers, L.C., Box 44. Examples of Richberg's publicity efforts are Richberg, "Railroad Valuation and the Public," 455–57, 460; Richberg, "The Great National Railroad Swindle: Gift, Graft, Guarantee," Address to the Conference for Progressive Political Action, St. Louis, Mo., Feb. 12, 1924, Richberg Papers, L.C., Box 19; Richberg, "Labor's Investment in Public Utilities," *Public Affairs*, March 1925, 15–16. Also see Richberg to the Editor, Chicago *Evening Post*, Jan. 18, 1924, Donald Richberg Papers, Chicago Historical Society, Box 3.

O'Fallon Railroad, a nine-mile coal-bearing line, for excessive profits allegedly collected over the 6 percent allowed by law. According to the Transportation Act of 1920, such excess profits were to be collected by the ICC and used to assist roads operating at a loss. The O'Fallon, however, maintained that its profits had not been excessive, on the grounds that the proper base for figuring valuation was primarily reproduction cost; using such a base, its profits did not even come up to the 6 percent allowed. The ICC, it claimed, had given undue weight to original cost in valuing its property and hence found its profits to be over 6 percent. Recognizing the case as a clear-cut presentation of the issues, one which would not be decided on technical rather than constitutional grounds, the Valuation Conference backed Richberg in defending the ICC valuation, while many of the nation's railroads united behind the O'Fallon defense against the original cost theory.

At the ICC hearing in July 1926 Richberg was the only representative to appear on behalf of the Commission's valuation, while approximately one hundred and fifty attorneys were present in defense of the railroad. The ICC's chief counsel had asked to be excused from the case; his assistant did speak in favor of the original cost theory, but in an independent and not an official capacity. At stake was billions of dollars, depending on which theory of valuation was upheld. To the dismay of the roads, the ICC upheld Richberg's arguments in a six-to-four decision, handed down February 15, 1927. The O'Fallon then took the case to the courts.[6]

In the meantime, Richberg lobbied for a congressional investigation into the whole matter of rate regulation and valuation. He suggested to Senator George W. Norris of Nebraska, who had succeeded La Follette as head of the National Valuation Conference, that plans for a government-sponsored transportation system be prepared as an aid in estimating the value of the nation's railroads; the concept was similar to the yardstick theory later utilized

---

[6] Richberg, *My Hero*, 121–22; Hugh Russell Fraser, "One Man Beats 150," *The Outlook* 145 (Oct. 5, 1927): 149–52. William F. Allen, "How One Man Single Handed Fought 'The Greatest Lawsuit in History,'" St. Louis *Post-Dispatch*, June 12, 1927.

by the Tennessee Valley Authority in competing with private electric power companies. Richberg did not actually envision setting
up a public transportation system, at least not in the foreseeable future, but suggested the idea as a way to "tear to pieces the valuation theories now being advanced by the railroads." The result
would make public ownership unnecessary: "If the cry were once
raised that a national transportation system should be constructed
and estimates were obtained of the cost, we would see a voluntary
reduction in the valuation of the railroads begin with a haste indicating panic." Norris, as one of a small group of progressives in
the Senate, was unable to undertake the project because he was already committed to a number of equally compelling causes. The
brunt of the battle would have to be borne by Richberg and the
Valuation Conference in the Supreme Court.[7]

Norris was able, however, to render limited assistance. Because
of a division within the ICC over the reproduction cost theory and
the original cost theory, the Commission was unable to agree upon
Richberg as its counsel in the O'Fallon case when it went to the
courts. As the successful defender of the ICC valuation in the original hearings, he would have been a logical choice, but was excluded because of the difference of opinion in the Commission.
The ICC selected Walter Fisher, former secretary of the interior
under President William Howard Taft, as its representative. Richberg petitioned the district court to allow him to intervene on behalf of the Valuation Conference, as it had been a party to the
original proceedings before the ICC, but the court would only allow
him to submit a brief; he did not participate in the oral arguments.
As a result, Richberg anticipated grave obstacles in gaining the right
to participate in the Supreme Court, especially since the O'Fallon
attorneys were opposed to his intervening. The case was scheduled
for the Court's October 1928 term.[8]

[7] Richberg to George W. Norris, Nov. 29, 1926; Norris to Richberg, Dec.
1, 1926; Richberg to Norris, Dec. 3, 1926; Norris to Richberg, Dec. 19,
1926, George W. Norris Papers, Library of Congress, Tray 8, Box 8.

[8] Richberg, *My Hero*, 122–23; Richberg to Norris, March 20, 1928,
Norris Papers, Tray 8, Box 8.

Fearing the worst, Richberg turned to Norris with a suggestion that the senator circulate a letter to be signed by members of the Congress urging the Court to hear Richberg. Norris was receptive to the idea, and soon it snowballed from a letter by concerned congressmen into an official Senate resolution. Richberg later related that it was Senator Burton Wheeler of Montana who first put forth the idea of a resolution. Though Richberg himself had raised the idea of bringing pressure on the Court, his original proposal did not contemplate official congressional action; he did not want to be put in the position of publicly forcing himself on the Supreme Court. Nevertheless, the Senate adopted the resolution on May 7, 1928, by a vote of forty-six to thirty-one after a debate in which the opposition challenged the propriety of congressional advice to the Supreme Court. Privately, Richberg was flattered.[9]

Though Richberg later asserted—at least for the public record —that he had been embarrassed by the idea of a Senate resolution on his behalf, he did feel that there was a precedent for such action and provided Norris with arguments to use in defending his recommendation to the Court. In brief, Richberg maintained that he was defending the legislature's prerogative, explicitly acknowledged by the courts, to determine public policy through agencies of its own creation, such as the ICC. Ratemaking and valuation were clearly matters of public policy, not subject to determination by judicial fiat. Therefore, the Senate had a direct interest in the O'Fallon proceedings and would be justified in asking the Court to hear a representative on its behalf. Richberg cited *Myers, Administratrix, v. United States* (272 U. S. 52, 65–88, 176–77 [1926]), where the Court itself had once sought representation from the Senate in a case involving the legislature's policymaking prerogatives.[10]

[9] Richberg to Norris, March 20, 1928; Norris to Richberg, March 26, 1928; Richberg to Norris, March 28, 1928; Richberg to [Norris], May 6, 1928, Norris Papers, Tray 8, Box 8; Richberg, *My Hero*, 122–23; Richberg, *Tents*, 154; U. S., *Congressional Record*, 70th Cong., 1st sess., 69, pt. 7: 7856–57, 7950–59; Chicago *Daily Tribune*, May 8, 1928.

[10] Richberg, *My Hero*, 123; Richberg to [Norris], May 6, 1928, Norris Papers, Tray 8, Box 8. See also Richberg, *Brief in Behalf of the National*

Richberg filed his petition to intervene, and the Supreme Court granted it, allowing him equal time with other supporters of the ICC valuation. Whether the Court had been persuaded by the Senate resolution or some other factor cannot be determined with certainty, although the deputy clerk of the Court later advised Richberg, "I wouldn't do it again if I were you."

Despite Richberg's efforts, the Supreme Court ultimately ruled against the ICC and reversed the O'Fallon decision in 1929. The Valuation Conference thus lost its most crucial test of the original cost theory. Yet with the onset of the Great Depression shortly afterward, valuation became a less urgent problem for the railway unions, which had been the chief backers of the Valuation Conference. Soon deflation, unemployment, and railroad mergers and consolidations became more relevant than valuation to Richberg and his clients. These were problems better handled through the Railway Labor Executives' Association.[11]

Besides the Valuation Conference, Richberg was involved in another attempt to organize labor power before the formation of the RLEA in 1926—this time, one avowedly political in both its purposes and methods. The Conference for Progressive Political Action had a brief life from 1922 to 1924 and was strongly supported by the railway labor unions, along with the Farmer Labor party, the Socialist party of America, and the AFL. Taking a major departure from the traditional nonpartisan political policy set by the AFL and generally followed by most of the labor movement, the railway unions backed what amounted to a third-party movement, fielding Senator Robert La Follette as a candidate for the presi-

---

Conference on Valuation of American Railroads, As Amicus Curiae, St. Louis & O'Fallon Railway Co. and Manufacturers Railways Co. v. United States of America and the Interstate Commerce Commission, Supreme Court of United States, October Term, 1928, No. 131 and 132, 1–13, printed brief in Norris Papers, Tray 8, Box 8.

[11] Richberg, *My Hero,* 123–24; Richberg to Norris, Jan. 1, 1929, Norris Papers, Tray 8, Box 8; Richberg, *Brief on Behalf of the National Conference on Valuation of American Railroads, As Amicus Curiae,* Supreme Court, October Term, 1928, No. 131–32; *St. Louis & O'Fallon Railway Company et al. v. United States et al.,* 279 U. S. 461, 478–88 (1929).

dency on the Progressive ticket in 1924. The AFL gave implicit support to the ticket, although its Executive Council never explicitly endorsed La Follette and his running mate, Senator Burton Wheeler of Montana.[12]

Richberg, as the railway unions' chief attorney in the shopmen's strike and their leading lobbyist on behalf of the Railway Labor Act, and as chief counsel of the Valuation Conference and a friend of La Follette, not surprisingly became chairman of the resolutions committee of the 1924 Progressive nominating convention. Before 1924, La Follette had tried to convince Richberg that he should run for the Senate in Illinois, not in the hope that he could win, but in order to begin marshaling votes for the future so that perhaps the Progressives might carry the state some day. Richberg was unable to consider the proposition for personal reasons—his divorce and remarriage in the fall of 1924—and so did not become a candidate for elective office but remained behind the scenes.[13]

The original plan for the convention, as drawn up by La Follette, called for Richberg to deliver the keynote address, but this was subsequently changed upon his arrival in the convention city, Cleveland, when it was decided he should take charge of the resolutions committee. Richberg and his committee prepared one of the shortest platforms on record. Four pages in length, it endorsed "the progressive principle of cooperation" against "monopoly," "autocracy," and "mastery" in economic affairs. Richberg regarded the party program of 1924 as essentially similar to that of 1912. Though he doubted that the old issues would arouse the electorate as they had before, Richberg had no choice except to defer to the political judgment of La Follette.[14] During the campaign itself, he served as the party's national counsel and devoted his time to seeing that candidates were placed on ballots in all the states. As always, Richberg worked up publicity material for the campaign, helped by his legal assistant, David E. Lilienthal.[15]

[12] Taft, *The A. F. of L. in the Time of Gompers*, 480–85.

[13] Richberg, *My Hero*, 136–38; Richberg, *Tents*, 133.

[14] Richberg, *My Hero*, 138; Richberg, *Tents*, 135–38; "Report of Committee on Resolutions," Cleveland, 1924, Richberg Papers, L.C., Box 33.

[15] Richberg, *My Hero*, 138; La Follette and La Follette, *Robert M. La*

Richberg had no illusions about the Progressives' chances for winning. His own belief was that La Follette was running not because of personal ambition but because 1924 was "his last chance to lead a great battle for the ideals to which he had given his life."[16] The nominees of the Democrats and Republicans had left him little choice. Once the election was over, an election in which La Follette polled about 4,800,000 votes to the Democrats' 8,400,000 and the Republicans' 15,700,000, Richberg saw little hope for the Progressive Conference. In an address entitled "Future Prospects of the Progressive Movement" he predicted that there were no future prospects unless the quality of American life underwent a drastic change. The prerequisite for a successful reform effort was a spiritual revolution against the "cynical materialism that dominates the Republican and Democratic parties." What a real reform movement required was a "religious purpose," one where life was treated as "divine" and hence where every man had worth and democracy was actually practiced. Instead, politics was dominated by the self-interest of an autocratic minority who reigned regardless of the effects of their selfishness on other people's lives. To Richberg, "the progressive movement [was] a political expression of spiritual unrest."

The vote at the November election held out little prospect that such an intangible revolution was in the offing. The voters apparently found comfort in the materialism of the New Era. Consequently, Richberg put aside any ideas of a permanent third party; though he had no faith in the Democrats and Republicans, after the election he likewise had "no interest in exerting myself in the organization of another party in which I shall equally lack faith but feel a greater sense of responsibility." On February 25, 1925, the railway labor unions, more interested in immediate gains than a spiritual revolution, pulled out of the Conference for Progressive Political Action, thereby abandoning efforts at reform

---

Follette, 2: 1121–24; David E. Lilienthal, *The Journals of David E. Lilienthal*, Vol. 1: *The TVA Years, 1939–1945, Including a Selection of Journal Entries from the 1917–1939 Period* (New York, 1964), 15.

[16] Richberg, *My Hero*, 138.

through a third party and sealing the fate of the 1924 movement.[17]

Of all the attempts at organizing railroad labor power, however, it was the Railway Labor Executives' Association, called into being by the need to defend the Railway Labor Act of 1926, that emerged as the most enduring alliance of the unions. Putting aside political programs like that of the Conference for Progressive Political Action, the RLEA was bipartisan in politics and dedicated to achieving the goals of railway labor through the courts, legislation, and publicity. Its objectives were anything but radical, and in a memorandum prepared on the occasion of the founding of the Association, Richberg described "the practical and dominating purpose of any labor organization" as being "to increase wages and to improve working conditions." He suggested that this could be done by defending the Railway Labor Act in the courts and by creating a research and statistical committee to provide the data needed to back up demands for increases in real wages and for maintaining the wage differentials between railroad workers and other trades. Richberg warned that "if the chief executives . . . have in mind only a limited cooperation to promote the separate objects of their organizations in special instances when temporarily joint action may seem helpful, this new association will add little to the existing powers of the component organizations." But if the several unions worked together instead of pursuing contradictory goals, "this association may inaugurate a development of the powers of the component organizations far beyond their previous possibilities."[18]

As chief counsel of the RLEA, Richberg's primary job was to make the Railway Labor Act work by promoting a friendly administration of the law and protecting it in the courts. Beyond this, most of his activity centered on developing programs for future action, preparing legislation, and lobbying on behalf of the unions.

The Railway Labor Act of 1926 did not depend as much on government initiative for its enforcement as on the willingness of

[17] Richberg, *Future Prospects of the Progressive Movement,* An Address to the City Club of Chicago, Nov. 20, 1924, 3–5, 12, Richberg Papers, L.C., Box 19; Taft, *The A. F. of L. in the Time of Gompers,* 485–86.

[18] Richberg, "A Memorandum for the Railway Labor Executives' Association," Aug. 16, 1926, 1, 3, Richberg Papers, C.H.S., Box 5.

labor and management to invoke the machinery provided for settling disputes. Because several of the railroads had accepted the bill with little enthusiasm, Richberg and the union executives had to be on constant guard against evasions of opportunities to utilize the law. Admittedly, they were handicapped by the law's nonpunitive character. In 1927, Richberg advised the Board of Mediation, which had consulted him concerning the construction of the Act, that the "law was not intended as compulsory arbitration . . . but that its proponents had taken [the] position that if parties could not agree themselves—or agree with the aid of mediators— then the pressure of facts—the logic of events—would practically compel them voluntarily to agree to submission of their disagreement to arbitration."[19]

Richberg's assumption that the "logic of events" would of itself provide sufficient pressure to bring about settlements soon proved unwarranted. In January 1928 the RLEA directed a subcommittee of four, headed by Bert Jewell of the AFL Railway Employees' Department, to consult with Richberg about preparing amendments to the Railway Labor Act. Two main problems had emerged in the first year-and-a-half of the operation of the new law: a breakdown in the system for creating Boards of Adjustment to settle grievances over the enforcement of contracts, and a continuation of company unions in the face of the statute's guarantee that employees had the right to organize free from employer interference.[20]

Richberg and the Executive Committee of the RLEA met on June 1, 1928, with members of the Board of Mediation to discuss the problem of creating Boards of Adjustment by agreement between management and labor as provided in the Railway Labor Act. Little progress had been made in establishing such Boards to handle grievances because the roads favored separate Adjustment Boards for each different railroad system, whereas the unions favored national or at least regional Adjustment Boards. The dis-

[19] Richberg, Memorandum, March 12, 1927, Richberg Papers, C.H.S., Box 5.

[20] Bert Jewell to Richberg, Jan. 21, 1928; J. G. Luhrsen to Richberg, Jan. 21, 1928; Richberg to Jewell, March 20, 1928, Richberg Papers, C.H.S., Box 6.

agreement was related to the problem of company unions. System Boards would provide a sphere of operations suited to the continuation of management-influenced company unions; national or regional Boards covering several railroad systems would mean a more general recognition of the standard railway unions, which were national in jurisdiction and far less susceptible to pressure from any one management. Since the Boards had to be created by agreement and were not to be set up at government initiative, the failure to agree simply meant that in most cases there were no Boards of Adjustment available to adjudicate grievances over the enforcement of contracts. Furthermore, the Mediation Board, to which appeals from Adjustment Boards might be sent, refused to take jurisdiction in any grievance case unless it had first gone through a Board of Adjustment. The failure to agree on Boards thus stymied the rest of the Act.[21]

Richberg vigorously dissented from the view that the Mediation Board could not consider grievances unless an Adjustment Board had previously attempted to bring about a settlement. But his argument at the June 1 meeting and his later efforts to convince the Mediation Board that it could intervene failed to alter its position.[22]

In fact, the reports Richberg received indicated that the Mediation Board was simply pursuing a holding action to avoid any substantial change in the labor situation on the railroads. His chief source of inside information was John Marrinan, secretary of the Board of Mediation, who resigned in late 1928 as a protest against the Board's " 'sit on the lid' performance." Though a disgruntled witness, Marrinan's picture of the Board's operations confirmed

[21] D. B. Robertson to Richberg, March 22, 1928; Richberg to Robertson, "Report of Conference with Board of Mediation Concerning Adjustment Boards Held in Washington, June 1, 1928," June 4, 1928, Richberg Papers, C.H.S., Box 6; Irving Bernstein, The Lean Years: A History of the American Worker, 1920–1933 (Boston, 1960), 218–20; Bernstein, The New Deal Collective Bargaining Policy (Berkeley, Calif., 1950), 42–43.

[22] Richberg to Robertson, "Report of Conference with Board of Mediation," June 4, 1928; Richberg to John Marrinan, Sept. 27, 1928; Merrinan to Richberg, Sept. 29, 1928, Richberg Papers, C.H.S., Box 6; Samuel E. Winslow to Richberg, Nov. 13, 1928; Winslow to Richberg, Dec. 1, 1928; Winslow to Robertson, Dec. 13, 1928, Richberg Papers, C.H.S., Box 7.

what Richberg already suspected. In a letter dated December 16, 1928, Marrinan reported, "At the recent [Mediation] Board meeting of some ten days duration a member of the Board informed me that nothing had been done about the adjustment board question." Similarly, the problem of recognition of independent unions over company unions "has never been given anything more than casual consideration." In sum, the record of the Board had been such that steps would have to be taken "to require the Board to function."[23]

Thus, a year after the RLEA had ordered Richberg to begin looking into the matter of amending the Railway Labor Act, the situation in regard to Adjustment Boards remained essentially unchanged. Amendments were clearly required in the face of the Mediation Board's unwillingness to break the logjam blocking the formation of grievance machinery. Richberg inaugurated what developed into a long campaign for amending the Act, a campaign that culminated in 1934, after he had left the railway unions to serve in the administration of Franklin D. Roosevelt. Others finished the work he had begun, though Richberg remained the unions' leading advocate in this as in other aspects of railway labor's legislative program right up until the spring of 1933. But much of this work lay in the future.[24]

Of more immediate concern was the second great problem faced by the RLEA: employee organization. Here court action seemed to be the most fruitful approach. The Adjustment Board question had depended upon the parties' willingness to agree, but the right of workers to form their own unions unhindered by management was clearly spelled out in the law. This provision of the Act did not depend on good will alone.

Richberg was not anxious to test the Railway Labor Act too soon, not because he had any doubt about its constitutionality, but because he wanted enough time to pass so that the law would have a chance to prove itself in operation. He hoped that a strong public

[23] Marrinan to Robertson, Dec. 4, 1928; Marrinan to Richberg, Dec. 16, 1928, Richberg Papers, C.H.S., Box 7.

[24] Bernstein, The New Deal, 42–56; Richberg, "Report of Donald R. Richberg to Meeting of Railway Labor Executives' Association," Cleveland, Ohio, July 24, 1930, Richberg Papers, L.C., Box 44.

sentiment would develop in its favor. Further, Richberg did not want to rush into a court test just for the sake of a test, preferring to wait until the best case came along, one that would require the railroads opposing employee organization to present their contentions on constitutional grounds. Consequently, after the Railway Labor Act had been in effect for over a year, Richberg recommended that the RLEA sponsor a test case that had arisen on the Texas and New Orleans Railroad, a subsidiary of the Southern Pacific Railroad Company. The T. & N.O. had conspired to avoid collective bargaining with the Brotherhood of Railway and Steamship Clerks. Instead, the road had established its own company union, the Association of Clerical Employees—Southern Pacific Lines, and had recognized it to the exclusion of the independent union. The company discharged members of the Brotherhood from its employ, while at the same time providing financial support and direction to its own organization.[25]

Richberg did not handle the case in the lower courts, but took over when it reached the Supreme Court. Nevertheless, he suggested a strategy for introducing into the record certain issues during the initial proceedings; his purpose was to lay the groundwork for raising constitutional questions later in the Supreme Court. First, there was the clear provision of the law itself, unambiguous in its assertion of the employees' rights. There were grounds for conspiracy charges against anyone who cooperated with others to deny a citizen his rights as guaranteed by the Constitution or laws of the United States. Second, Richberg believed that denying workers the right to organize freely deprived them of property rights—those growing out of their right to work, those had by virtue of a contract with an employer, and those "as members of an organization which the carrier is seeking to destroy." These property rights might be "as much entitled to the protection of a court of equity as the property rights of an employer in his business."

[25] Richberg, *My Hero,* 142–43; Richberg to E. H. Fitzgerald, June 27, 1927, quoted in Fitzgerald to Robertson, June 30, 1927, Richberg Papers, C.H.S., Box 5; Bernstein, *The Lean Years,* 218; *Texas & New Orleans Railway Company et al.* v. *Brotherhood of Railway & Steamship Clerks et al.,* 281 U. S. 548, 554–57.

Finally, Richberg saw grounds for a case in court precedents which prevented unions from seeking to persuade employees to violate yellow-dog contracts, in that the same reasoning might be applied to employers, who thereby could not seek to induce employees to break faith with their independent unions by joining another organization, the company union.[26]

The Clerks went to court and won a temporary and a permanent injunction against the railroad, ordering the disbanding of the company union. The Fifth Circuit Court upheld the ruling on June 10, 1929, by a vote of two to one. Richberg then went on to win what was the single most important decision sustaining the validity of the Railway Labor Act. Richberg felt that the recent controversy over the appointment of Charles Evans Hughes as chief justice may have helped his cause. Labor generally had opposed the Hughes nomination on grounds that he had long represented big business in his legal practice. Richberg was sure that the dispute tended to guarantee Hughes's objectivity in hearing a case involving management-labor conflicts. On May 26, 1930, the Court handed down a unanimous decision, written by Hughes. The heart of the Railway Labor Act was secure, the Court holding that "the entire policy of the Act . . . must depend for success on the uncoerced action of each party through its own representatives to the end that agreements satisfactory to both may be reached and the peace essential to the uninterrupted service of the instrumentalities of interstate commerce may be maintained."[27]

Although the Railway Labor Executives' Association was nonpartisan, its plans for developing a legislative program necessitated becoming involved in the political process. It made a difference who was elected to office. In 1928, the RLEA endorsed several mem-

[26] Richberg to Fitzgerald, June 27, 1927, quoted in Fitzgerald to Robertson, June 30, 1927, Richberg Papers, c.h.s., Box 5.

[27] Edward Berman, "The Supreme Court Interprets the Railway Labor Act," *The American Economic Review* 20 (Dec. 1930): 619–39; Bernstein, *The Lean Years*, 218; Richberg, *My Hero*, 143–44; Richberg, *Interpretation of the Railway Labor Act* ([Washington, D. C.], 1931), in Richberg Papers, l.c., Box 6; *T. & N.O. v. Brotherhood of Railway and Steamship Clerks*, 281 U. S. 548, 554–57, 569 (1930).

bers of Congress without regard to party label and solely on the basis of their labor records. It took a neutral position on the presidential race, since there was a division of allegiance among the union executives themselves, but allowed each executive to work as an individual for whichever candidate he chose. Richberg and D. B. Robertson, president of the RLEA, were both enthusiastic backers of Secretary of Commerce Herbert Hoover—even before the Republican convention—and worked actively for his nomination and election. They felt Hoover could be relied on as a progressive.[28]

Robertson made contact with Hoover about securing a satisfactory labor plank and vice-presidential candidate, and directed Richberg to prepare a draft statement for consideration by the Republican platform writers. Bert Jewell of the AFL Railway Employees' Department assisted Richberg, also at Robertson's request. The result of Richberg and Jewell's handiwork—a reaffirmation of the principles of employee organization and collective bargaining— was turned over to John Marrinan, secretary of the Board of Mediation under the Railway Labor Act and a Hoover promoter. Marrinan presented the plank to Hoover and also cleared it with Frank Morrison and William Green of the AFL. It seemed that the Hoover forces were receptive to suggestions from Robertson and that he might play a larger role in the campaign.[29]

Consequently, Richberg undertook to serve as the go-between to bring Marrinan and Robertson together for organizing the labor vote on Hoover's behalf. Except for their efforts before the convention, however, neither Robertson nor Richberg played a major part

[28] Robertson to Herbert C. Hoover, Feb. 1, 1929, Richberg Papers, C.H.S., Box 7; Robertson to Jewell, Aug. 7, 1928; Robertson, "Statement by D. B. Robertson, Chairman, Railway Labor Executives' Association, and President, Brotherhood of Locomotive Firemen and Enginemen," Aug. 6, 1928, Richberg Papers, C.H.S., Box 6.

[29] Marrinan to Richberg, May 28, 1928; Robertson to Jewell, June 1, 1928; Jewell to Richberg, June 7, 1928; Richberg to Martin F. Ryan and J. A. Franklin, June 4, 1928; Ryan to Richberg, June 6, 1928; Jewell to Richberg, June 12, 1928; Jewell to Members, Railway Labor Executives' Association, June 13, 1928; [Richberg and Jewell], "Proposed Labor Plank for Presentation to Republican Convention," Richberg Papers, C.H.S., Box 6.

in the subsequent presidential race, as William Doak of the Brotherhood of Railroad Trainmen took over the management of the labor side of the Republican campaign instead, despite Hoover's apparent interest in Robertson initially. Doak had a longstanding ambition to become secretary of labor in the new administration and succeeded in being selected to head up the Republican labor campaign—according to Robertson—partly through misrepresenting the labor situation to Hoover. Doak apparently maintained that Roberston was unacceptable to a large part of the labor movement and would therefore lose rather than gain votes. As a result, Robertson and Richberg found themselves on the sidelines for the 1928 campaign.[30]

By election time, Hoover's stance on questions important to railway labor had alienated Richberg anyway, so that he went over to the Democratic camp at the last moment. At the beginning of the campaign, Richberg was inclined to regard the friendly labor statements of Alfred E. Smith, the Democratic candidate, as so much rhetoric not likely to be followed up with action. He felt Smith's entire political career revealed a tendency for a gap to develop between promises and deeds. Hoover had a better record, in Richberg's opinion, on delivering what he promised. In time, Richberg became more friendly to Smith because Hoover seemed to be making no important commitments to labor at all; instead, Richberg felt he was "excessively desirous of not offending ultra conservative people" whereas Smith was "willing to risk offending them." Smith had even endorsed the efforts of railway labor to obtain a bill outlawing injunctions in labor disputes. In the end, Richberg voted for Smith. Robertson likewise was disappointed in Hoover's performance.[31]

[30] Robertson to Richberg, July 4, 1928; Jewell to Robertson, July 16, 1928; Robertson to Richberg, Aug. 5, 1928; Robertson to Richberg, Aug. 31, 1928; Robertson to Richberg, Sept. 19, 1928, Richberg Papers, C.H.S., Box 6; Marrinan to George Barr Baker, Oct. 5, 1928; Robertson to Hoover, Feb. 1, 1929; Robertson to Richberg, Feb. 27, 1929, Richberg Papers, C.H.S., Box 7.

[31] Richberg to Frederic C. Howe, Aug. 30, 1928; Richberg to Robertson, Aug. 28, 1928; Robertson to Richberg, Aug. 31, 1928; Richberg to Robert-

The Republican victory in 1928 consequently was not a step forward for labor, at least as Richberg viewed it. Hoover's noncommital attitude toward the labor movement in general during the campaign was an accurate foreshadowing of what Richberg and the railway labor executives would be up against during his tenure in the White House. Though at the beginning of the campaign Richberg had high hopes that he could count on Hoover as a progressive, his disappointment at Hoover's failure to enunciate a clear-cut labor program meant that his battles on behalf of the railroad unions probably would be as tough as ever.[32] Despite the progress of the past several years, with the passage of the Railway Labor Act, the organization of the National Conference on Railroad Valuation, and the creation of the Railway Labor Executives' Association, Richberg was to face the same opposition forces that he had encountered prior to the Hoover administration. As the Adjustment Board dispute and the O'Fallon and T. & N.O. cases showed, the opposition was not going to surrender without a struggle. Consequently, Richberg's work was far from done.

---

son, Sept. 10, 1928; Richberg to Howe, Sept. 24, 1928; Richberg to Robertson, Sept. 27, 1928; Richberg to Marrinan, Sept. 27, 1928; Marrinan to Richberg, Oct. 1, 1928, Richberg Papers, c.h.s., Box 6; Richberg to Marrinan, Oct. 31, 1928; Marrinan to Richberg, Nov. 3, 1928; Mrs. Glenn E. Plumb to Richberg, Nov. 6, 1928; Richberg to Marrinan, Nov. 5, 1928, Richberg Papers, c.h.s., Box 7; Bernstein, *The Lean Years*, 395.

[32] Richberg to Marrinan, Sept. 27, 1928, Richberg Papers, c.h.s., Box 6.

CHAPTER V

Consolidation

The inauguration of the Hoover administration, something that Donald Richberg had worked for almost to the end of the 1928 campaign, brought little in the way of change as far as railway labor was concerned. The kinds of problems and the nature of the opposition that Richberg encountered remained much the same as before. Most of his work continued to be concentrated in the Railway Labor Executives' Association, though again he became involved in related but separate reform projects, such as a Conference of Progressives called by Senator George Norris of Nebraska in 1931. Richberg's RLEA work followed the pattern that had already been established, fighting court battles and formulating new legislation, although in the latter regard the RLEA moved significantly to broaden its overall program, especially with the onset of the Great Depression in 1929.

For Richberg, the greatest legislative battle of this period was the movement to win legislation limiting the use of injunctions in labor disputes—a movement sparked principally by George Norris. The plight of the coal miners had motivated Norris initially, but his bill was intended to benefit the labor movement as a whole and he was strongly supported by Richberg and other leading legal experts throughout the country. Norris consulted Richberg not as an official representative of the RLEA, though it was vitally interested in the outcome and supported his contributions, but as a labor lawyer of high repute in his own right.[1]

Norris invited Richberg, Felix Frankfurter and Francis Sayre of Harvard Law School, E. E. Witte of the Wisconsin Legislative Reference Library, and Herman Oliphant of Columbia University to come to Washington and write a substitute anti-injunction bill to replace one that he and his colleagues on a Senate Judiciary Sub-Committee, Thomas Walsh of Montana and John J. Blaine of Wisconsin, had decided to reject. The original measure, S. 1482, had been presented by Senator Henrik Shipstead of Minnesota and limited the jurisdiction of equity courts to protecting property defined only as something "tangible and transferable."[2]

The Shipstead bill was really the brainchild of Andrew Furuseth, president of the International Seamen's Union and a friend of the Minnesota senator.[3] Furuseth was without any legal education and failed to comprehend the havoc his proposal would create if, in an effort to protect employee organization against injunctions, property ceased to be defined as an intangible right and was limited exclusively to concrete things. Despite Richberg's opinion that Furuseth "doesn't know what he is talking about," he was destined to create considerable difficulties for the substitute bill. Furuseth's persistence attested to his sincerity if not to his legal understanding. He steadfastly opposed the bill written in response to Norris's plea by Richberg, Frankfurter, Oliphant, Witte, and Sayre, and temporarily swayed the AFL.[4]

The Norris group gathered in Washington for two days of intensive consultation at the beginning of May 1928 and produced the first draft of a new law. There then followed several weeks of correspondence among the conferees to hammer the language into

[1] George W. Norris, *Fighting Liberal* (New York, 1945), 308–10; Irving Bernstein, *The Lean Years: A History of the American Worker, 1920–1933* (Boston, 1960), 391–95, 415; Donald Richberg to George W. Norris, Feb. 11, 1930, George W. Norris Papers, Library of Congress, Tray 79, Box 7.

[2] Bernstein, *The Lean Years,* 395–97; Norris to Felix Frankfurter, April 21, 1928, Felix Frankfurter Papers, Library of Congress, Box 29.

[3] Bernstein, *The Lean Years,* 395; Norris to Frankfurter, June 11, 1928, Frankfurter Papers, Box 63.

[4] Bernstein, *The Lean Years,* 396–97; Richberg to Norris, June 18, 1928; Frankfurter to Norris, June 21, 1928, Frankfurter Papers, Box 29; Richberg to Frankfurter, June 18, 1928; Frankfurter to Richberg, June 20, 1928, Frankfurter Papers, Box 32.

final shape.[5] The object of these efforts, as stated by Witte, was not geared primarily to formulating revisions of the substantive law, because "the courts will hold them unconstitutional" anyway, but to attacking the problem of injunctions "through procedural changes" designed to protect the rights of the workers. Such procedural revisions would "stand a good chance of being enacted into law and also of being sustained by the courts." Frankfurter and Richberg seconded this view.[6] Although all the conferees contributed to the refinements of the original draft, the final touches were made by Frankfurter and Oliphant because further personal conferences were not possible and because Richberg and Witte were located too far away to make frequent consultation feasible. Everyone, however, kept in close touch by mail and all approved the ultimate version.[7]

Norris introduced the draft bill into the Senate on May 29, 1928. In brief, it made yellow-dog contracts unenforceable in federal courts as contrary to a statement of public policy set forth in the bill. The new law would deny the federal courts jurisdiction to issue injunctions in labor disputes under several enumerated conditions; no injunction might be issued to enjoin workers from refusing to work, joining or remaining a member of a labor organization, paying strike benefits from union treasuries, aiding others involved in a labor dispute by any lawful means, giving publicity

[5] Norris, *Fighting Liberal*, 312–13; Frankfurter to Richberg, April 24, 1928; Richberg to Frankfurter, April 26, 1928, Frankfurter Papers, Box 32; Norris to Frankfurter, May 5, 1928, Frankfurter Papers, Box 29; E. E. Witte to Frankfurter, May 12, 1928; Witte to Richberg, May 12, 1928; Frankfurter to Richberg, May 14, 1928; Richberg to Frankfurter, May 16, 1928; Richberg, "Memorandum for Messrs. Oliphant, Frankfurter, and Witte," May 16, 1928; Witte to Richberg, May 17, 1928; Frankfurter to Herman Oliphant, May 18, 1928; Oliphant to Frankfurter, May 21, 1928; Oliphant to Norris, May 25, 1928, Frankfurter Papers, Box 63.

[6] Witte to Francis B. Sayre, May 26, 1928; Frankfurter to Witte, May 29, 1928, Frankfurter Papers, Box 63; Richberg, "Comment upon Briefs (for Employer Organizations) Filed in Opposition to the Sub-Committee Anti-Injunction Bill," May 5, 1930, Norris Papers, Tray 85, Box 4.

[7] Richberg to Frankfurter, May 16, 1928; Witte to Richberg, May 17, 1928; Witte to Frankfurter, May 17, 1928; Oliphant to Frankfurter, May 21, 1928, Frankfurter Papers, Box 63.

to the dispute by any means except force or violence, assembling peaceably, or cooperating with others to do such acts. A separate provision specifically directed that no injunction could be issued on grounds of unlawful combination or conspiracy in carrying out any of the above. Union officials and members were exempted from liability for unlawful acts in a strike unless it could be shown that they actually authorized or participated in such crimes. Definite guidelines were laid down prescribing the procedure for issuing an injunction; these attempted to insure that no order would be issued unless substantial injury would otherwise ensue, and then only after personal notice had been given to those against whom the injunction was directed. Temporary restraining orders might not be effective longer than five days. Those who failed to comply with the law in a labor conflict would be ineligible for injunctive relief. Criminal contempt cases arising out of an injunction would be subject to jury trial.[8]

No action was taken on the Norris bill at the first session of the Seventieth Congress, but after Congress adjourned, the 1928 AFL convention met in New Orleans. Largely through Furuseth's influence, the Norris bill was not endorsed but instead referred to a special committee headed by Matthew Woll of the Photo-Engravers Union. In June 1929 Woll and his colleagues recommended that the Norris bill be endorsed in amended form. The AFL Executive Council approved the Committee report on August 16. In October the AFL's Toronto convention backed a revised version of the Norris bill.[9]

Norris now had to decide how, or whether, to reconcile his bill with that of the AFL. Again he turned to Richberg, Frankfurter, Oliphant, Witte, and Sayre. Though differing on specifics, they all agreed that the proposed amendments would weaken rather than strengthen the Norris bill.[10] It was Frankfurter, however, who

---

[8] Bernstein, *The Lean Years*, 397–400.

[9] Ibid., 400–403.

[10] Ibid., 403; "Comparison of Anti-Injunction Bills," n.d., Norris Papers, Tray 42, Box 8; Oliphant to Norris, Dec. 2, 1929; Witte to Norris, Dec. 6, 1929; Witte to Frankfurter, Dec. 6, 1929; Oliphant to Frankfurter, Dec. 9, 1929; Richberg to Frankfurter, Jan. 7, 1930; Witte to Frankfurter, Jan. 21,

pointed out the crucial role that Richberg would have to play in placating organized labor. Frankfurter felt it "undersirable that Senator Norris' Committee should so much as appear to be introducing a bill precisely in the form in which the A.F. of L. drew it, as the Senate Committee would be merely a conduit for the A.F. of L." Its amendments would in some cases weaken the bill; in others, they would be harmless, but of no great advantage either; in all events, full acceptance by the Senate Judiciary Committee would be a major liability in getting the bill through Congress. As a representative of the RLEA and the AFL Railway Employees' Department, Richberg could make the AFL see the problem; Frankfurter believed this was the "one thing which you can say that none of us can say."[11]

Taking up Frankfurter's suggestion, Richberg advised Norris against giving the appearance of capitulating to organized labor, urging that "if the committee on the judiciary should report out a somewhat revised bill there would be more disadvantage than advantage in incorporating *all* the suggestions of the A.F. of L." As a friend of labor, Richberg could and did criticize what he and the legal experts had decided were ill-founded or pointless amendments, politically inexpedient at best.[12]

Norris introduced a revised bill on May 19, 1930. The law was now substantially in its final form; he had not incorporated the AFL amendments. In a Washington conference of December 1931,

---

1930; Frankfurter to Norris, Jan. 28, 1930, Frankfurter Papers, Box 63; Frankfurter, Oliphant, and Witte, "Observations on Amendments Proposed by the American Federation of Labor to the Injunction Bill Drafted by the Sub-Committee of the Senate Committee on the Judiciary," n.d., Norris Papers, Tray 79, Box 7; Frankfurter to Richberg, Jan. 28, 1930, Frankfurter Papers, Box 32; Richberg to Frankfurter, Feb. 6, 1930, Frankfurter Papers, Box 78; Richberg to Norris, Feb. 11, 1930, Norris Papers, Tray 79, Box 7; Richberg, "Memorandum Concerning Amendments to Anti-Injunction Bill Suggested by the American Federation of Labor," n.d., Norris Papers, Tray 42, Box 8; Norris to Richberg, March 6, 1930; Frankfurter to Norris, March 11, 1930; Witte to Norris, March 13, 1930; Witte to Richberg, March 13, 1930; Witte to Frankfurter, March 13, 1930, Frankfurter Papers, Box 63.

[11] Frankfurter to Richberg, Jan. 28, 1930, Frankfurter Papers, Box 32.

[12] Richberg to Norris, Feb. 11, 1930, Norris Papers, Tray 79, Box 7.

Richberg and Norris met with AFL chiefs and ironed out their differences. The AFL agreed to eliminate most of its suggestions,
though some would be offered from the floor of the Senate as
amendments to the Norris bill when it came up for consideration.
The bill could not thereby be labeled as an AFL ultimatum. It
would be more than a year and a half after its introduction, however, before the revised Norris bill was reported out of committee
favorably.[13]

In defense of the proposed bill, Richberg sent Norris a commentary on briefs submitted in the spring of 1930 by counsel representing management, James A. Emery, Daniel Davenport, and
Walter Gordon Merritt. As was his customary strategy when backing new legislation, Richberg emphasized that the bill did not de-
part from established principles of jurisprudence. In attacking the
injunction and yellow-dog contract, he argued that he was simply
defending the right of workers to make legally binding contracts.
Agreements made under compulsion of any kind would be invalid
anyway. Richberg affirmed that "to write this doctrine into the law
is not to propose anything novel."

Richberg denounced the idea implicit in the arguments of management that "innocent acts done in combination may constitute a
conspiracy." Such an idea indicated a failure to understand "the
original and time-honored definition of a conspiracy" as essentially
combining for "the accomplishment of a lawful purpose by unlawful means; or, the accomplishment of an unlawful purpose by lawful means." But the object of the labor movement was hardly unlawful, nor could the constitutional rights of free speech and
assembly be transformed into unlawful acts by a court decree simply because these rights were invoked by a combination of men

[13] Bernstein, *The Lean Years*, 403, 411; Legislative Representative of
AFL to Alexander Fleisher, Nov. 9, 1931; Fleisher to Edward F. Mc-
Grady, Dec. 8, 1931, American Federation of Labor Papers, Wisconsin
State Historical Society, Series 11, File B, Box 4; Roger Baldwin to Frank-
furter, Dec. 8, 1931; Richberg to Baldwin, Dec. 12, 1931, Frankfurter Pa-
pers, Box 55; Frankfurter to Baldwin, Dec. 9, 1931; Norris to Baldwin,
Dec. 12, 1931; Baldwin to Norris, Dec. 14, 1931, Norris Papers, Tray 79,
Box 7.

rather than individuals acting alone. Richberg concluded that employer "hostility to the proposed legislation provides strong evidence that it is soundly conceived to compel the courts of equity to relinquish the exercise of unfair partisan powers which they have been induced to assume and to exercise under the persuasion of the attorneys who now oppose this bill."[14]

At the suggestion of Richberg and Alexander Fleisher, prominent in the work of the American Civil Liberties Union, the ACLU in mid-1930 formed a special Committee on Labor Injunctions to marshal support among eminent liberals on behalf of the Norris bill. Roger N. Baldwin, leader of the ACLU, and especially Fleisher were active in carrying out the Committee's work.[15]

In the meantime, Richberg found himself the object of attempts to bring about a compromise in Senator Norris's position. On January 3, 1931, Secretary of Labor William Doak, formerly of the Brotherhood of Railroad Trainmen, telephoned Richberg in Chicago and asked him to come to Washington. Doak claimed that he was acting at the suggestion of President Hoover. Despite heavy commitments to other clients, Richberg agreed to meet the secretary on January 7. Doak led Richberg to believe that the president was concerned that the Norris bill would be pressed for passage at the current session of Congress, and therefore wanted to bring the opposing forces together in the hope of effecting compromises satisfactory to both sides. Accordingly, the secretary of labor had arranged for a conference that same day between Richberg and the management representatives, James Emery and Walter Gordon Merritt. Doak and counsel from his department would also attend. Richberg objected that such a conference would be useless, as Emery and Merritt were representing forces opposed to any compromise with organized labor. Further, Richberg feared that such a conference would put him in a false position as one of the authors of the bill and as one intimately connected with the Judiciary Com-

[14] Richberg, "Comment upon Briefs (for Employer Organizations) Filed in Opposition to the Sub-Committee Anti-Injunction Bill," May 5, 1930, Norris Papers, Tray 85, Box 4.

[15] Bernstein, *The Lean Years*, 410; Fleisher to Norris, June 19, 1930, Norris Papers, Tray 79, Box 7.

mittee, the RLEA, and the AFL Railway Employees' Department.
But Doak was insistent.

As Richberg had anticipated, the meeting proved fruitless. He
found Emery and Merritt still opposed to the basic objects of the
proposed bill. They were only out to get concessions. Equally important, Richberg "was constantly oppressed with the feeling that
merely engaging in such a debate might be subject to future mis-
representation." This feeling was confirmed later when he received
a memorandum summing up the exchange of views that had taken
place. Richberg thereupon consulted Norris and learned that there
was little likelihood of the bill passing at the current session of
Congress. He informed Doak of this and used it as an excuse to
avoid any further conferences. Richberg left Washington on January 8.

That Secretary Doak was out to make a bargain was even more
clear from a question he put to Richberg during the course of their
conference. As Richberg recalled it, Doak inquired whether he
"would be interested in an appointment to the Federal bench,"
perhaps a district judgeship. Doak made no offer of a specific trade
of a judicial post in exchange for scuttling the injunction bill, but
simply indicated "that he might be able to exert considerable influence in this direction." Richberg did not see the suggestion as an
outright bribe, but believed that Doak "was merely using the common political method of inducing a helpful attitude by holding out
the possibility of a future favor." Norris thought the offer sufficiently incriminating, however, to use it against Hoover in the 1932
presidential campaign, and Richberg backed up his efforts in statements to the press.[16]

Despite the administration's hostility, events were moving toward passage of the bill. The Depression of 1929, of course, was
forcing both the electorate and its leaders to the left, so that the
shibboleths of the business community against labor legislation no

[16] The quotations and general outline of facts are from Richberg to Norris, Sept. 27, 1932, Norris Papers, Tray 1, Box 3. Also see Norris to Richberg, Sept. 17, 1932; Richberg to Norris, Sept. 23, 1932; John P. Robertson
to G. M. Johnson, Dec. 31, 1932, Norris Papers, Tray 1, Box 3; New York
Times, Oct. 21, 1932.

longer seemed as convincing as in the past. The 1930 congressional elections gave the Democrats a slim majority in the House of Representatives and reduced the Republican majority in the Senate to one. The side-effects of the election resulted in a reorganization of the Senate Judiciary Committee to the advantage of the Norris bill. A growing sympathy for the anti-injunction movement was likewise apparent in the states, where a number of new labor laws dealing with injunctions and yellow-dog contracts were in the works. Furthermore, two of Hoover's judicial nominations resulted in severe criticism and drew public attention to injunction abuses and the need for remedial legislation. On March 21, 1930, the president recommended Judge John J. Parker for a vacancy on the United States Supreme Court, and on January 12, 1932, he sought Senate approval of Judge James Wilkerson for a place on the Seventh Circuit Court of Appeals. Richberg actively lobbied against his old enemy Wilkerson, who had granted the Daugherty injunction in the 1922 shopmen's strike. Parker had issued the so-called Red Jacket injunction of 1927 against organizing efforts and strikes by the United Mine Workers in West Virginia on grounds that the miners were bound by valid yellow-dog contracts. The Senate rejected Parker, and the opposition to Wilkerson was such that he requested that Hoover withdraw his name from consideration.[17]

With the opposition crumbling, the Norris bill was finally reported out of committee favorably on January 27, 1932, at the height of the Wilkerson controversy. It passed the Senate with only token opposition, 75 to 5. House action followed much the same course, and the vote was 362 to 14. Hoover reluctantly signed the bill on March 23, 1932, because—as Norris told Richberg—"he lacked the courage to veto it" and knew that the majorities in both Houses were sufficient to override him if he balked. In spite of itself, the Hoover administration had witnessed a long step forward in labor relations.[18]

[17] Bernstein, *The Lean Years*, 406–12; E. J. Manion, form letter to members of the United States Senate, Jan. 15, 1932; Richberg to Norris, March 18, 1932; Richberg to Norris, April 28, 1932, Richberg Papers, C.H.S., Box 14.
[18] Bernstein, *The Lean Years*, 410, 412–15; Norris, *Fighting Liberal,*

Despite heavy commitments to the RLEA throughout these years, Richberg still found time to devote to other pursuits. In 1930, he published his first autobiographical effort, *Tents of the Mighty*. It was not a simple recitation of the facts of his own life, but rather the story of a larger theme: the conflict between a public policy based on individual self-interest and one based on a scientific determination of the needs of the whole community. As such, it represented another attempt on Richberg's part to examine his own individual existence in terms of what he could contribute to the larger public good. He placed his career in the context of what he believed was a long-range trend toward the scientific analysis and solution of social problems.[19]

Richberg did more than just write about this ideal. He tried to apply it to the realities of the political process by responding to a call for a Conference of Progressives issued by Senators George Norris of Nebraska, Edward Costigan of Colorado, Bronson Cutting of New Mexico, Robert La Follette, Jr., of Wisconsin, and Burton Wheeler of Montana. The Conference took place in Washington. D. C., on March 11 and 12, 1931, with the announced purpose of "discussing and outlining a program of legislation to be presented at the next session of Congress."[20]

Norris was chairman of the meeting, which was nonpartisan and not called with the idea of founding any third party. The conferees were impelled by the Great Depression which had begun in 1929 and which they believed the Hoover administration was incable of reversing. They undertook to prepare programs in five subject areas: unemployment and industrial stabilization, public utilities, agriculture, tariffs, and representative government. David Robertson, head of the RLEA, participated along with Richberg and

---

313–15; John P. Robertson to William J. Froelich, March 15, 1932, Norris Papers, Tray 79, Box 7. The quotation is from Norris to Richberg, Sept. 17, 1932, Norris Papers, Tray 1, Box 3.

[19] Richberg, *Tents of the Mighty* (New York, 1930).

[20] Progressive Conference, 1931, *Proceedings of a Conference of Progressives to Outline a Program of Constructive Legislation Dealing with Economic and Political Conditions for Presentation to the First Session of the Seventy-Second Congress,* 3, pamphlet in Norris Papers, Ac. 6900, Tag No. 49, Box 20.

addressed the meeting on unemployment. Richberg, because of his experience in utility rate regulation and railroad valuation, chaired and addressed the session on public utilities. He also prepared a report on the conclusions of his session, aided by a Committee on Public Utilities made up of eminent experts in the field and including Paul U. Kellogg, editor of *Survey*, William E. Mosher of Syracuse University, James C. Bonbright of Columbia University, Theodore Kronshage and David Lilienthal of the Wisconsin Public Service Commission, Amos Pinchot, the old Progressive, and several others.[21]

The report of the Public Utilities Committee recommended stronger state and federal regulation and the creation of publicly owned enterprises to compete with private utility companies and establish standards of rates and services. Pinchot and Norris wanted to come out unreservedly for an all-inclusive public ownership of electrical and other utilities. As chairman of the Committee, Richberg resisted outright public ownership, believing instead that "the only effective method of regulation which has been found is competition and that the government should definitely adopt the policy of public competition as a policy of regulation," much on the model of the Tennessee Valley Authority to be instituted during the administration of Franklin Roosevelt largely through Norris's efforts. He felt "wholesale public ownership" was "impractical," and yielded no farther than the yardstick idea of the future TVA in preparing the Committee report.[22]

Though the Richberg Committee succeeded in submitting a report to Norris, it produced nothing in the way of specific legislation for recommendation to Congress. Despite the proclaimed purpose of the 1931 Progressive Conference, the idea of formulating

[21] Ibid., 3, 109–11, 135–40; "The members of the Committee on Public Utilities appointed by the Progressive Conference, which met at Washington in March, 1931," mimeographed list in Richberg Papers, C.H.S., Box 11.

[22] Richberg, "Report of Committee on Public Utilities of the Progressive Conference," Oct. 8, 1932, Richberg Papers, C.H.S., Box 11; Amos Pinchot to Richberg, Aug. 3, 1931; Norris to Richberg, Aug. 13, 1931; Pinchot to Norris, Aug. 19, 1931, Norris Papers, Tray 8, Box 4; Norris to Richberg, Oct. 14, 1931, Richberg Papers, C.H.S., Box 12. The quotation is from Richberg to Norris, Aug. 15, 1931, Norris Papers, Tray 8, Box 4.

legislation did not even come up. Much like the National Progressive Service of an earlier day, the Committee found that devising concrete legislative proposals would prove far more difficult than enunciating general principles. Besides, the Committee was an informal organization working completely through correspondence rather than personal conferences. Largely for this reason, the final report was the work of Richberg, and his ideas prevailed, though most of the Committee approved his efforts.[23]

Despite outside activities, including continued participation in Chicago affairs, Richberg devoted by far the greatest part of his energies to developing the program of the Railway Labor Executives' Association and to fighting its battles in the courts and at the negotiating table. Especially with the onslaught of the depression, it was crucial to expand railway labor's legislative program into areas hitherto left unexplored. New crises had to be faced while at the same time preventing the worsening of old ones.

The usual procedure in formulating a new plank in the RLEA platform was for the union executives to decide among themselves the broad outlines of policy and then turn the problem over to Richberg as general counsel for further analysis and suggestions, and ultimately for the construction of a concrete proposal either in the form of legislation or unilateral RLEA action. Richberg was thus as much involved in the internal functioning of the RLEA as in lobbying in the halls of Congress. Furthermore, he had the opportunity to initiate ideas as well as to carry them out.[24]

[23] Norris to Richberg, March 21, 1931; Richberg to Norris, March 30, 1931; Alice Houlihan to S. Burton Heath, June 6, 1931, Richberg Papers, c.h.s., Box 11; Richberg to Norris, Oct. 1, 1931; Richberg to Norris, Oct. 9, 1931, Richberg Papers, c.h.s., Box 12.

[24] For a sampling of how Richberg and the RLEA executives worked together, see J. A. Farquharson to Richberg, May 23, 1931, Richberg Papers, c.h.s., Box 11; "Memorandum Concerning Work on Federal Workmen's Compensation and Retirement Insurance—(Old Age Pensions)," Dec. 28, 1931, Richberg Papers, c.h.s., Box 12; Richberg to David B. Robertson, March 1, 1932, Richberg Papers, c.h.s., Box 14. Examples of Richberg's initiation of policy or suggestions are in Richberg to George M. Harrison, May 19, 1931; S. N. Berry to Richberg, May 27, 1931, Richberg Papers, c.h.s., Box 11; Richberg to "Dear Sir" [selected members of the RLEA], Aug. 5, 1932, Richberg Papers, c.h.s., Box 15.

Of primary concern to the RLEA as a result of the depression was management's proposal that several railroad lines be merged or consolidated as a step toward economizing operating expenses, a step forced by the drastic decline in railroad revenues. What might happen to thousands of jobs, to seniority rights, and to contracts protected by the Railway Labor Act of 1926 were life-and-death questions for railway workers.

Richberg and the labor leaders of the RLEA lobbied vigorously against any plans for reducing the work force in the name of economy. They believed that such a step was particularly misleading in that the economies thereby created were false because they reduced the available consuming power needed to support prosperity. To destroy jobs while dividends were still being paid on railroad stocks flew in the face of common sense; such a policy would only increase over-saving by the well-to-do and further withdraw consumptive power from the one sector of the economy—the working people— where it would surely be used, thereby creating markets and jobs. Furthermore, too often mergers were for the benefit of the financiers who would profit from organizing the new combinations. Consolidation would likewise mean reduced or canceled railroad service to some communities, further spreading the depression by destroying jobs and creating obstacles to the exchange of goods. To the railroad employees, this not only meant unemployment and displacement but also raised the risk that railroad service to many communities might permanently be replaced by trucking.[25]

[25] Richberg, *Memorandum Brief in Support of S. J. Res. 161,* April 16, 1930, including "Statement of Railway Labor Executives' Association Concerning Railroad Consolidation" of March 31, 1930, Richberg Papers, L.C., Box 6; U. S., Congress, Senate, 72nd Cong., 1st sess., Committee on Manufactures, *Emergency Financing for Unemployed Workers,* Hearings on S. 4947 (1932), 7–20, copy in Richberg Papers, L.C., Box 43; Richberg, "Report of Donald R. Richberg to Meeting of Railway Labor Executives' Association, Cleveland, Ohio, July 24, 1930," 1–3, and Richberg, "The Spread-Work Folly," Aug. 17, 1932, Richberg Papers, L.C., Box 44; David B. Robertson, "In Re: Subject of Legislation Affecting Railroad Consolidation," April 18, 1929, Richberg Papers, C.H.S., Box 7; Timothy Shea to Members, Railway Labor Executives' Association, April 15, 1930, Richberg Papers, C.H.S., Box 9; Richberg to David B. Robertson, March 1, 1932, Richberg Papers, C.H.S., Box 14.

On much the same grounds, Richberg also spoke out against the so-called spread-work movement for increasing employment by reducing the hours of the workday and making up the difference by hiring more workers. Unless the plan envisioned paying the same wages for a six-hour day as for an eight-hour day, it would only spread poverty around. What was really needed, Richberg believed, were not plans to spread the same total wages among more people, but some way to increase total wages and consequently consuming power. When the RLEA supported proposals for the six-hour day, it was on the understanding that the same wages would be paid for less work.[26]

Railroad consolidations and unemployment were thus the most immediate crises facing the RLEA as the depression deepened. Richberg and David Robertson sought to marshal management cooperation on the consolidation question through Alfred P. Thom, general counsel of the Association of Railroad Executives, but made little headway.[27] Consequently, much of Richberg's energy was devoted to preparing legislative programs to block sanctioning by the Interstate Commerce Commission of consolidations that would violate contracts or procedures for negotiation as guaranteed by the Railway Labor Act; this would at least assure that labor would be consulted before changes were introduced. Richberg supported these efforts by testifying before congressional committees and working closely with friendly members of Congress, such as Senators George Norris, Edward Costigan, James Couzens, Robert Wagner, and Robert Howell, and Representative Fiorello La Guardia.[28]

[26] Richberg to members of the RLEA, Aug. 5, 1932, Richberg Papers, C.H.S., Box 15; Richberg, "The Spread-Work Folly," Aug. 17, 1932, Richberg Papers, L.C., Box 44.

[27] David B. Robertson to Richberg, March 28, 1929; David B. Robertson, "In Re: Subject of Legislation Affecting Railroad Consolidation," April 18, 1929, Richberg Papers, C.H.S., Box 7.

[28] Richberg to A. G. McKnight, April 9, 1930, Richberg Papers, C.H.S., Box 9; Richberg, Memorandum Brief in Support of S. J. Res. 161, April 16, 1930, 3–10, Richberg Papers, L.C., Box 6; Richberg, "Report of Donald R. Richberg to Meeting of Railway Labor Executives' Association, Cleveland, Ohio, July 24, 1930," 1–3, Richberg Papers, L.C., Box 44; Richberg to David B. Robertson, March 1, 1932, Richberg Papers, C.H.S., Box 14; U. S.,

Ultimately, two pieces of legislation, which took cognizance of the arguments he and the labor executives had made, passed before Richberg left the RLEA to serve in the Franklin D. Roosevelt administration. The first was the Bankruptcy Act of 1933, signed by President Hoover on March 3. Largely because of the concern of the railway labor unions that economies would be made at their expense, Senator George Norris introduced a series of amendments to the original bill which Congress accepted and which required receivers in corporate reorganizations to conform to the terms and procedures of the Railway Labor Act in renegotiating contracts with employees. Financial reorganization of bankrupt roads thus might not provide an excuse for unilateral cancellation of contracts or reduction of wages. Furthermore, the principle of employee organization free from management coercion or influence as set forth in the Railway Labor Act was reasserted, as was the mandate of the Norris-La Guardia Act against yellow-dog contracts.

The second piece of legislation was the Emergency Transportation Act approved by President Franklin Roosevelt on June 16, 1933. This was the last major legislative project that Richberg worked on before severing his ties with the RLEA and moving into the new administration. The new law created a Federal Coordinator of Transportation empowered to eliminate waste and duplication in rail service by promoting consolidation and financial reorganization. Partly in response to the fears of railway labor as articulated by Richberg and the union executives in congressional hearings on the bill, guarantees were written into the law to protect jobs, to improve the grievance provisions of the Railway Labor Act by creating regional Adjustment Boards, and to assure compliance with the terms of the Bankruptcy Act.[29]

While the Emergency Transportation Act represented a forward

Congress, Senate, 73rd Cong., 1st sess., Committee on Interstate Commerce, *Emergency Railroad Transportation Act, 1933*, Hearings on S. 1580 (1933), 77–129; U. S., Congress, House, 73rd Cong., 1st sess., Committee on Interstate and Foreign Commerce, *Emergency Railroad Transportation Act, 1933*, Hearings on H.R. 5500 (1933), 69–113, 161–88; Irving Bernstein, *The New Deal Collective Bargaining Policy* (Berkeley, Calif., 1950), 43–47.

[29] Bernstein, *The New Deal*, 44–47.

step in labor's attempt to hold the line against unemployment, it was of only one year's duration. What was needed was permanent legislation, a need met by amending the Railway Labor Act in 1934. For several years Richberg had been working on amendments to the 1926 Act at the direction of the railway labor leaders. Although he did not participate in the final successful thrust which began in the fall of 1933, after he joined the Roosevelt administration, he had laid the groundwork for the ultimate result. By October 1932 Richberg had formulated a labor program in the form of several specific amendments to the Railway Labor Act providing for strengthened guarantees of unhindered employee organization, empowering the Board of Mediation to determine the accredited representatives of either the carriers or the employees (by elections if necessary), granting district courts the power to issue orders enforcing the procedures for negotiation defined in the Act, providing penalties for carriers who conspired to violate the Act and to deny employees their rights of collective bargaining and freedom of representation, and requiring all district attorneys to institute prosecutions against carriers violating the law. Equally important, grievances arising out of the failure of disputants voluntarily to create Adjustment Boards could be referred to the Board of Mediation even though such Boards had not considered the question initially as contemplated in the original Act; this would break up one of the worst roadblocks in the functioning of the grievance machinery of the Act.[30]

Fighting consolidations and amending the Railway Labor Act were not the only remedies to railway labor's problems; an expanded RLEA program, negotiations with management, and court action provided additional solutions to additional problems. The enlarged program of the RLEA required Richberg to develop analyses and proposals dealing with truck and bus transportation, hours of work, workmen's compensation, employers' liability, old-age pensions, public works, and emergency financing for unemployed workers.

[30] Ibid., 47–56; A. F. Whitney to Members, RLEA, Oct. 12, 1932, Richberg Papers, C.H.S., Box 16; Richberg, "Report of Donald R. Richberg to Meeting of Railway Labor Executives' Association, Cleveland, Ohio, July 2, 1930," 3, Richberg Papers, L.C., Box 44.

While few concrete proposals for legislation emerged from these discussions for which Richberg and the RLEA could claim exclusive credit, these concerns did indicate a significant broadening of perspective by the railway organizations. And Richberg made sure that the views of the RLEA were well known in the halls of Congress.[31]

Additionally, Richberg took part in numerous negotiations, arbitrations, and mediations under the Railway Labor Act. He also engaged in extensive litigations to enforce state laws limiting the length of trains and providing for minimum numbers of men on crews operating trains. This work took Richberg all over the country; as general counsel of the RLEA he was called upon by rail unions from east to west to assist them in local or state as well as national controversies.[32]

Of all the collective bargaining Richberg took part in, perhaps the most significant was that leading to a 10 percent wage cut for railway employees in 1932. Faced with declining revenues and the need to meet interest payments and other obligations on capital in-

[31] Richberg, "Report of Donald R. Richberg to Meeting of Railway Labor Executives' Association, Cleveland, Ohio, July 24, 1930," Richberg Papers, L.C., Box 44; Richberg to David B. Robertson, April 10, 1931, Richberg Papers, C.H.S., Box 11; Richberg to B. M. Jewell, Manion, J. G. Luhrsen, July 16, 1931, enclosing Richberg, "Report of Old Age Pensions to the Railway Labor Executives' Association"; "Memorandum concerning Work on Federal Workmen's Compensation and Retirement Insurance— (Old Age Pensions), " Dec. 28, 1931, Richberg Papers, C.H.S., Box 12; Richberg to David B. Robertson, Feb. 22, 1932; Richberg to David B. Robertson, March 1, 1932, Richberg Papers, C.H.S., Box 14; Richberg to David B. Robertson, July 27, 1932; [Richberg] to Robert M. La Follette, Jr., June 25, 1932, Richberg Papers, C.H.S., Box 15; Whitney to Members, RLEA, Oct. 12, 1932; Richberg, "Workmen's Compensation for Railway Employees," Dec. 29, 1932, Richberg Papers, C.H.S., Box 16; Richberg, "Financing a Public Works Program," March 31, 1933, Richberg Papers, L.C., Box 44.

[32] Richberg, "Report of Donald R. Richberg to Meeting of Railway Labor Executives' Association, Cleveland, Ohio, July 24, 1930," 4–7, Richberg Papers, L.C., Box 44; Richberg, "Memories for My Grandchildren," 17–24, Manuscript in possession of Mrs. John H. Small III, Charlottesville, Va.; Richberg, "My Hero," Draft #2, chapt. 10, 4–12, Richberg Papers, L.C., Box 14; Richberg, My Hero: The Indiscreet Memoirs of an Eventful but Unheroic Life (New York, 1954), 141–46.

vestment, the railroads proposed increased rates and a wage cut as the solution. Exploratory talks got underway in the fall of 1931; most of the rest of the year was spent in maneuvering over the agenda of a proposed national conference which would deal not only with the wage question but also with consolidations, the six-hour day, stabilization of employment, pension plans, employment bureaus, motor transportation, and other grievances. Another issue in the preliminary arrangements was the question of obtaining assurances from the management side that its representatives would be empowered to make a binding agreement when the conference was finally held; the unions had been disappointed in a meeting of November 1931 when the management spokesmen appeared without power to conclude agreements. When railway labor obtained such assurances in December 1931, it had passed a landmark in management-labor relations. The proposed conference was to be the first time in railroad history that nationwide collective bargaining was agreed to by management. The RLEA had succeeded in winning over management to the position it had taken in a resolution of November 2, 1931, that "both the managements of the railroad systems and their employees are organized so that they are able to deal nationally with problems and emergencies affecting the entire transportation industry."[33]

Although the union leaders themselves determined policy throughout the conference, Richberg was close at hand and assisted both in the planning of long-range strategy and in the negotiations themselves. In January 1932 the 1,200 railway delegates at the conference authorized him to formulate their agreement to take a

[33] Daniel Willard to David B. Robertson, Nov. 14, 1931; David B. Robertson to Willard, Nov. 17, 1931; Willard to David B. Robertson, Nov. 21, 1931; David B. Robertson to Willard, Nov. 21, 1931; C. E. Seehorn, W. C. Keiser, A. B. Miller, B. L. Summers, R. B. Wilkins, W. G. Metcalfe, to General Chairmen and Local Chairmen, Brotherhood of Locomotive Firemen and Enginemen, in U. S., Dec. 16, 1931; Willard to David B. Robertson, Dec. 18, 1931; "Press Notice," Dec. 18, 1931; David B. Robertson to Willard, Dec. 21, 1931, Richberg Papers, C.H.S., Box 12; Bernstein, *The Lean Years*, 314–16. The quotation is from "Resolution Adopted by Railway Labor Executives' Association," Nov. 2, 1931, enclosed in David B. Robertson to R. H. Aishton, Nov. 2, 1931, Richberg Papers, C.H.S., Box 12.

10 percent wage cut. Richberg viewed this as a realistic step taken in recognition of the exigencies of the railroads' financial situation, and he strongly supported the action. On the management side, it was Daniel Willard, president of the Baltimore and Ohio and chairman of the employer representatives, who induced the chief recalcitrants—the Union Pacific, the Burlington, and the Southern Pacific—to go along with a 10 percent cut rather than hold out for the 15 percent which they originally sought. As a result of the efforts on both sides, an agreement was reached mutually, thus avoiding the likelihood of unilateral action by the railroads had the conference failed.[34]

Though the railway workers accepted a wage cut, they had prevented the roads from acting separately in serving notice, under the terms of the Railway Labor Act, of an intention to change the existing contracts. Some roads did give notice, but the successful involvement of the managements of most of the country's railroads in a nationwide collective bargaining session was a major victory for railway labor. Furthermore, the roads had wanted a 15 percent cut; the compromise that came out of the January 1932 conference resulted in a 10 percent cut to be restored automatically within one year unless extended by mutual agreement. At a time when workers in other industries were suffering reductions in pay imposed unilaterally by management, the railway unions established a precedent for nationwide collective bargaining and succeeded in limiting the extent of their losses. They also procured promises from management to take all possible steps to stabilize employment and to investigate a number of the complaints that had been discussed in the course of the conference.[35]

Before the railway wage question came to a culmination, Rich-

[34] Richberg, "My Hero," Draft #2, chapt. 10, 19–25, Richberg Papers, L.C., Box 14. In addition, see Richberg, "Memories for My Grandchildren," 28–31; Richberg, My Hero, 147–48; Bernstein, The Lean Years, 315–16.

[35] Bernstein, The Lean Years, 313–16; C. M. Rodgers, Seehorn, Miller, Fred R. Bean, H. H. Burnett, R. L. Glenn, T. M. Spooner to General Chairman, BLFE et al., Jan. 12, 1932; "Report of Railway Labor Executives' Association with Reference to Negotiations with Committee of Railway Presidents concerning Questions of Unemployment and Wages," Feb. 1, 1932, Richberg Papers, C.H.S., Box 14.

berg's own financial status came under review—at his own instigation. Years after he had severed his ties with the RLEA, Richberg took pride in the fact that he had never held a permanent retainer from the unions; he always worked on a job-by-job basis. This, he believed, enabled him both then and later to look upon labor questions with a detachment and objectivity not possible to one permanently dependent on one group of clients.[36] This thought may very well have been simply an unconscious rationalization of his later anti-union outlook, for in 1930–1931 he attempted to procure just such a retainer from the RLEA, albeit unsuccessfully.

The issue arose when Richberg was offered an opportunity to undertake work for another client, not connected with the railway unions, on a permanent, full-time basis. He anticipated that the new work would be acceptable to him and would enable him to spend more time with family and friends in Chicago than was possible while representing the unions. In the hope of having the RLEA equal this other bid for his services, which thus far had been on a per diem basis, Richberg suggested several propositions for a retainer, with the definite implication that he might not continue to represent the RLEA unless "a satisfactory, permanent relationship" could be worked out. Financial difficulties prevented the RLEA from settling the question, so the union executives continued their previous per diem arrangement. Nevertheless, Richberg did not leave. He preferred to work for clients he could identify with the public interest; this identification provided a justification for his work which could never be equaled by service to strictly private clients. This need for justification, as well as the many personal relationships he had built up over the years in union circles, plus the small amount of public attention that his work sometimes brought, probably helped to keep Richberg in the service of the railway unions for a while longer despite other offers. His relationship with the RLEA continued as before.[37]

[36] Richberg to the Editor, Chicago *Journal of Commerce,* July 8, 1933, Richberg Papers, L.C., Box 1; Richberg, *My Hero,* 162.

[37] Martin F. Ryan to Richberg, Feb. 14, 1931; Richberg to Ryan, March 5, 1931; Jewell to Ryan, March 10, 1931, Richberg Papers, C.H.S., Box 11. The quotation is from Richberg to David B. Robertson, Jan. 23, 1931, Richberg Papers, C.H.S., Box 11.

As the depression deepened, it became clear to Richberg that he and railway labor would have to look elsewhere if the Republican party renominated President Hoover in 1932. In the preconvention campaign of 1928, Richberg and David Robertson had sought to marshal railway labor behind Secretary of Commerce Hoover, only to be disappointed in his failure to enunciate a progressive labor program during the course of the election campaign. Developments in the years that followed confirmed the worst fears of Richberg that Hoover's commitment to labor was lukewarm at best. The administration had resisted the movement to pass an antiinjunction bill despite widespread support for the measure once the abuses of judges such as Wilkerson and Parker became generally known. Informal, nongovernmental efforts at reform, such as the 1931 Progressive Conference sponsored by Senator George Norris, resulted in rhetoric rather than accomplishment. The development of an enlarged RLEA program signified not only a broadening perspective on the part of railway labor but also an increasing need. The wage cuts suffered by rail and other industrial workers as the decade of the 1930s opened were symbolic of the need for a new approach to the problems of the depression.

Although Richberg personally was tempted to take up a more economically secure occupation than representing railway labor, his need to be part of a movement he believed was graced with the public good, and his rapture with participating in public or semipublic work, helped to keep him receptive to calls for service. He continued to work for railway labor, and thus was in a strategic position to participate in the new administration when the opportunity came. In fact, his association with the new regime began during the campaign, well before the election of 1932. When the call came, Richberg was ready.

CHAPTER VI

The Door to Preferment

After the disappointments of the Hoover years, Donald Richberg was receptive to any sign that the Democrats rather than the Republicans would carry on his concept of the progressive tradition. Hoover's desire for vindication and his control of the party machinery virtually assured that he would be the Republican nominee in 1932. To Richberg, the Republican party could only promise more of the same. The Democrats thus became the center of his interest. Of course, after the initial phase of Hoover's 1928 campaign, Richberg had no personal stake in the administration, and this undoubtedly was a factor in turning him toward the Democrats. His disillusionment with Hoover's labor policy, the prospect that a second term for the president would mean no new ideas in dealing with the depression, and his personal career situation made it all but certain that 1932 would find Donald Richberg in the Democratic camp.

Richberg's initial contact with the Democratic organization occurred in July 1932, after Governor Franklin D. Roosevelt of New York had won his party's presidential nomination. Roosevelt took the initiative by asking Richberg to arrange for a conference with members of the Railway Labor Executives' Association. As in the 1928 campaign for Hoover, he served as the go-between for the nominee and David B. Robertson, chairman of the RLEA. Richberg's involvement with the candidate was the result of his official position as general counsel of the RLEA, for he and Roosevelt were not personally acquainted and knew each other only by reputation prior to the summer of 1932.[1]

The conference took place on August 29 with Richberg and representatives of fifteen of the railway labor organizations present. The union executives provided Roosevelt with a capsule summary of the RLEA program, including their position on railroad consolidation, retirement insurance and pensions for railway workers, the six-hour day, and unemployment relief. Richberg considered the meeting a success in more ways than one. Not only did the RLEA have an opportunity to present its views to the Democratic candidate as a guide to developing his labor platform, but Richberg himself established personal contact with the probable victor in the coming elections. As Richberg later fondly recalled, Roosevelt told one of his associates after the meeting that he was "a man I want to have near me in Washington."[2]

Richberg was anxious to participate in the campaign and was alert to the opportunities that came his way. He acquired what he called an "associate membership" in the Brain Trust, Roosevelt's informal policy committee headed by Raymond Moley of Columbia University, when he offered to help on railroad questions. Richberg was an ideal counselor in view of his reputation as one of the country's leading labor lawyers and his part in bringing Roosevelt and the RLEA together for their August conference. Roosevelt readily accepted his offer. Along with Adolph Berle of Columbia, future Secretary of the Treasury William Woodin, Joseph B. Eastman of the Interstate Commerce Commission, Ralph Budd of the Burlington Railroad, House Interstate and Foreign Commerce Committee counsel Walter Splawn, and other experts, he participated in the preparation of a railroad speech for Roosevelt under Moley's supervision.[3]

[1] Donald Richberg to Louis McHenry Howe, July 14, 1932, Donald Richberg Papers, Chicago Historical Society, Box 15; Richberg, *My Hero: The Indiscreet Memoirs of an Eventful but Unheroic Life* (New York, 1954), 154.

[2] "Memorandum for Conference with Governor Roosevelt on August 29, 1932," and "Representatives of Standard Railway Labor Organizations," Aug. 29, 1932, Richberg Papers, C.H.S., Box 15. The quotation is from Richberg, *My Hero*, 155.

[3] Richberg, *My Hero*, 155; Raymond Moley, *After Seven Years* (New York, 1939), 45; Richberg to Moley, Sept. 30, 1932; "Copy of Revision of

Another avenue of approach to the Roosevelt campaign organization was the National Progressive League for Franklin D. Roosevelt. Senator George Norris of Nebraska became honorary chairman and Senator Edward Costigan of Colorado was honorary vice-chairman. Though he lacked enthusiasm for the project initially, Richberg was made executive chairman of the group. The purpose of the Progressive League was to mobilize support among former Progressives, especially those who left the Republican party in 1912, on behalf of the Democratic ticket. At first, Richberg felt that the results of such an effort would not be worth the trouble and expense, and further raised the possibility that the Republicans might try the same tactic and conceivably marshal more support from old Progressive-Republicans than the Democrats. But the group's possibilities for giving him access to Roosevelt were ultimately compelling. Richberg had no intention of consciously using the League for his own private ends, but his desire to do battle for reform causes undoubtedly supplied much motivating power and made him willing to become active in the project. It was a handy outlet for his desire to participate in the campaign. The League itself was of little consequence in the election, but as a vehicle for Richberg's ambitions it served him well.[4]

With the predictable Democratic victory at the November elections, Richberg's name became the subject of speculation as to a possible appointment in the new administration. He was one of many figures on the outer fringes of the Roosevelt group, though in private he grossly exaggerated the possibility of a high-level appointment for himself. Publicly, he would have nothing to do with talk about appointments, whether for himself or for anyone else. He even refused to recommend those who sought his support for their own ambitions, including his former law partner, Harold Ickes. One of the apparent reasons for his public reluctance regarding himself was his financial situation. Even a top-level post in

9/12/32," draft speech on railroads for Franklin D. Roosevelt, Richberg Papers, c.h.s., Box 15.
    [4] Richberg, *My Hero*, 156–57; Basil Manly to Richberg, Aug. 26, 1932; Richberg to Manly, Sept. 3, 1932; Richberg to Manly, Sept. 26, 1932; Richberg to Manly, Sept. 30, 1932, Richberg Papers, c.h.s., Box 15.

government would mean a drastic cut in income. Richberg still had
several relatives dependent upon him for support; this was an old
problem made more acute by the depression.[5]

Privately, however, Richberg hoped that such obstacles somehow could be overcome. While not openly seeking an appointment,
nor wishing to force himself upon the president, he worked behind
the scenes and hoped that he would be drafted for a suitable position. For much of the winter and spring, Richberg set his sights on
the cabinet itself, and at various times had dreams of the Interior,
Labor, and Justice departments. He was sorely disappointed at the
selection of Harold Ickes as secretary of interior. Afterwards, he
scolded Ickes for having sought his support for the job; Richberg
wrote Ickes that such a request amounted to asking "me to take
myself entirely out of the cabinet picture so that you might put
yourself in." Richberg reasoned that if the cabinet was to be politically and geographically balanced, there would not be enough room
for two Progressive lawyers from Chicago. Furthermore, Richberg
explained, to back Ickes for a position would repudiate "the efforts
of my friends to obtain my appointment." Richberg's hopes rose
briefly later in the spring of 1933. The unexpected death of Senator
Thomas Walsh of Montana, who had been Roosevelt's first choice
for attorney general, seemed to reopen the door to preferment, however tenuously. Despite the backing of the railway labor executives, Richberg lost out again.[6]

[5] Richberg to A. F. Whitney, Nov. 21, 1932, Richberg Papers, C.H.S.,
Box 16; Richberg to Felix Frankfurter, Jan. 14, 1933, Felix Frankfurter
Papers, Library of Congress, Box 32; Richberg, *My Hero*, 158–60.
[6] David Lilienthal to Richberg, Dec. 8, 1932; Richberg to Lilienthal,
Dec. 19, 1932, Richberg Papers, C.H.S., Box 16; Richberg to Frankfurter,
Jan. 14, 1933, Frankfurter Papers, Box 32; Gilson Gardner to Roosevelt,
Jan. 19, 1933; [Richberg] to Clarence N. Goodwin, Jan. 27, 1933; Rich-
berg to Ickes, Feb. 24, 1933, C.H.S., Box 17; Ickes to Richberg, Feb. 20,
1933; Richberg to Ickes, Feb. 20, 1933; Richberg to Moley, Feb. 20, 1933,
Donald Richberg Papers, Library of Congress, Box 1; Richberg to Manly,
March 7, 1933; "Wire sent to all Chief Executives by Mr. A. F. Whitney,"
March 7, 1933; Bert Jewell to Whitney, March 7, 1933; J. G. Luhrsen to
Roosevelt, March 7, 1933; E. J. Manion to Roosevelt, March 7, 1933;
Leo J. Hassenauer to Richberg, March 8, 1933; Jewell to George Norris,
March 10, 1933, Richberg Papers, C.H.S., Box 17; Richberg, *My Hero*,

Actually, the cabinet was beyond Richberg's grasp. Raymond Moley relates in his memoirs that Richberg was considered for three positions, none of cabinet rank.[7] Though hardly a disinterested witness, Harold Ickes later recorded in his *Secret Diary* that Roosevelt never had any intention of appointing Richberg to a cabinet position. One day in September 1933 Ickes had been talking to Roosevelt about Richberg and mentioned "that Richberg thought he was being seriously considered for the Cabinet and might have landed it if I hadn't crowded him out." According to Ickes, "The President threw back his head and laughingly said that he had never for a moment thought of Richberg in connection with the Cabinet."[8] But in view of the almost fortuitous manner in which Ickes himself had gained appointment, largely because of Roosevelt's inability to find a suitable man willing to undertake the Interior post and despite his lack of any prior acquaintance with Ickes, the possibility—remote though it was—that Richberg might have been offered a place in the cabinet was not to be ruled out in such a facile manner.

There were other, more realistic opportunities besides the cabinet available to Richberg. The most desirable was the job of solicitor general. Roosevelt had already offered the position to Felix Frankfurter of Harvard Law School, but he turned it down, feeling that he could be of greater assistance to the president by remaining outside the administration. Roosevelt asked him to recommend someone else, so Frankfurter decided to sound out Richberg as a possibility. Richberg's immediate response was negative because the job's low salary would not cover his financial and family obligations. Yet on the very day of his refusal, he changed his mind and tried to reach Frankfurter to tell him that he wanted to reconsider his decision. Frankfurter seemed reluctant to recommend him, however, and Richberg was always mystified as to the reason.

157–59. The quotations are from Richberg to Ickes, Feb. 24, 1933, Richberg Papers, c.h.s., Box 17; a copy of this letter has recently been placed in the Richberg Papers at the Library of Congress.

[7] Raymond Moley, *The First New Deal* (New York, 1966), 290 n.

[8] Ickes, *The Secret Diary of Harold L. Ickes,* Vol. 1: *The First Thousand Days, 1933–1936* (New York, 1953), 87.

Frankfurter had decided that Richberg could render greater service to the Roosevelt administration by retaining his position as counsel to the railway labor executives.[9] Roosevelt considered Richberg for other posts as well, among them comptroller of currency and counsel of the Bureau of Internal Revenue. None of these proposals ever came to fruition.[10]

Richberg's eventual draft into administration service came about as the result of his assistance in preparing the president's legislative program during the "Hundred Days," the first three months of Roosevelt's tenure during which the basic measures of the early New Deal were drawn up, sent to Congress, and signed into law. Richberg was frequently in Washington on RLEA business and was requested to assist with the administration program, as he reported to A. F. Whitney, Robertson's successor as chairman of the RLEA, "particularly so far as it concerns the railroads." He was especially interested in the legislation that eventually emerged as the Emergency Transportation Act of 1933. In addition, Senators La Follette and Costigan called on him to help draw up a program for the progressive group in Congress to supplement the administration's ideas on recovery. Thus, Richberg was much in demand and found himself in an excellent position to keep track of developments regarding a possible appointment. For the time being, his situation remained indefinite, and as late as March 22, 1933, he was still considering whether to renew the lease on his Chicago office. Yet conditions were fluid, and on March 28 Richberg wrote to David Lilienthal, "Regarding the Washington situation—the picture is still blurred. But every now and then, as in a mirror, one seems to see a face."[11]

[9] Richberg, *My Hero*, 159; Frankfurter to Roosevelt, March 14, 1933, and Frankfurter, memorandum, March 15, 1933, Frankfurter Papers, Box 34. The quotations are from Lilienthal, *The Journals of David E. Lilienthal*, Vol. 1: *The TVA Years, 1939–1945, Including a Selection of Journal Entries from the 1917–1939 Period* (New York, 1964), 155.

[10] Richberg, *My Hero*, 159–60; Moley, *First New Deal*, 290 n; Ickes, *Secret Diary*, 1:6–7.

[11] Edward P. Costigan and Robert M. La Follette, Jr., to Richberg, March 6, 1933; Frances Perkins to Richberg, March 22, 1933; Richberg to Moley, March 27, 1933, Richberg Papers, L.C., Box 1; Richberg to Alice Houlihan,

What led Richberg into greater and greater involvement in the administration was not his interest in railroad legislation but the assistance he lent on an industrial recovery bill. Although Roosevelt had no intention of presenting Congress with a comprehensive measure for dealing with the business depression when he called a special session for March 9, his hand was forced when a proposal by Senator Hugo Black of Alabama to limit the workweek to thirty hours passed the Senate on April 6, 1933.

Prior to this, the president had ordered his chief policy adviser, Raymond Moley, to study the innumerable plans for restoring prosperity that had flowed into Washington since the inauguration. But Moley later recalled that as of April 4, "thinking in business and government circles on the subject had not crystallized sufficiently to justify any further moves at the time." One of Moley's associates, James Warburg, had prepared a detailed analysis of the several plans, but Moley decided that the results of Warburg's study were inadequate. Roosevelt agreed and told Moley to shelve further work on the problem for the future.[12]

The passage of Senator Black's thirty-hour bill changed everything. Considerable support was gathering behind the measure, and Roosevelt would have to act quickly to regain the initiative. Otherwise, he ran the risk of seeing a recovery bill pass without his having had a hand in it. Yet he was reluctant to rally behind Black. As Secretary of Labor Frances Perkins hopefully interpreted the president's position, Roosevelt was "committed to the idea of a dynamic economy, an economy of greater expansion of production and distribution than we had known, rather than an economy of curtailment of production"; therefore, he doubted that a simple spread-work movement without any concomitant increase in purchasing power would solve the unemployment problem. And something had to be done to rid the proposal of its rigidity. Every kind of work, whether in industry or agriculture, could not be

---

March 22, 1933, Richberg Papers, c.h.s., Box 17. The quotation to Whitney is from Richberg to Whitney, March 6, 1933, and the quotation to Lilienthal is from Richberg to Lilienthal, March 28, 1933, both in Richberg Papers, c.h.s., Box 17.

[12] Moley, *After Seven Years*, 184–86.

tied to a six-hour day and a thirty-hour week; as Roosevelt put it in regard to the dairy industry, "There have to be hours adapted to the rhythm of the cow." Furthermore, there were grave doubts about the constitutionality of the Black bill.

For the time being, Roosevelt authorized Secretary Perkins to submit amendments to the Black bill designed to introduce a measure of flexibility and discretion in applying the thirty-hour standard. She also proposed minimum-wage standards to be recommended by special industrial boards on which labor, management, and government would be represented. Another board might consider limited exemptions from the law, and the secretary of labor would have discretion to impose machine-hour limitations. Perkins's amendments for saving the bill, however, caused as much controversy as the original measure itself. Opposition came from both labor and business quarters, and Roosevelt regarded the support of both, but especially the latter, as essential for any recovery bill. Before the Black bill got any farther, the administration withdrew its backing for the Perkins amendments and set forth an entirely new plan.[13]

At the same time that the president had allowed the secretary of labor to try amending the Black bill, he reversed his decision of April 4 not to press the preparation of a comprehensive industrial recovery measure, and on April 11 put Moley back to work coordinating the several proposals that had been suggested. Without informing Moley, Roosevelt also encouraged a number of others to try a hand at solving the same problem. Senator Wagner of New York was working on a draft recovery bill, assisted by former New York congressman Meyer Jacobstein, Harold Moulton of the Brookings Institution, David Podell and Gilbert Montague, two trade association lawyers, Fred Kent of the Bankers Trust Company, Malcolm Rorty and James Rand, two progressive business

[13] Frances Perkins, *The Roosevelt I Knew* (New York, 1946), 192–97. The quotation from Roosevelt is cited by Perkins, 194. Also see Irving Bernstein, *The New Deal Collective Bargaining Policy* (Berkeley, Calif., 1950), 29–31; Moley, *After Seven Years*, 186–87; Moley, *First New Deal*, 284, 287–88; Ellis Wayne Hawley, *The New Deal and the Problem of Monopoly: A Study in Economic Ambivalence* (Princeton, N. J., 1966), 21–23.

executives, W. Jett Lauck, a labor economist for the United Mine Workers, and members of Congress such as M. Clyde Kelly and Robert La Follette, Jr. Undersecretary of Commerce John Dickinson also had a proposal; from time to time he had worked on this problem with Jerome Frank and Rexford Tugwell of the Department of Agriculture and Labor Secretary Frances Perkins. Eventually, Dickinson and Wagner got together and produced a common draft.[14]

In the meantime, Moley was making little headway; he was already overburdened with several other equally important projects. By April 25, he realized that he could not deliver a recovery bill in time to block the Black bill or the Perkins substitute, and would have to assign the task to someone else. By chance, Moley ran into Hugh Johnson in a hotel lobby in Washington. Johnson was an economic adviser to business tycoon Bernard Baruch and an ex-cavalry officer and General in the Army. During the First World War, he had helped to organize the draft and served as army liaison with the War Industries Board. He later went into the agricultural implement business. After Roosevelt won the nomination in 1932, Baruch loaned Johnson to the Democratic campaign organization, and he became a full-fledged member of the Brain Trust, specializing on farm and business policy. Moley now turned to Johnson for help. He found him an office in the old State, War, and Navy Building and put him in charge of writing an industrial recovery bill. Johnson, eager to participate in the administration, needed no encouragement, and plunged right into a task that would keep him in Washington for the next year and a half.[15]

Johnson had well-developed ideas as to what was needed. He had frequently discussed the problem of industrial recovery with Baruch and Alexander Sachs of the Lehman Corporation. In addition, his service with the War Industries Board during the First World War provided him with experience in the only comparable effort to mobilize the economy for a national objective. Johnson's

[14] Moley, After Seven Years, 186–88; Hawley, The New Deal, 23–25.
[15] Moley, After Seven Years, 188; Moley, First New Deal, 283–85; Hugh S. Johnson, The Blue Eagle from Egg to Earth (Garden City, N. Y., 1935), 193.

first draft of a bill proposed suspending the antitrust laws, empowering the president to sanction business agreements on labor and competitive standards, and providing for federal licensing as a means of insuring compliance with the law. The version being developed by Senator Wagner's group, with the cooperation of Undersecretary of Commerce Dickinson, suggested combining a program of public works and government loans with industrial self-government through trade associations; it also guaranteed labor's right to collective bargaining.[16]

Neither Moley nor Johnson felt competent to deal with the labor provisions of a comprehensive recovery bill, nor did they consider them central to their objectives. Consequently, Moley suggested that Johnson get help from Donald Richberg as a gesture to win labor support for the measure. In view of his help in the campaign and his current work on railroad legislation, it was not surprising that Moley should think of Richberg rather than someone else. Though officially he represented only the railroad brotherhoods, Richberg seemed to have the confidence of the labor movement generally and would serve as a good spokesman to represent its interests, thereby encouraging labor to support the resulting bill.[17] Furthermore, Richberg's ideas about industrial recovery generally conformed to those then circulating within the administration and among its friends. Though differing on particulars, he was thinking along the same lines as Moley and Johnson and saw the solution to the depression in proposals that would "recognize the necessity of a planned economy."[18]

Richberg had well-developed ideas about industrial recovery and had worked them out in the form of a program which he presented before the Senate Committee on Finance in February 1933. Testifying on the causes and remedies of the depression, he em-

[16] Hawley, *The New Deal*, 23–25; Johnson, *Blue Eagle*, 193, 196–97; Bernstein, *The New Deal*, 31–32.

[17] Moley, *First New Deal*, 290; Johnson, *Blue Eagle*, 201; Richberg, *The Rainbow* (Garden City, N. Y., 1936), 107; Bernstein, *The New Deal*, 32.

[18] Richberg, *Depression Causes and Remedies*, Testimony before the Committee on Finance, U. S., Congress, Senate, Feb. 23, 1933, 12–15, 25, pamphlet in Richberg Papers, L.C., Box 19.

phasized the need for business-government planning to bolster consumption through higher wages and lower prices rather than retrenchment through cutting production and raising prices; in other words, he emphasized moving toward an economy of plenty and away from an economy of scarcity.

To accomplish this objective, Richberg enumerated several proposals. "Self-Government in Industry" was one answer. Once the working classes were adequately organized, it would be practical "to create industrial councils composed of representatives of managers, investors and workers and then to create a national council composed of similar representatives of all essential industries." The workers would double as consumer representatives, so that "ultimately, in the national council, all producing and consuming interests would be so represented that one group could hardly obtain sanction for a policy clearly contrary to the general welfare." Profiteering would be eliminated by "a legal limitation upon profit-making in the essential industries"; profits should be adequate only to meet the interest charges necessary to attract capital for investment. Profit limitation could be effected through the taxation system.

Though investors and government were already adequately organized to participate in such a scheme, unionization had not yet advanced to the point where labor could play its part in a national council to determine national economic policy. The Richberg plan thus called for encouraging and protecting the right of labor to organize free from interference by other interest groups. Richberg did not want others to speak on behalf of labor, but wanted it to be able to stand up for its own interests. Therefore, he saw unionization as the *sine qua non* of any plan for industrial self-government through a national economic council.

In the meantime, while this fundamental reorganization of interest groups was being carried out, Richberg proposed that several ameliorative actions be put into effect immediately: 1) appropriations for direct relief to supplement and maintain the work of state welfare agencies; 2) a program to create mass purchasing power and to increase employment quickly, by extending credit to unemployed heads of households and to industries willing to resume or increase employment and production; 3) creation of a national council to plan further emergency measures on an experimental, trial-and-error basis as a way of developing proved recovery devices until fundamental reform could be realized.[19] In addition, prior to testifying before the Senate Finance Committee, Richberg had worked with Senators La Follette, Costigan, and Cutting on a public works bill, and so could be numbered among those sympathetic to pump-priming as a way to revive the economy.[20]

It was obvious that Moley could count on Richberg as one attuned to what he and Johnson were trying to do in their proposed National Industrial Recovery bill. Richberg agreed to help out, and drafted a labor provision for the bill based on his experiences with the Railway Labor Act of 1926 and the Norris–La Guardia Anti-Injunction Act of 1932.[21]

By early May, the Wagner-Dickinson and the Johnson-Richberg drafts had progressed to a point where either one or the other would have to be selected or the two reconciled. Roosevelt thereupon held a conference with everyone working on the problem to decide the main points to be included in an administration bill. Having worked on both the industrial recovery measure and, prior to that, a public works bill, Richberg expressed confidence during the meeting that the two different approaches could be reconciled in a comprehensive program. He subsequently was included in a committee appointed by the president to combine the principal features of the two drafts in a single bill.[22]

The joint drafting committee appointed by Roosevelt included Richberg, Hugh Johnson, Senator Wagner, Budget Director Lewis Douglas, John Dickinson, Rexford Tugwell, and Frances Perkins. After Tugwell smoothed over a few misunderstandings present at the outset, he, Dickinson, and Perkins dropped out of the picture, leaving the rest of the committee free to draw up a compromise bill, assisted (in Johnson's words) only by "a few 'horners-in' from

[19] Ibid., 14–26.

[20] Richberg, The Rainbow, 106; Richberg, My Hero, 163.

[21] Richberg, The Rainbow, 107; Richberg, My Hero, 164; Bernstein, The New Deal, 32.

[22] Richberg, The Rainbow, 107–108; Richberg, My Hero, 164.

time to time." The resulting bill directed that the attack on the depression be carried out on two coordinated fronts: business-government cooperation to control the damaging effects of unrestrained competition, and public works to prime the pump of the economy. Title I of the National Industrial Recovery Act (NIRA) allowed each industry, as an ad hoc group or through trade associations, to propose a code of fair competition governing trade and labor practices, which upon approval by the president would be exempt from the antitrust laws and would have the authority of law in the codified industry. The Act empowered the president to license businesses to secure compliance. Title II set up a Public Works Administration with an appropriation of $3.3 billion to provide a spur to production and, in turn, consumption.[23]

The bill that was signed into law on June 16, 1933, contained the soon-to-be-famous Section 7a of Title I, the clause requiring that every code of fair competition guarantee the right of collective bargaining and unimpaired union organization. Richberg later claimed that 7a originated in the draft prepared by himself and General Johnson.[24] Although Moley and Johnson had called upon Richberg for help as a labor expert, the evolution of Section 7a was a far more complex undertaking. Certainly the Wagner group was thinking along similar lines. In the process of drafting and redrafting, individual contributions were reworked and sometimes altered beyond recognition. And given the concessions to business, it would have been difficult to enact the program without labor provisions, so that some sort of Section 7a was likely to be drafted by someone.

In view of the general consensus in administration circles, the question of individual authorship was less crucial than if there had been sharp divergences of opinion among those whom Roosevelt

[23] Richberg, *The Rainbow*, 107–10; Richberg, *My Hero*, 164–65; Moley, *After Seven Years*, 188–89; Moley, *First New Deal*, 290–92; Hawley, *The New Deal*, 25. For the text of the law as passed by Congress, see U. S., *Statutes at Large* (1933), 48:195. The quotation is from Johnson, *Blue Eagle*, 204.

[24] Richberg to Natasha von Hoershelman, Sept. 26, 1933, with "Memorandum concerning Section 7(a)," National Recovery Administration Papers, Record Group 9, National Archives, Series 47, Box 581; U. S., *Statutes at Large* (1933), 48:195, 198–99.

relied on. The truly significant fact was that opinion in the administration had coalesced behind a series of related ideas which were brought together in the final bill: business-government cooperation, reliance on trade associations for implementing the program, temporary suspension of the antitrust laws, imposition of trade and labor standards through codes of fair competition, and public works. As Moley later recalled, it was probable that a recovery bill would have evolved even if he had never run into Hugh Johnson in a hotel lobby and turned the job over to him; so many people were working on relatively similar projects that some kind of a law was almost bound to develop.[25]

The bill that emerged from the joint drafting committee and passed through Congress by mid-June was thus the product of a growing consensus in the business community and the nation at large. And so were Richberg's own ideas about industrial recovery; originality was not one of his strong points. As Henry I. Harriman, president of the United States Chamber of Commerce, described the situation to Roosevelt, "The psychology of the country is now ready for self-regulation of industry with government approval of agreements reached either within or without trade conferences."[26]

Richberg's initiation into the new recovery administration grew directly out of his association with Johnson. The General was hard at work drawing up a plan of organization and recruiting personnel even before the bill passed Congress; in fact, he moved in this direction before any orders to do so had been issued from the White House, and simply assumed that he would be in charge of the agency he had helped to create. The crusty ex-cavalryman had taken a liking to the Chicago labor lawyer and determined to have him in the National Recovery Administration (NRA), as the agency for implementing Title I was to be called. Besides, Richberg apparently had the confidence of the labor movement and would satisfy the AFL. At the same time, he was no radical and seemed to subscribe to most of the ideas and assumptions of Johnson and Moley. Ultimately, after much haggling, Johnson and Richberg

[25] Moley, *After Seven Years*, 188.
[26] Henry I. Harriman to Roosevelt, May 11, 1933, Franklin Roosevelt Papers, Franklin D. Roosevelt Library, Official File 466.

were to agree on the job of general counsel as most appropriate.[27]

Richberg was anxious to have a part in the experiment; as he later recalled, "There was the lure of a great adventure and the possibility of sharing in a great achievement." Furthermore, his position was not unlike that of Johnson. Having contributed to planning the NRA he regarded it with something of a paternal interest. But Richberg was still confronted with the obstacle of his family obligations; a government salary would simply not meet his needs.[28] In order to get Richberg, Johnson took an extraordinary step to meet his wage demands and accepted a lower wage for himself, even though the post of general counsel was subordinate to that of administrator. The NRA general counsel thus received $14,120 per year (before Roosevelt's economy program effected a 15 percent reduction). Except for the president and his cabinet, Richberg was the highest paid member of the administration.[29]

Johnson went farther. Perhaps realizing that Richberg needed to justify his work as something special and as contributing to the public interest, Johnson emphasized that the president also wanted him to join the NRA. This was just the sort of appeal to which Richberg was vulnerable. He later fondly recalled that he had "a direct understanding with the President himself" and agreed to serve only at Roosevelt's "personal request." Roosevelt was willing to give Richberg the attention and assurances that he wanted, but may have created a misunderstanding in doing so. The president confided that he needed a watchdog on Johnson, not being sure what kind of an administrator he was going to make. Richberg was thus given the definite impression that he enjoyed a special relationship to the president and that actual authority in the NRA was divided between him and Johnson—at least unofficially. Whether this was a correct interpretation of Roosevelt's assurances or not, it was the

[27] Johnson, *Blue Eagle*, 201, 212; Richberg, *The Rainbow*, 110–12; Richberg, *My Hero*, 165; "Proceedings of Meeting No. 1 of the Special Industrial Recovery Board," June 19, 1933, 21, Franklin Roosevelt Papers, OF 466.

[28] Richberg, *The Rainbow*, 110–12.

[29] Alvin Brown to Richberg, Oct. 16, 1933, Richberg Papers, L.C., Box 47; Richberg, *My Hero*, 166–67.

one Richberg carried away from his meeting with the president.[30] Although the future difficulties that would someday develop between Richberg and Johnson were based on actual differences of opinion over policy and administration, Richberg's concept of his watchdog role in the NRA undoubtedly contributed to Johnson's later fears that Richberg was after his job.

Richberg thus entered the NRA with an exaggerated sense of his own importance. Furthermore, having been involved in the project from its inception, he came to regard the NRA uncritically. From the first, this approving attitude blinded him to dangers which he should have noticed as the tacit representative of the labor interest at the policy level of the NRA organization.

Moley and Johnson originally had turned to Richberg for help in drafting the NIRA as one who had the confidence of labor and could speak on its behalf. This same reasoning played a part in Johnson's desire to see Richberg join the NRA organization once the drafting process was over. Many in the railway brotherhoods and the AFL likewise looked on Richberg as a labor man in the new setup. And so did many in the industrial community, as Hugh Johnson found out when he was swamped with protests from businessmen upon announcing Richberg's appointment as general counsel. Grace Abbott of the Department of Labor, who was worried whether there would be adequate protection for labor in the code-making process, sought the counsel of Felix Frankfurter as to what might be done about the problem; Frankfurter's response typified the way in which many authorities regarded Richberg's position: "The inclusion of Donald Richberg as general counsel goes a long way to introduce the interests committed to the Secretary of Labor at the policy-making stages of what will be done under the Act."[31]

[30] Richberg, *The Rainbow*, 111–12; Richberg, *My Hero*, 165–66.

[31] Moley, *First New Deal*, 290; Johnson, *Blue Eagle*, 201, 212; Arthur M. Schlesinger, Jr., *The Age of Roosevelt*, Vol. 2: *The Coming of the New Deal* (Boston, 1959), 162–63; Miss Grace Abbott, "Memorandum for F. F. re: the Labor Department and the Administration of the Industrial Recovery Bill," May 25, 1933, and Frankfurter to Abbott, May 30, 1933, both in Frankfurter Papers. Box 62

Yet Richberg's view turned out to be different. Once he was appointed, he did not conceive of his role as being an unofficial representative and protector of labor. Instead of forthrightly facing the fact that everyone expected him to be labor's man in the NRA, Richberg perceived himself as playing what he regarded as a higher role: that of a disinterested arbiter smoothing over the conflicts among business, labor, and government.[32]

Richberg had always resented the idea of the lawyer as the representative of private or special interests. In place of such a concept, he saw the lawyer as an officer of the court, a public official bound to serve the general good. But in an organization like the NRA where most of the officeholders regarded themselves as the agents of opposing interests, labor could not afford to have a representative who was going to try to be impartial. Herein lay the seeds of the eventual estrangement between organized labor and Donald Richberg.

Even before the new organization officially got underway, Richberg's favorable identification with the NRA and his role in it interfered with his perception of what was happening. In staffing the NRA, Johnson got Bernard Baruch, his former boss, to mobilize what he dubbed "the very Brahmins of Big Industry" for help in recruiting the "best material in industry" to man the new organization.[33] Johnson's almost complete indifference to the labor movement as a source of personnel set the tone of the project from the first and should have alerted Richberg to the direction NRA was taking. Labor was going to need a protector. But if Richberg perceived what was happening, he failed to react. Wishing the best for a project he had helped to launch, and concerned with finding a niche in it for himself, his senses were dulled to the dangers that lay ahead.

Richberg thus began his tenure in the administration under two misconceptions: he perceived his relationship to Johnson as administrator in a way that was likely to lead to a clash at both the policy

[32] Richberg to the Editor, Chicago *Journal of Commerce*, July 8, 1933, Richberg Papers, L.C., Box 1; Richberg, *My Hero*, 162–63; Richberg, *The Rainbow*, 101–105, 115–21, 252–59, 275–84.

[33] Johnson, *Blue Eagle*, 206, 212–19; Hawley, *The New Deal*, 56–57.

and the personal levels; and he failed to understand that he was supposed to be a labor representative in the NRA and instead abdicated this role in favor of an Olympian concept of representing all economic interests, even though the assumptions underlying the NRA and the way it was staffed made it clear that business interests would be dominant and that labor would need defending. Having misconstrued his role-situation, Richberg was almost bound to run into trouble.

In some ways, Richberg's personal experiences were symbolic of what was happening to the National Recovery Administration itself. Vaguely defined in the law, with few policy standards or organizational guidelines, the NRA was all things to all men. Each could interpret the law according to his own predilections. Advocates of contrary approaches to industrial recovery could read their own ideas into the Act. It seemed to satisfy everyone in the beginning, but for the same reason was destined to satisfy no one in the end. Like Richberg, most of the supporters of the NRA launched the experiment amid a series of misunderstandings and a failure to perceive the realities of the situation.[34] To them, it hailed a new era of business-government cooperation that had in fact not yet arrived, as was to become all too evident in the subsequent history of the NRA.

As the NRA proved to be founded upon an uncertain dream, so too Richberg's belief that he could stand above the clash of selfish interests was to prove equally ephemeral. When he spurned the role of defending labor's interests and ignored the dangers of business dominance of the NRA in favor of seeking an unattainable level of impartiality, he sealed his own fate. Richberg was like most men and just as incapable of achieving perfect objectivity. Turning away from labor influences in a gesture of fair-mindedness to all interests, he was destined to succumb to business influences—which, after all, were the stronger of the two in the NRA. But it was this last point that Richberg failed to take adequate account of.

[34] Hawley, *The New Deal*, 26–52.

CHAPTER VII

The President's Counselor I

Donald Richberg's understanding of the task facing the National Recovery Administration was ambivalent and sometimes contradictory. On the one hand, he condemned the business community for bringing the country to the verge of economic disintegration, and on the other, he believed that the answer to the depression lay in combined action, under a government watchdog, among these same businessmen to control the destructive characteristics of competition and to set fair labor standards.[1] What Richberg did not count on was that the businessmen would make friends with the government watchdog, so that the NRA did not keep the upper hand in guarding against abuses of the privileges it allowed by temporarily suspending the antitrust laws.

Richberg's vacillation between a punitive and a benevolent attitude toward business collusion was apparent in his first major address as general counsel of the National Recovery Administration, a speech that Felix Frankfurter of Harvard Law School especially liked because it was "an admirable blend of *suaviter* and *fortiter,* the more so because the *fortiter* has slightly the edge on the *suaviter* in the cocktail."[2] In what was advertised as "officially approved by Administrator Hugh S. Johnson as a statement of Administration policy,"[3] Richberg warned his listeners at the Merchants' Association of New York on July 6, 1933, that the depression had taught the American people a lesson they would not soon forget. They would not keep in power "men who have no plan, no program for the general welfare, no understanding of the obligations to the common good that arise out of power to control the industries of the nation." While Richberg had no desire to see "the political socialization of industry," he prophesied that "unless industry is sufficiently socialized by its private owners and managers so that the great essential industries are operated under public obligations appropriate to the public interest in them—the advance of political control over private industry is inevitable."

Believing that the responsible businessman had been sufficiently chastened by the depression, Richberg assured the Merchants' Association that "the National Industrial Recovery Act was written in the confident belief that the great majority of businessmen are ready to take intelligent action, to accept their responsibilities courageously, and to cooperate with their fellows and with their government." This was the rationale of the whole NRA scheme, for the codes of fair competition would "not be in any sense the product of a dictatorship." Instead, industry itself would prepare the codes, so that they "will represent the uncoerced desire of . . . industry to govern itself wisely and in the public interest." By writing such a law as the NIRA, the New Deal reaffirmed its faith in the capitalist system, for "one of the primary purposes of the law is to avoid any necessity for government control of business; to encourage private initiative, to rely on self-discipline; to put faith in voluntary, collec-

[1] Donald Richberg, "Gold-plated Anarchy: An Interpretation of the Fall of Giants," *The Nation* 136 (April 5, 1933): 368–69; Richberg, *Depression Causes and Remedies,* Testimony before the Committee on Finance, U. S., Congress, Senate, Feb. 23, 1933, 7, 14, 16–17, 20–22, pamphlet in Donald Richberg Papers, Library of Congress, Box 19; Richberg, "Mutualism," *Proceedings of the Academy of Political Science* 13 (June 1928): 185–94; Richberg, *Laborism in This Changing World,* Address before the Brotherhood of Locomotive Firemen and Enginemen, Erie, Pa., Aug. 28, 1932, pamphlet in Richberg Papers, L.C., Box 19; Richberg, *The Rainbow* (Garden City, N. Y., 1936), 106–44.

[2] Felix Frankfurter to Richberg, July 7, 1933, Richberg Papers, L.C., Box 1.

[3] National Recovery Administration Release No. 29, July 3, 1933, Franklin D. Roosevelt Papers, Franklin D. Roosevelt Library, Official File 466.

tive agreements as the means of fixing and stabilizing human relations in and between units of industry." The burden of justifying the faith of the administration thus rested with business itself.[4]

The reaction to Richberg's policy pronouncement was generally unfavorable, and the New York *Herald Tribune* detected "the distinct touch of the iron hand beneath the velvet glove."[5] Yet such a reaction misinterpreted the trend of Richberg's thinking since the days of the Progressives. He conceived of the Railway Labor Act of 1926, for example, not as a measure to wield government force on behalf of labor, but simply as a device to guarantee that labor would have the opportunity to run its own affairs by being allowed to organize itself and bargain collectively. The law was a way of freeing labor to do something for itself, not to force the government to take over its functions.

Despite his frequently impassioned denunciations of the abuses of the capitalist system, there was no doubt in Richberg's mind that the private sector of the economy was to be the dominant element in NRA. And within the private sector, it was to be the managerial elements, exercising the traditional rights of property, rather than labor or the consumer, that would initiate and administer the codes in most instances. Although Richberg believed that "self-government in industry" meant "an adequate representation" of management, labor, and consumers "in the control of industry," he added a crucial qualification to this definition:

That doesn't mean the substitution of government control for management. Nor does it mean labor participation in management. On the contrary, I not only think there is a fundamental inconsistency in that conception, but curiously enough, the American labor movement itself has never been very keen about guiding and participating in management. They have as a rule rather objected to the possibility of their being asked to accept such responsibilities. But it does mean that management, while exercising its proper prerogatives, must take into con-

---

[4] Richberg, Address to Merchants' Association of New York, July 6, 1933, NRA Release No. 30, in Richberg Papers, L.C., Box 19.

[5] New York *Herald Tribune*, July 7–8, 1933; Philadelphia *Ledger*, July 9, 1933; New York *Evening Post*, July 7, 1933. The quotation is from the *Herald Tribune* of July 7, 1933.

sideration and must have a basis of conference and some corrective force for its own judgment on behalf both of those who do the manual or minor intellectual work of the industry, and of the public whose support must be obtained by the industry in the disposition of its products.[6]

Presumably, collective bargaining and the free choice of the marketplace would be sufficient to insure participation by labor and the consumers, rather than a more direct role in writing and enforcing the codes. Government's role in the NRA scheme would be to serve as a court of last resort for driving recalcitrants into line and for protecting labor and the consumer where private action proved inadequate. Richberg firmly believed in the NRA as an experiment in self-regulation, not government-regulation.[7]

Richberg's commitment to capitalism was evident in his acute sensitivity to his reputation as a radical, a reputation that had grown out of his representation of the railway labor unions and was wholly out of proportion to reality. Richberg seemed to feel somewhat guilty about his past connections, and took special precautions to explain that he was by no means a roistering revolutionary and was undeserving of the name "Comrade Richbergski" given him by a West Coast trade magazine.[8] He vehemently protested a description of him as a "lobbyist at large for organized labor" by the Chicago *Journal of Commerce*.[9] And in the autumn of 1933, he com-

[6] [Richberg], "Sunday Breakfast Club," Philadelphia, Pa., Nov. 5, 1933, 4, mimeographed speech in Richberg Papers, L.C., Box 19.

[7] Richberg, "Progress of the National Recovery Administration," Address over Columbia Broadcasting System, July 26, 1933, NRA Release No. 93; Richberg, Address over National Broadcasting Company, July 31, 1933, NRA Release No. 145; Richberg, "The Background of the N.R.A.," Address at Ottumwa, Iowa, Sept. 4, 1933, NRA Release No. 624; Richberg, "The Great Adventure of the N.R.A.," Address at Memphis, Tenn., Sept. 4, 1933, NRA Release No. 617; Richberg, "Underlying Principles of the National Industrial Recovery Act," Address at Babson Institute, Wellesley Hills, Mass., Sept. 8, 1933, NRA Release No. 628, all in Richberg Papers, L.C., Box 19.

[8] "Comrade Richbergski Issues Another Threatski," *Crow's Pacific Coast Lumber Digest*, April 15, 1935, 15.

[9] Richberg to the Editor, Chicago *Journal of Commerce*, July 8, 1933, Richberg Papers, L.C., Box 1.

plained of finding himself "constantly facing the difficulty of getting to an understanding with people who are perfectly sure that I am headed in a direction which is exactly opposite from the direction in which I am headed." Richberg felt compelled to use his public addresses as a platform for defending his "economic faith" in the hope of countering rumors that he was "some sort of wild radical, or a Socialist, with probably strong communistic leanings." Instead, he presented himself as "a convinced opponent of state socialism," one who did not "believe in the efficacy of state regulation of industrial operations" but did "believe very much in democratic processes and in the value of what I would call competitive individualism." Although the latter "must be qualified by a social conscience and a social responsibility," this was a matter of private morality and not something imposed by government decree. To Richberg, the NRA was "the half way house" between "undisciplined individualism" and "state socialism" that would save the free enterprise system from its self-destructive tendencies.[10]

This anxiety to explain away his apparent radical reputation and his labor affiliations revealed Richberg's deep-seated need for acceptance. It undoubtedly played a part in bringing him more and more under business influences in the NRA as he tried to justify his career to his colleagues and the business community. Johnson's policies in selecting personnel for NRA meant that Richberg daily brushed shoulders with men from the business world. As he sought and won their acceptance, he toned down his former labor bias more and more. Despite the sometimes melodramatic rhetoric condemning businessmen for leading the United States into the depression, Richberg's belief in the fundamental rationality of man, his faith in the possibility of cooperative efforts among opposing interests, his commitment to private rather than political domination of business, plus his sensitivity about his radical reputation revealed a trend in his thinking which the business community had no need to fear. Here was another element in the eventual estrangement between Richberg and organized labor.

Strictly speaking, Richberg's duties as NRA general counsel were

---

[10] [Richberg], "Sunday Breakfast Club," Philadelphia, Nov. 5, 1933, 1–3, Richberg Papers, L.C., Box 19.

those of a technical legal expert charged with interpreting the law for the administrator, Hugh Johnson.[11] But his understanding with the president, upon accepting appointment, involved a much larger role, one in the policy-making sphere. Most of the day-to-day administrative matters of the NRA Legal Division were left to his assistant, Blackwell Smith, and a growing army of young lawyers who had come to Washington to join the New Deal. Always fascinated by questions of theory and principle, Richberg concentrated on mastering the larger issues which bore on policy. Even had he chosen, he could not have supervised everything in the Legal Division, as the mass of detail in writing and administering the several hundred codes that eventually were approved was simply too great. Instead, Richberg devoted most of his time to working with Johnson, mediating special problems in code writing or industrial disputes, and making speeches in defense of a planned economy and the NRA.[12]

In the realm of policy, Richberg's interpretation of Section 7a of the National Industrial Recovery Act proved to be the acid test of his shifting attitude toward labor-management relations. Early in July, General Johnson in an NRA press release moved to counter propaganda emanating from organized labor that the only way workers could benefit from the NRA was by joining unions; at the same time, he challenged a similar advertising campaign sponsored by management that the company union was the workers' salvation. Johnson denounced both as "incorrect," "erroneous," and intended "to foment misunderstanding and discord." Furthermore, he declared, "It is not the function or the purpose of the Administrator to organize either industry or labor."[13] As Johnson confided to the

[11] Dudley Cates to Hugh Johnson, Aug. 21, 1933, Richberg Papers, L.C., Box 45.

[12] Thomas I. Emerson, "The Reminiscences of Thomas I. Emerson," 1:239, 244–46, 261–62, 265–66, 269–74, Oral History Research Office, Columbia University; Richberg, The Inside Story of the N.R.A., Address to Massachusetts State Recovery Board and County Chairmen, Dec. 15, 1933, pamphlet in Richberg Papers, L.C., Box 19. For an example of the struggles involved in writing one code, that for the bituminous coal industry, see James P. Johnson, "Drafting the NRA Code of Fair Competition for the Bituminous Coal Industry," Journal of American History 53 (Dec. 1966): 521–41.

[13] Johnson, NRA Release No. 34, July 7, 1933, NRA Papers, Series 223.

Special Industrial Recovery Board, the supervisory body appointed by the president to oversee NRA policy, on August 14, 1933, "This law should bring about open shops—shops where a man will be employed regardless of whether he belongs to any union or not," although Secretary Perkins prodded him into admitting that it need not "force open shops."[14] Despite this concession, Johnson's position was clear.

Richberg was in wholehearted agreement. The Johnson-Richberg position was soon elaborated in one of several policy statements interpreting Section 7a. Issued August 23, 1933, over the signatures of both General Johnson and Richberg, it purported to outline "the plain meaning of Section 7(a)." The words "open shop" and "closed shop" were banned from all codes and from "the dictionary of the N.R.A.," but only because they had "no agreed meaning." Employee rights of organization and collective bargaining as guaranteed by 7a meant "only one thing, which is that employees can choose anyone they desire to represent them, or they can choose to represent themselves." The ramifications of this were that "employers . . . can make collective bargains with organized employees, or individual agreements with those who choose to act individually." The representatives of the majority of the workers would not speak on behalf of all the workers; individuals and minorities could do their own bargaining and make their own separate contracts.

The August 23 statement went farther. The NIRA injunction against an employer's requiring a worker to join a company union as a condition of employment did not preclude company unions altogether: "The law does not prohibit the existence of a local labor organization, which may be called a company union and is composed only of the employees of one company." What management must avoid was maintaining such an organization by "interference, restraint or coercion," or forcing a worker to join the company union or to refrain from joining a different union. Though a man could not be compelled to join a local or company union, he could

[14] "Proceedings of Meeting No. 9 of the Special Industrial Recovery Board," Aug. 14, 1933, 9–10, Office of Government Reports Papers, Record Group 44, Federal Records Center, Suitland, Md., Series 10, Box 57.

do so if he freely chose it.[15] Lest there be any misunderstanding, Richberg reiterated this policy a few days later over a nationwide radio hookup on the National Broadcasting Company: "The law is not intended to enthrone any national labor organizations or to dissolve any local organization."[16] But the Johnson-Richberg stand against the majority rule principle seriously undermined the benefits organized labor could expect to obtain from 7a's guarantees of organization and collective bargaining. And their approval of the company union offered management an opportunity for evading the provisions of the law for protecting independent labor organization.

Johnson and Richberg thus emerged early in the life of the NRA as spokesmen for a compromising approach to labor policy. Although they definitely respected the legal right of union organization and collective bargaining, they appeared to suggest little that would threaten established relations between management and labor. The rights guaranteed by 7a did not compromise those of an employer so long as he did not interfere with unions or refuse to bargain with them. Even in the latter regard, bargaining did not mean that agreement must be reached. In the words of Richberg and Johnson, "The N.R.A. will not undertake in any instance to decide that a particular contract should be made, or should not be made between lawful representatives of employees and employers."[17] As had always been Richberg's point of view, labor conditions and wages were a matter for private determination between managers and workers.

The fate of the National Labor Board (NLB), created on August 5, 1933, revealed in stark terms the dilemma created by the Johnson-Richberg policy. The NLB had no powers of enforcement, but was to serve as a vehicle for adjusting industrial disputes and

[15] Johnson and Richberg, Joint Statement of Aug. 23, 1933, Richberg Papers, L.C., Box 45. Another copy and several drafts are in National Recovery Administration Papers, Record Group 9, National Archives, Series 47, Box 581. Also see New York *Times*, Aug. 24, 1933.

[16] Richberg, "Capital and Labor under the N.R.A.," Address over National Broadcasting Company, Aug. 29, 1933, Richberg Papers, L.C., Box 19.

[17] Johnson and Richberg, Joint Statement of Aug. 23, 1933, Richberg Papers, L.C., Box 45.

as a way of bringing publicity to bear on those who defied Section 7a. The most the Board could do was to ask NRA to remove a recalcitrant employer's Blue Eagle, the special insignia of compliance displayed by those who adhered to a code or signed an agreement with the president to maintain minimum labor standards. It might also recommend that the Justice Department look into possible violations of the law.

In a series of interventions and decisions, the National Labor Board evolved a policy on the question of determining employee representatives for collective bargaining with management. The NLB favored free elections utilizing secret ballots. More important, it favored having representatives of the majority speak on behalf of all the workers in negotiations—i.e., the principle of majority rule. This ran directly counter to the Johnson-Richberg position in favor of proportional representation. The NLB felt that majority rule was simply a commonsense approach to making collective bargaining effective.

While the Board enjoyed some early successes in winning employer acceptance of its position, they were short-lived. By fall, the National Association of Manufacturers launched a campaign against the NLB and such companies as Weirton Steel and Budd Manufacturing openly resisted NLB efforts to hold free elections to determine employee representation. By early 1934, the Board's authority, which never had depended on anything more than the good will of management and labor, was seriously eroded. President Roosevelt moved to clarify and strengthen the Board's duties in Executive Orders issued on December 16, 1933, February 1, 1934, and February 23, 1934. The latter two gave the NLB specific authority to hold elections and to present its findings to the Justice Department for possible prosecution of violators of Section 7a. No instructions were issued as to whether the principle of majority rule or proportional representation should guide the Board in determining employee spokesmen. But a few days after the February 1 Order had been promulgated, Johnson and Richberg stepped in and issued an interpretation which seemed to undercut the president's attempts to bolster the NLB's prestige. Roosevelt probably did not intend to make the Board too powerful, as he still harbored a hope that he could win the cooperation of the business community in making the NRA a success. The Johnson-Richberg statement served to reassure industry.[18]

Johnson and Richberg explicitly reaffirmed the position taken in their joint communiqué of August 23, 1933. They asserted that the president's Order of February 1 empowering the NLB to hold elections simply provided "a method whereby any specific group of employees or all the employees of a plant or of one employer may select, by a majority vote, representatives clearly empowered to act for the majority in their relations with their employer." Yet this "does not restrict or qualify in any way the right of minority groups of employees or of individual employees to deal with their employer." The president's "affirming this right of collective action" placed "no limitation upon individual action." Furthermore, it was not true that "employees if permitted to act in their own free choice, may not select a company union (meaning local plant union)." Although Roosevelt's Executive Order was accompanied by a press release asserting that its issuance had been inspired by the spread of company unions and their use as camouflage by management for anti-union activities, Johnson and Richberg mitigated the impact of this accusation: "In so far as the statement in the press release might be read as saying that employees' representatives in all company unions are chosen by employers it was not so intended as there is no evidence that such is the case."[19]

Despite the president's Orders, the confusion in administration circles negated whatever gains might have been made. Reacting to pressure from at least two sides, the president wanted a Board better able to deal with labor disputes, yet at the same time did not wish to alienate the business community. Roosevelt's uncertainty opened

[18] Irving Bernstein, *The New Deal Collective Bargaining Policy* (Berkeley, Calif., 1950), 57–62; Arthur M. Schlesinger, Jr., *The Age of Roosevelt*, Vol. 2: *The Coming of the New Deal* (Boston, 1958), 144–51; Samuel I. Rosenman, ed., *The Public Papers and Addresses of Franklin D. Roosevelt with a Special Introduction and Explanatory Notes by President Roosevelt*, Vol. 2: *The Year of Crisis, 1933* (New York, 1938), 318–19, 524–25.

[19] Johnson and Richberg, NRA Release No. 3125, Feb. 4, 1934, NRA Papers, Series 223.

the breach that Richberg and Johnson slipped into, and neither received a presidential rebuke. It also spelled doom for the National Labor Board.

The deterioration of the NLB's position was apparent to no one more than to Senator Robert Wagner of New York. As chairman of the NLB he had fought to win presidential support for a more forceful stand against abuses of Section 7a. Defeated by the ambiguities of the president's own policy, and by the business bias of Johnson and Richberg, in early 1934 he proposed new legislation to create a board that would have real power to make binding decisions. Wagner consulted neither Johnson nor Richberg in drafting the legislation, and he failed to win Roosevelt's support. In the face of administration reluctance, Wagner accepted a compromise backed by the president, Public Resolution No. 44, which authorized the creation of a National Labor Relations Board similar in structure and power to the old National Labor Board. The president turned to Richberg and Labor Solicitor Charles Wyzanski, Jr., for aid in preparing the proposal, and the result was a holding device which failed to settle the question of majority rule or proportional representation. With the off-year elections coming up, Roosevelt was really postponing a decision on the main issue; many congressmen were equally anxious to do so, and Public Resolution No. 44 passed in June. The real question was left unresolved with the prospect that a stalemate over NRA labor policy would continue.[20]

The ambiguities and contradictions surrounding the evolution of NRA labor policy were duplicated in other areas of activity as well, though Richberg figured most prominently in labor questions. Trade practices, price fixing, and monopolies, as well as the writing and enforcement of the codes themselves, all opened up a Pan-

[20] Bernstein, *The New Deal*, 62–83; Schlesinger, *The Age of Roosevelt*, 2:150–51; Frances Perkins, Robert F. Wagner, Charles E. Wyzanski, Jr., and Richberg to Franklin D. Roosevelt, June 21, 1934, Franklin Roosevelt Papers, OF 716; Samuel I. Rosenman, ed., *The Public Papers and Addresses of Franklin D. Roosevelt with a Special Introduction and Explanatory Notes by President Roosevelt*, Vol. 3: *The Advance of Recovery and Reform*, 1934 (New York, 1938), 322–27.

dora's box. Although the greater part of Richberg's energy was devoted to labor-management relations, his support of General Johnson and his positive identification with the NRA implicated him in all its policies. This was not something he acknowledged reluctantly, but with enthusiasm. Although prepared to own up to faults of execution and administration, Richberg defended the fundamentals of NRA policy on virtually every question. In fact, he exhibited far too much sensitivity to criticism and took much of it personally. This is a critical weakness in any public official, and in Richberg's case, with his high-strung personality and need for approval, was especially trying.

Richberg's reaction to the report of a special NRA review board was illustrative. In the spring of 1934, General Johnson recommended the appointment of a National Recovery Review Board to investigate alleged monopolistic tendencies in the operation of the codes of fair competition. This was in response to criticisms of NRA made most vocally by Senators Gerald Nye of North Dakota, George Norris of Nebraska, and William Borah of Idaho. Johnson and Richberg agreed to appoint Clarence Darrow, a renowned civil libertarian and an old friend of Richberg's from Chicago, chairman of the Review Board. They soon regretted their choice. Darrow produced an openly partisan and biased report after perfunctory hearings in which the NRA was given little chance to defend itself and in which critics of economic planning were given free rein to denounce the NRA as a conspiracy of the large corporations against small business.[21]

Richberg gave as good as he received and pilloried Darrow for conducting "a haphazard, one sided investigation" designed "to justify a preconceived opposition to the fundamental theories and purposes of the National Industrial Recovery Act." Holding the report up to ridicule, he pointed out glaring inconsistencies. The most important was its assertion that "all competition is savage, selfish and relentless," so bad that "one may as well dream of mak-

[21] Johnson, *The Blue Eagle from Egg to Earth* (Garden City, N. Y., 1935), 271–76; Schlesinger, *The Age of Roosevelt*, 2:132–35; Ellis Wayne Hawley, *The New Deal and the Problem of Monopoly: A Study in Economic Ambivalence* (Princeton, N. J., 1966), 82–85, 95–97.

ing war lady-like as of making competition fair." Contrasted with this was the report's proclamation that "a return to the antitrust laws for the purpose of restoring competition" was "one of the great needs of the times."[22]

Richberg was hurt all the more by the report because Darrow was an old friend. His reaction to a good-natured comment by H. L. Mencken measured the depth of his disappointment. Mencken thought the Darrow Report "a masterpiece of transparent sophistry," so well-calculated to fail in its purpose of indicting the NRA that he wrote Richberg, "In the Baltimore Sun of today I am suggesting maliciously that you wrote the report yourself, and palmed it off on those poor innocents." Richberg revealed the strain on his sense of humor when he shot back, "I think it particularly malicious of you to suggest that I wrote the Darrow Report in the same paragraph in which you proclaim it to be a masterpiece of transparent sophistry." Mencken had to explain, "But there is manifestly an enormous difference between unconscious sophistry and the kind that takes in and flabbergasts an antagonist! My charge was that you concocted the latter variety."[23]

Richberg was not the only one under a strain after a year of NRA. The Blue Eagle campaign to bring all employers under a special President's Reemployment Agreement establishing minimum labor standards, the preparation and approval of hundreds of codes, the mediation and settlement of numerous strikes, and the conflict between NRA and NLB over labor policy had brought Hugh Johnson to the end of his tether. Both men were the victims of overwork, but whereas Richberg manifested this in hypersensitivity to criticism and worry over the future of NRA and his place in it, Johnson took refuge in drink, periodic explosions of temper, and occasional unexplained absences from work.

Under a great deal of pressure himself, Richberg tended to see all the troubles of NRA in terms of Johnson's breakdown. He as

[22] Richberg, "Commentary on majority report of National Recovery Review Board," n.d., Richberg Papers, L.C., Box 46.

[23] H. L. Mencken to Richberg, June 4, 1934; Richberg to Mencken, June 5, 1934; Mencken to Richberg, June 7, 1934, all in NRA Papers, Series 47, Box 582.

well as others in the administration determined to do something about Johnson, for his failings were real enough. But given Richberg's position in the NRA and his own ambitions, it was not surprising that Johnson questioned his motives. What had begun as a highly compatible relationship between the two men by the spring of 1934 deteriorated into rivalry and mistrust.[24]

The president was reluctant to make a move. As David Lilienthal later recorded in his diary, Roosevelt hoped that "some eleventh hour miracle would intervene to save him the painful necessity of pulling Johnson out." He tended to avoid decisions of a difficult nature that had a personal side to them, and excused many of Johnson's shenanigans with the comment, as Harold Ickes recalled it, that "every Administration had to have a Peck's Bad Boy."[25]

But the signs of Johnson's breakdown became more and more apparent as time went on. Rumors circulated that the General enjoyed an illicit relationship with his secretary, Miss Frances Robinson, popularly known as "Robbie." A more serious charge was that she and not the General made policy decisions when Johnson was on one of his binges. The General took Robbie with him everywhere and they shared an apartment, apparently to save living expenses. Robbie figured in the deteriorating relationship between the NRA administrator and general counsel. Richberg remembered a number of occasions when he and Robbie had clashed, and he definitely considered her a disruptive factor in the functioning of the NRA.[26]

---

[24] Hawley, *The New Deal*, 104–105; Schlesinger, *The Age of Roosevelt*, 2: 152–55; Richberg, *My Hero: The Indiscreet Memoirs of an Eventful but Unheroic Life* (New York, 1954), 174–75; Johnson, *Blue Eagle*, 212, 371–76, 382–91.

[25] David E. Lilienthal, *The Journals of David E. Lilienthal*, Vol. 1: *The TVA Years, 1939–1945, Including a Selection of Journal Entries from the 1917–1939 Period* (New York, 1964), 99; Harold L. Ickes, *The Secret Diary of Harold L. Ickes*, Vol. 1: *The First Thousand Days, 1933–1936* (New York, 1953), 147–48.

[26] Schlesinger, *The Age of Roosevelt*, 2:152–54; Johnson, *Blue Eagle*, 214, 372–73; Raymond Clapper, diary, Nov. 15, 1933, May 3, 5, 1934, all in Raymond Clapper Papers, Library of Congress, Box 8; Clapper, reference file, March 2, 1936, Clapper Papers, Box 160.

Far more important than the possibility of scandal was the simple fact that Johnson's periodic incapacity interrupted the smooth functioning of NRA. As Richberg confided to David Lilienthal in May of 1934, "Johnson has worn himself out, to the point where he doesn't want to work," but "the whole thing is built up so that only he can decide." As Lilienthal recorded in his diary, Richberg felt himself compelled to take "the bit in his teeth frequently to straighten things out."[27] Richberg's feeling of duty to the president, who had from the beginning given him special assurances of his watchdog role in the NRA, plus his positive identification with the administration and his place in it, all provided him with a convincing rationale to move against Johnson before he wrecked the NRA.

By June of 1934, both Johnson and Richberg were talking about a drastic reorganization for NRA. Johnson believed that most of the code writing was nearly concluded, so that the NRA could turn more of its energy to code administration—supervising and participating in the actual process of industrial self-government. Richberg believed that the main problem was Johnson himself; if he would leave, everything would work out. Richberg and Secretary of Labor Perkins, who bore a grievance against the General over labor policy and temporarily allied herself with the NRA general counsel, made certain that Roosevelt was apprised of the allegedly deteriorating conditions in NRA.[28]

Richberg and Johnson discussed the possibility that both might resign and leave the president free to bring in a new management. In these conversations, Johnson told Richberg that he would probably have to stay on duty for a while longer to see the reorganization plan through, but implied that it would be acceptable for Richberg to resign anyway. On the other hand, as Richberg later recalled, "In long talks with the President he made me clearly understand that he thought General Johnson should retire." Furthermore, Roosevelt "wanted me to continue in the service to

[27] Lilienthal, *Journals*, 1:42.
[28] Schlesinger, *The Age of Roosevelt*, 2:154–55; Johnson, *Blue Eagle*, 373–81; Johnson to Roosevelt, June 26, 1934, Richberg Papers, L.C., Box 45; Richberg, *My Hero*, 174–75; Frances Perkins, *The Roosevelt I Knew* (New York, 1946), 235–49.

aid in the reorganization," though both the president and Richberg agreed that he could not actually succeed Johnson as administrator.[29]

Deciding that something must be done about the General, Roosevelt tried the indirect approach first. He turned to Bernard Baruch with the suggestion that Johnson take a trip to Europe and leave a committee in charge of running NRA. When he found out about this, Johnson exploded. The General harbored suspicions against Richberg and credited him with scheming for his dismissal. Richberg was worried that Johnson suspected something and tried to assure him that there was no conspiracy afoot.[30] But after raising the matter of his own resignation in a preliminary way with the president on June 4, Richberg sent in an official resignation to both Roosevelt and General Johnson on June 26. He gave a pointed summary of his personal situation to Roosevelt:

Recently . . . my position has become intolerable. Many persons have been urging that General Johnson should take a long over-due vacation and because of my position I have been mentioned as one of several persons who might be made, individually or jointly, responsible temporarily. This being brought to the attention of the General, he quite evidently regards me as engaged in undermining his position. I would not think of continuing to work under anyone holding that attitude. The only way to clear up the situation and maintain self-respect is for me to resign forthwith. I cannot see that I can be of any future service to anyone if I permit my reputation to be destroyed and myself placed in the false position of being forced out because of an intrigue against my superior.[31]

Roosevelt tried to calm both Johnson and Richberg. But he was determined to reform the NRA; the only question was how to do it. For the time being, he urged the General to take a much needed vacation and consulted with Richberg about reorganizing the in-

[29] Richberg, My Hero, 174–75.
[30] Schlesinger, The Age of Roosevelt, 2:154–55; Ickes, Secret Diary, 1:172; Johnson, Blue Eagle, 373–75, 382–85.
[31] Richberg to Marvin McIntyre, June 4, 1934; Richberg to Roosevelt, June 4, 1934, Franklin Roosevelt Papers, OF 466; Richberg to Johnson, June 26, 1934; Richberg to McIntyre, June 26, 1934; Richberg to Roosevelt, June 26, 1934, Richberg Papers, L.C., Box 2.

dustrial recovery program. In fact, Richberg included with his letter
of resignation a plan outlining the ideas he and the president had
been discussing. Johnson and Robbie would take a vacation for
thirty to sixty days, and an "Acting Board of Administration"
would guide the NRA in his absence. A new "Industrial Council"
would be created and temporarily replace the National Emergency
Council, an agency set up in 1933 to coordinate all recovery activities. The director of the proposed Industrial Council would carry
out the instructions of the president "in approving codes or prescribing regulations, or otherwise in the exercise of the powers conferred upon the President in the National Industrial Recovery Act,
which have not been already delegated by the President to the Administrator for Industrial Recovery." According to the final phase
of the plan, the director of the new Industrial Council would be
Richberg.[32]

Richberg prepared a draft Executive Order implementing the
plan, and Roosevelt issued the Order with only inconsequential
changes on June 30, 1934. Richberg was made director of the new
council, called the Industrial Emergency Committee, and appointed
executive secretary of the Executive Council, another previously
established coordinating agency, and executive director of the National Emergency Council. In addition, the Order granted Richberg a leave of absence as NRA general counsel, though he retained
the title of that office as well. In effect, all coordinating activities
had been consolidated in Richberg's hands, at least on paper, and
later in the year some of these agencies would be consolidated in
name as well as in fact.[33]

Johnson also submitted a proposal for NRA reorganization on
June 26. The most important of his recommendations was an idea
for replacing the administrator by a board of directors with its own
chairman and president. The board would decide policy questions

[32] Richberg to Roosevelt, June 26, 1934, with attached "Outline of a
Program," and draft "Executive Order," Richberg Papers, L.C., Box 2. Also
see Richberg, draft of "Outline of Program," June 26, 1934, Franklin
Roosevelt Papers, OF 466.
[33] Ibid.; "Executive Order: Creating the Industrial Emergency Committee," June 30, 1934, National Emergency Council Release, July 2, 1934,
mimeograph copy in OGR Papers, Series 76, Box 749.

and its president would execute them. His ideas were not incompatible with Richberg's feeling that one-man rule in the NRA should end. In fact, Johnson said as much himself.[34]

The president had thus taken the first step toward replacing Johnson, and the General went off on a vacation in the West for several weeks. Richberg was not entirely satisfied, for officially the solution was a temporary one, and the General might yet return to power in the NRA. Johnson's status as administrator remained intact. In the meantime, Richberg took a short vacation in July. His absence undoubtedly eased the General's fears about leaving Washington himself.[35] But throughout the summer, Richberg's reports to the National Emergency Council as executive director emphasized the deteriorating situation regarding NRA presumably arising out of uncertainty over its reorganization. Richberg painted a picture of unrest, indecision, and lack of compliance with the codes, and attributed it to the failure to settle the NRA crisis once and for all. His reports would become more optimistic as autumn and Johnson's demise drew nearer.[36]

By mid-August, Richberg increased the pace of his campaign to unseat Johnson. He saw the president personally and prepared memoranda outlining the situation and its solution. On August 16, he emphasized the need for action on several grounds: 1) "Major matters of policy are pressing so for decision that the alternative is confusion and disintegration for lack of decision, or a grave risk of decisions which will cause increased difficulty"; 2) "Distrust and dissatisfaction throughout the country are increasing daily the resistance to the program"; 3) "The quality of N.R.A. personnel is steadily declining. Important officials are leaving"; 4) "The General himself is, in the opinion of many, in the worst physical and mental condition and needs an immediate relief from responsibil-

[34] Johnson to Roosevelt, June 26, 1934, Franklin Roosevelt Papers, OF 466.

[35] Schlesinger, *The Age of Roosevelt*, 2:154–55; Richberg, *My Hero*, 178–81; Johnson, *Blue Eagle*, 375; Roosevelt to Johnson, July 2, 1934, Franklin Roosevelt Papers, President's Personal File 702.

[36] Memoranda from Donald Richberg to Members of the National Emergency Council, dated July 10, 24, Aug. 7, Oct. 2, 16, 1934, all in OGR Papers, Series 1, Box 5.

ity." Richberg recommended a conference between himself, Johnson, and the president to settle on a plan of permanent reorganization, to arrange a further leave for the General, and to give out a face-saving understanding that Johnson might still do some work for the administration in the future.[37] Unless the plan were carried out, Richberg wrote on August 18, "A violent slide down hill for the Industrial Recovery Program is inevitable." In addition, Richberg was "holding up the renting of a house after October 1," and hinted that he would leave the administration unless something were done soon. If the president would dispose of Johnson, everything would be all right: "At present *one* man by personal obstinacy and for *personal* reasons is absolutely blocking a reformation that *every* other informed person knows is necessary to save the N.R.A."[38] Besides Secretary Perkins, Treasury Secretary Henry Morgenthau, Jr., and Rexford Tugwell of the Agriculture Department, among others, supported this viewpoint.[39]

Once again the president attempted to make a move. He called Johnson to a conference at the White House on August 20, along with Perkins and Richberg. The president suggested that the General go abroad with a commission to study recovery programs in Europe; he could take Bernard Baruch, Gerard Swope of General Electric, or other industrialists with him. Roosevelt assured Johnson that he need not worry about what would happen to NRA, but the General was convinced that Richberg and Perkins had succeeded in deposing him at last. Johnson left the White House and within a matter of hours placed a letter of resignation in Roosevelt's hands. Still reluctant to hurt the General, Roosevelt asked Johnson back for another conference and tried to smooth things over. For the time being, he would continue in office, though Roosevelt advised him that he would take over the NRA personally for a while to learn its problems firsthand. In the meantime, Johnson was to for-

[37] Richberg to McIntyre, Aug. 16, 1934, Richberg Papers, L.C., Box 45.
[38] Richberg to McIntyre, Aug. 18, 1934, Richberg Papers, L.C., Box 45.
[39] Schlesinger, *The Age of Roosevelt*, 2:155; Henry Morgenthau, Jr., "Diaries of Henry Morgenthau, Jr.," Record Group 23, Franklin D. Roosevelt Library, 2:17; Rexford Tugwell to Roosevelt, Sept. 5, 1934, and Tugwell to Roosevelt, Sept. 7, 1934, both in Franklin Roosevelt Papers, OF 466.

mulate his plan of NRA reorganization. In reality, Johnson was through as administrator.[40]

In the meantime, the press had a field day in rumor mongering. Presidential Secretary Steve Early suspected that Johnson's secretary, Robbie, was responsible for some of the stories. She seemed to be working with a publicity agent, James Cope, formerly employed by the Associated Press, and together they were giving out items that Early felt should not be released. He wanted Johnson to be ordered to stop this. Rumors circulated that Robbie was urging Johnson to walk out on NRA without further ado. On the other side, there were stories that Blackwell Smith, acting chief of the Legal Division, and Leon Henderson, chief of the Research and Planning Division, were prepared to resign in protest over Johnson's reluctance to get out of NRA. Somehow, Richberg managed to keep from saying anything for publication which would have added fuel to the fire.[41]

Privately, Richberg continued to press Roosevelt for a final determination of the question of Johnson's status. On September 5, he prepared a memorandum once again describing the desperate condition of the NRA. He was encountering difficulties in retaining and adding high quality personnel; plans for the efficient administration of NRA were all ready to go, if only the word were given; until Johnson was removed, no plan would be availing, for "a team of horses can't be driven in harness with a wild bull." Richberg painted the picture in terms which revealed his own tensions and nervousness, as he told how "the people intimately concerned with this situation in Washington are struggling against inclinations to hysteria," and how "those responsible for keeping N.R.A. going talk to me with tears in their voices and sometimes actually in their eyes." He advised the president to stop wasting time by allowing Johnson to draw up an elaborate plan of reorganization. Richberg

[40] Schlesinger, The Age of Roosevelt, 2:155–56; Johnson, Blue Eagle, 377–97; Richberg, My Hero, 175–76; Elliott Roosevelt, F.D.R.: His Personal Letters, 1928–1945 (New York, 1950), 3:412–13.

[41] Stephen Early to McIntyre, Aug. 27, 1934; Early to McIntyre, Aug. 30, 1934; Early to McIntyre, Aug. 31, 1934, Franklin Roosevelt Papers, OF 466.

had all the plans that were needed; the only obstacle was Johnson.[42]

At Roosevelt's direction, Rexford Tugwell took a sampling of opinion among Richberg, Perkins, Agriculture Secretary Henry Wallace, Harry Hopkins, the head of the Federal Emergency Relief Administration, and Secretary of Interior Harold Ickes. The consensus seemed to be that Johnson had outlived his usefulness and that his continued presence in NRA would only be a disruptive factor. They recommended that an administrative board be set up to run NRA and to supervise its reorganization.[43] On September 9, Johnson submitted his plan for a reorganized NRA, also recommending a board to replace the single administrator. In the meantime, Richberg was working on drafts of the necessary Executive Orders for implementing reform and preparing lists of candidates for the new board. Johnson finally yielded to the inevitable on September 24, and submitted his resignation effective October 15. This time Roosevelt accepted it.[44]

On September 27, the president issued an Executive Order creating a new National Industrial Recovery Board (NIRB) and appointing Clay Williams of Reynolds Tobacco, Arthur D. Whiteside of Dun and Bradstreet, Sidney Hillman of the Amalgamated Clothing Workers of America, and two college professors, Leon Marshall and Walton Hamilton. Two Richberg allies, Leon Henderson and Blackwell Smith, were made economic adviser and legal adviser to the Board. As director of the Industrial Emergency Committee, Richberg would remain influential in NRA policy, for the president's Order authorized the new NIRB to administer NRA "subject to the general approval of the Industrial Emergency Committee."

[42] Richberg to McIntyre, Sept. 5, 1934, with attached "Memorandum," Sept. 4, 1934, Franklin Roosevelt Papers, OF 466.

[43] Tugwell to Roosevelt, Sept. 5, 1934; Tugwell to Roosevelt, Sept. 7, 1934, Franklin Roosevelt Papers, OF 466; Ickes, Secret Diary, 1:195.

[44] Johnson to Roosevelt, Sept. 9, 1934, Franklin Roosevelt Papers, OF 466; Johnson, Blue Eagle, 391–97; McIntyre to Early, Sept. 13, 1934; Richberg to Roosevelt, Sept. 14, 1934, with attached "Memorandum on President's Special Board," "Tentative Draft of Statement," and "Tentative Draft of Letter" to Johnson, all in Franklin Roosevelt Papers, OF 466; Richberg to McIntyre, Sept. 15, 1934, with attached "Memorandum," Richberg Papers, L.C., Box 46.

Furthermore, Richberg had personal ties with some members of the Board, especially Williams and Whiteside.[45]

Richberg had to withstand one further challenge to his influence before the situation stabilized. Secretary of Interior Ickes and Labor Solicitor Charles Wyzanski, Jr., suggested to Roosevelt that Robert M. Hutchins, president of the University of Chicago, be made chairman of the NIRB; they felt his appointment would allay the bad publicity attendant on Johnson's resignation by bringing an effective administrator to the leadership of the new Board. Roosevelt directed Ickes to sound Hutchins out. He was able to obtain a leave of absence from the University's Board of Trustees, but Richberg stepped in and blocked his appointment. Richberg protested on the grounds that Hutchins would not appeal to the business community, whose cooperation was essential for the success of NRA. The NIRB threatened to resign en masse if the appointment went through. Ickes blamed the Board's attitude on Richberg, firmly believing that the NIRB "has been carefully hand-picked by himself," so that he might control NRA "in his devious, indirect way since there is not a strong or outstanding man on it." In the face of the possible resignation of the NIRB, Roosevelt backed down, and Hutchins gradually lost interest. Eventually Clay Williams became chairman of the NIRB. As Ickes, by now no friend of Richberg, summed it up, "Richberg, through his self-appointed N.R.A. Committee, is in pretty firm control of the situation and he will fight any man who threatens to jeopardize that control."[46] Yet Ickes's perception was distorted by his own ambitions, and Richberg's actual power position turned out to be much more vulnerable than he estimated.

[45] Rosenman, *Public Papers of Roosevelt*, 3:405–407; Schlesinger, *The Age of Roosevelt*, 2:157; Richberg, *My Hero*, 186, 298.

[46] Schlesinger, *The Age of Roosevelt*, 2:157–58; Robert M. Hutchins to Roosevelt, Oct. 4, 1934; Hutchins to Roosevelt, Oct. 5, 1934; Early to Roosevelt, Oct. 15, 1934, all in Franklin Roosevelt Papers, OF 466; Richberg to Early, Oct. 17, 1934, and Richberg to Roosevelt, Oct. 17, 1934, both in Richberg Papers, L.C., Box 45; Ickes, *Secret Diary*, 1:197–98, 200–201, 208–11, 219–21, 235–36, 242–43. The quotations are from Ickes, *Secret Diary*, 1:210, 220.

CHAPTER VIII

The President's Counselor II

Donald Richberg's emergence as chief coordinator of the recovery program and overseer of the National Recovery Administration not surprisingly inspired an outpouring of political commentary about his rising fortunes. He appeared on the cover of *Time* magazine for the week of September 10, 1934, and was soon dubbed "Assistant President," much to his outward displeasure. His various coordinating assignments were further consolidated on October 31, 1934, when the Executive Council was merged with the National Emergency Council, and the Industrial Emergency Committee was made a subcommittee of the National Emergency Council. Richberg continued as director of NEC, while still holding the title of NRA general counsel and remaining on leave from that post. The official duties of the NEC were "to provide for the orderly presentation of business to the President"; "to coordinate inter-agency problems of organization and activity of Federal agencies"; "to coordinate and make more efficient and productive the work of the field agencies of the Federal Government"; "to cooperate with any Federal agency in performing such activities as the President may direct"; and "to serve in an advisory capacity to the President and to the Executive Director."[1]

In his November 4 diary entry, Secretary of Interior Harold Ickes recorded that the newspaper stories of Richberg as "sort of an Assistant President," who "outranks the whole Cabinet," had begun to "annoy the President very much indeed." As Ickes re-called with relish, "To listen to the President, one would never think that Richberg was more than an exalted messenger boy, but to read the newspapers, one would think that the President really shares his power with him." He suspected that Richberg's staff was responsible for many of the news items and concluded, "There seems to be little doubt that Richberg is reaching out in every di-rection for all the power he can possibly gather unto himself."[2] After reading one of columnist Arthur Krock's pieces about Rich-berg, Roosevelt himself complained to Steve Early, "Tell [Krock] that this kind of thing is not only a lie but that it is a deception and a fraud on the public. It is merely a continuation of previous lies such as the headlines that Moley was running the government; next that Baruch was Acting President; next that Johnson was the man in power; next that Frankfurter had been put over the Cabinet and now that Richberg has been put over the Cabinet."[3]

If Richberg had any illusions of grandeur, he was soon disap-pointed. Whatever influence he had as executive director of NEC depended on the confidence the president placed in him. To co-ordinate Cabinet officers and the heads of independent agencies, all superior to him in real political power, required the authority of the presidency itself. To succeed, Richberg had to enjoy a greater intimacy with the president than anyone else. But he did not pos-sess this kind of contact. However close he may have been to Roosevelt, it was not close enough.[4] Except on NRA policy where

[1] *Time* 24 (Sept. 10, 1934): cover; Donald Richberg, *My Hero: The In-discreet Memoirs of an Eventful but Unheroic Life* (New York, 1954), 183; Samuel I. Rosenman, ed., *The Public Papers and Addresses of Frank-lin D. Roosevelt with a Special Introduction by President Roosevelt*, Vol. 3: *The Advance of Recovery and Reform, 1934* (New York, 1938), 441–44.

[2] Harold L. Ickes, *The Secret Diary of Harold L. Ickes*, Vol. 1: *The First Thousand Days, 1933–1936* (New York, 1953), 220–21.

[3] Franklin Roosevelt to Stephen Early, Nov. 3, 1934, Franklin D. Roose-velt Papers, Franklin D. Roosevelt Library, Official File 788. A perceptive contemporary assessment of Richberg's actual position is Mark Sullivan, "Richberg's New Duties Expected to Relieve Burden So President May Concentrate on Big Affairs," New York *Herald Tribune*, Nov. 11, 1934.

[4] Herman Miles Somers, *Presidential Agency: The Office of War Mo-*

he carried great weight with the National Industrial Recovery
Board because of his previous position and his friendship with
Board members, Richberg lacked the authority to meet his responsi-
bilities.

Despite Ickes's worst fears, which were undoubtedly a product
of his own jealousy, the most that Richberg could do was to conduct a holding action to keep the Recovery Administration functioning smoothly, make reports and prepare an agenda for the
president's consideration at NEC meetings, and carry out whatever
specific instructions Roosevelt might issue. Richberg had no source
of power apart from the president, so unless Roosevelt gave him
specific authority to act, he was stymied.

Even if Richberg had been in a position to reshape the recovery
program, it was unlikely that he would have done so. Despite the
less-than-successful results of the NRA's first year of operation, Richberg believed as firmly as ever in the original assumptions underlying the plan of recovery through industrial self-government.
Richberg believed that the NRA's troubles were primarily administrative in nature, so that he was not the man to seek a revision of
the basic principles guiding the experiment.

As it turned out, the new recovery regime inaugurated by the
National Industrial Recovery Board and the National Emergency
Council proved remarkably similar to the old Johnson regime. Conflicts over basic policy questions which had developed in the first
year of NRA continued unresolved into its second year. Minor improvements had been made and would continue to be made in such
areas as price fixing, consumer and labor representation on code
authorities, and supervision of code enforcement. But so much of
the pressure for change had developed only after most codes were
already written that it proved difficult to extend reform retroac-
tively to a significant segment of industry. Furthermore, earlier attempts to meet criticism through new policy guidelines had often

---

bilization and Reconversion (Cambridge, Mass., 1950), 206–207. Richberg
sometimes had difficulty in obtaining appointments of adequate duration to
discuss National Emergency Council business with the president. See Richberg to Marvin McIntyre, Nov. 10, 1934, and Richberg to McIntyre, Dec.
8, 1934, Franklin Roosevelt Papers, OF 788.

inspired a reaction among interests opposed to change, causing the NRA to draw back from its own announced reforms. Caught in the middle of conflicts among industry, labor, and consumers, the administration faced a genuine dilemma in finding policies satisfactory to all its constituents. The new arrangement under Richberg at the head of the NEC and Clay Williams at the head of the NIRB would ultimately fail to break the impasse in the recovery program.[5]

Symptomatic of the continuing stalemate was labor policy. The old Johnson-Richberg theory of proportional representation of all workers in collective bargaining remained NRA policy, despite the efforts of the new National Labor Relations Board (NLRB) to promote majority rule. The same old arguments between NRA and NLRB were thrashed out all over again. The basic conflict was defined in the late summer of 1934, when the NLRB ruled in the Houde Engineering Corporation case that employee representation in collective bargaining should be on the basis of majority rule, even though earlier in the year the president had settled a strike in the auto industry by putting into effect a plan of proportional representation and creating a special Automobile Labor Board which would adjust disputes.[6]

A related but distinct controversy centered on the Newspaper Industrial Board. Provision for the Board had been written into the newspaper publishing code to handle labor complaints, but it failed to function smoothly and was in a constant state of deadlock. The result was a major policy confrontation between Richberg and the National Industrial Recovery Board on one side and the National Labor Relations Board on the other. Because of the failure of the Newspaper Industrial Board to function, the NLRB accepted an appeal from Dean Jennings, who had been dismissed from the San

[5] Arthur Schlesinger, Jr., *The Age of Roosevelt*, Vol. 2: *The Coming of the New Deal* (Boston, 1959), 158–61; Ellis Wayne Hawley, *The New Deal and the Problem of Monopoly: A Study in Economic Ambivalence* (Princeton, N. J., 1966), 72–110.

[6] Irving Bernstein, *The New Deal Collective Bargaining Policy* (Berkeley, Calif., 1950), 60, 84–86; Schlesinger, *The Age of Roosevelt*, 2:397–98; New York *Times*, Sept. 4, 1934; New York *Journal of Commerce*, Sept. 15, 1934; New York *Evening Post*, Nov. 22, 1934; *Wall Street Journal*, Dec. 3, 1934.

Francisco *Call-Bulletin* for union activities, and ruled that he should be reinstated. A great outcry from publishers greeted the decision, and Richberg bombarded the president with requests that he prevent the NLRB from intervening in codes that had their own machinery for handling labor questions. But in view of the NLRB's stand on the majority rule principle, Richberg's objections had far more significance than jurisdictional concerns. Eventually he won out, and Roosevelt instructed the NLRB not to consider labor disputes in industries where codes provided adjustment machinery like the Newspaper Industrial Board.[7]

Equally significant in Richberg's drift toward the businessman's point of view in labor relations was his role in extending the automobile code in the spring of 1935. Despite the objections of organized labor to proportional representation and NIRB reservations about the functioning of the Automobile Labor Board, the president decided to extend the code beyond its expiration date until June 1935. The prospect of continuing the status quo in the auto industry was unacceptable to the American Federation of Labor, especially since it felt that the president had given assurances that there would be no extension without consultation with the unions. John L. Lewis of the United Mine Workers pronounced the judgment of organized labor on Richberg's role in the extension: "Mr. Richberg secretly conspired with the leaders of the automobile industry to deceive the President and bludgeon labor. Like medieval ruffians, they lay in secret during the day and emerged after nightfall to perpetrate their deeds and announce the consummation of

[7] Schlesinger, *The Age of Roosevelt,* 2:398–400; Richberg to McIntyre, Dec. 13, 1934, Franklin Roosevelt Papers, OF 788; Richberg to Louis McHenry Howe, Dec. 18, 1934, Franklin Roosevelt Papers, OF 466; Richberg to Howe, Dec. 21, 1934, with attached draft letter from Roosevelt to National Labor Relations Board; Elisha Hanson, "Memorandum on Exclusive Jurisdiction of Newspaper Industrial Board in Labor Controversies Arising under Code for Daily Newspaper Publishing Business," Jan. 4, 1935; "Proposal agreed to by Mr. Richberg and Mr. Hanson in conference, January 11, 1935"; Richberg to Howe, Jan. 12, 1935, Louis McHenry Howe Papers, Franklin D. Roosevelt Library, Box 83; Richberg to McIntyre, Jan. 14, 1935, with attached draft statement; Roosevelt to Francis Biddle, Jan. 22, 1935, Franklin Roosevelt Papers, OF 716.

their plot." He could imagine "the giggling falsetto cackles of Mr. Richberg when the strain was over and the deed was done."[8]

Richberg perhaps incautiously responded to the "personal attack" of the AFL. But in doing so, he revealed much about the way he perceived his role in government and how he saw himself standing above the clash of selfish interests in the name of the public good: "The charge that I am a 'traitor to organized labor' amounts to the demand that as a public official I should put subservience to the policies of a particular labor organization, above loyalty to the Government and to my conception of the public interest. If a refusal to yield to such a demand be treason, let those who charge it make the most of it." Richberg argued that because "each party naturally seeks to protect self-interest and declines to yield its convictions," ultimately "the representatives of the government always must make a decision." Though Richberg believed he was dealing out even-handed justice to both management and labor, the latter viewed his recommendation for extending the auto code as the last straw.[9]

The stalemate in NRA labor policy induced Senator Robert Wagner to renew his movement for legislation creating an effective labor relations board with power to enforce the majority rule principle in matters of employee representation for collective bargaining purposes. Eventually he succeeded, but won the president's backing only after it was clear that the NRA labor provisions had broken down under industry subversion and the Johnson-Richberg interpretation of representation questions. Roosevelt's ambivalence was the product of his continuing reluctance to alienate the business community. He regarded its cooperation as essential to any plan of recovery he might propose. But by the spring of 1935, business

[8] Lewis quoted in Schlesinger, *The Age of Roosevelt*, 2:163–64; Sidney Fine, *The Automobile under the Blue Eagle* (Ann Arbor, Mich., 1963), 370–76; Roosevelt to Richberg, Jan. 15, 1935, Franklin Roosevelt Papers, OF 466; Press Release, Feb. 5, 1935, containing correspondence, Charlton Ogburn to Roosevelt, Jan. 28, 1935, and Roosevelt to Ogburn, Feb. 4, 1935, in National Recovery Administration Papers, Record Group 9, National Archives, Series 7, Box 21.

[9] Richberg, National Emergency Council Release, Feb. 4, 1935, Office of Government Reports Papers, Record Group 44, Federal Records Center, Suitland, Md., Series 76, Box 750.

adamance on price fixing, monopoly, code enforcement, and labor policy made the president feel more and more that winning its loyalty was a futile hope. Roosevelt finally announced administration support for the principles of Wagner's National Labor Relations Act a few days before the Supreme Court did away with the NRA altogether and after the Senate had already passed the bill. Political necessity more than conviction won the Roosevelt administration over to the idea of a strong labor board.[10]

As the labor camp became alienated from Richberg, the business community began to realize that he was committed to the preservation of the rights of employers as well as employees, and to the resolution of labor disputes primarily through private rather than government mechanisms. His stand against the majority rule principle helped to pull the fangs from Section 7a; his fight over the newspaper code protected labor-management relations from greater encroachments of federal authority through the NLRB. What Richberg had been saying in speeches since the inception of NRA was now borne out in deeds.

Harold Ickes noted the change in Richberg, and in his diary recorded rumors that Richberg "was swinging further to the right all the time and that business was strong for him." He had heard that the job of general counsel of the Iron and Steel Institute had been offered to Richberg. Ickes talked to Felix Frankfurter about his former law partner and recorded that "he can't understand what has happened inside of Richberg, but he feels that something has gone wrong and that he is a real danger to the Administration." Frankfurter presumably expressed the opinion that "Richberg now represents exactly the opposite point of view from that which was supposed to be the one of this Administration." Ickes claimed that Justice Louis Brandeis, Senator George Norris, Senator Robert La Follette, Jr., Treasury Secretary Henry Morgenthau, Jr., relief administrator Harry Hopkins, and Charles E. Merriam of the University of Chicago distrusted Richberg and were worried about his apparent change.[11]

[10] Schlesinger, The Age of Roosevelt, 2:400–406; Bernstein, The New Deal, 88–128.

[11] Ickes, Secret Diary, 1:210–11, 221, 246–48. The quotations are from

Arthur D. Whiteside of Dun and Bradstreet, who served on the National Industrial Recovery Board until the spring of 1935, was one of Richberg's staunchest admirers. In May 1934 he had urged Richberg to remain in the administration for as long as possible. As usual, Richberg was concerned about his financial problems, and Whiteside wrote to Richberg urging him to stay in office and observing that his forced withdrawal because of monetary difficulties would represent a serious setback for the ideals which he represented in the NRA. Whiteside even offered to help underwrite Richberg's expenses should that become necessary to keep him on the job; he invited Richberg to call upon his office for funds in an emergency. Furthermore, he asked Richberg to think about associating professionally with him when he finally did decide to leave the administration.[12]

Richberg was receptive to Whiteside's overtures, though for the time being he could continue in government service without outside help. Nonetheless, he found comfort in the knowledge that "if I should find myself in unexpected difficulties there would be somewhere I could turn for a temporary lift." He assured Whiteside that "it would be a great pleasure to me to enjoy a further association with you," although no commitments of a professional nature were concluded at this juncture.[13] After Richberg retired from the NRA in June 1935, however, he made a temporary arrangement with Dun and Bradstreet to hold a retainer for a minimum of two months at $2,500 per month; this involved some vaguely defined

210, 247. In addition, see Philadelphia *Record*, Dec. 8, 1934; New York *Journal of Commerce*, Dec. 7, 1934; William G. Woolfolk to Richberg, Aug. 30, 1933; Willard M. Kiplinger to Richberg, Sept. 23, 1933, Richberg Papers, L.C., Box 1; Daniel Willard to Richberg, Sept. 29, 1934; Henry I. Harriman to Richberg, Oct. 6, 1934; J. Howard Pew to Richberg, Oct. 6, 1934; R. Douglas Stuart to Richberg, Oct. 12, 1934; Daniel Willard to Richberg, Nov. 19, 1934; Harold Boeschenstein to Stephen Early, Dec. 31, 1934, all in Richberg Papers, L.C., Box 2.

[12] Arthur D. Whiteside to Richberg, May 9, 1934, formerly in the possession of Mrs. John H. Small III (Mrs. Donald R. Richberg), Charlottesville, Va., and recently deposited in the Richberg Papers, L.C.

[13] Richberg to Whiteside, May 16, 1934, formerly in the possession of Mrs. John H. Small III and recently deposited in Richberg Papers, L.C.

duties such as serving as an adviser on some publicity matters.[14]

Richberg's break with organized labor and his initiation into the business camp were thus clearly evident in NRA policy. At the same time, his newspaper reputation as "Assistant President" underwent a severe test as he tried to administer the National Emergency Council. His lack of the requisite authority for coordinating the activities of Cabinet officers and agency heads was starkly apparent in the minutes of the NEC itself. Richberg's role at the meetings was limited to technical matters such as preparing the agenda and giving progress reports on the recovery program, and rarely involved policy decisions. The latter were left to the president, members of the Cabinet, and agency heads, all of whom regularly attended the NEC sessions. The meetings reflected Richberg's total dependence on the president for his authority.[15] Except in regard to the NRA, where he had strong ties of friendship and loyalty among the members of the National Industrial Recovery Board, Richberg was primarily a technician carrying out the orders of the president and taking care of numerous details of administration. He did not really coordinate the other members of the NEC even though he was executive director; instead, many—such as Ickes—successfully resisted what they regarded as his encroachments on their administrative preserves. Despite all the publicity, Richberg's power position was exceedingly vulnerable.[16]

Nevertheless, there was no doubt that Richberg took himself seriously and felt that the burdens of the whole administration rested on his shoulders.[17] Ickes believed that "Richberg is a dan-

[14] Whiteside to Richberg, June 17, 1935, formerly in possession of Mrs. John H. Small III and recently deposited in Richberg Papers, L.C.

[15] Lester G. Seligman and Elmer E. Cornwall, Jr., *New Deal Mosaic: Roosevelt Confers with His National Emergency Council* (Eugene, Ore., 1965), 232–474 (minutes of NEC meetings for July 10, 1934, to April 23, 1935).

[16] Ickes, *Secret Diary*, 1:221, 242–43, 245–47; Ickes to Richberg, Feb. 25, 1935; Richberg to Ickes, Feb. 28, 1935; Ickes to Richberg, March 15, 1935, OGR Papers, Series 3, Box 16; Somers, *Presidential Agency*, 207.

[17] For a picture of the nature of Richberg's duties, see Richberg to Rudolph Foster, Aug. 16, 1934, with attached draft Executive Order and press statement; Roosevelt to Richberg, Aug. 22, 1934, Franklin Roosevelt Pa-

gerous man for the Administration" because "he is utterly selfish, and undoubtedly his great ability is being used to build himself up." Equally important, Ickes observed, "He is highly temperamental and nervous and likely to go off at half cock."[18] Although Ickes could not hide his own jealousy, his comments had some ring of truth. Richberg was under a great deal of pressure in a situation that was inherently unstable, and he showed the effects of the strain. He realized the vulnerability of his position and felt a need for vindication. This was amply evident in an ill-humored exchange with Hugh Johnson in December 1934, when Richberg learned that the General planned to serialize his NRA memoirs in the *Saturday Evening Post*.

Without having seen the manuscript of Johnson's memoirs, Richberg sent a protest to George Horace Lorimer, editor of the *Post*: "I have been told by several persons, seeming to have sources of accurate information, that this book includes certain definitely described attacks upon me, which, if made, would be untrue, maliciously libelous and designed wholly for the purpose of doing me harm." He informed Lorimer that "there is nothing lower in the scale of publishing than the publication of character assassination for the purpose, either of venting personal spleen, or building circulation." If Lorimer went ahead, he would have to "accept the full legal responsibility" for any statements "derogatory to me and obviously designed as destructive of my personal and professional

pers, OF 285; Executive Director, NEC, to Attorney General, Oct. 26, 1934; Richberg to McIntyre, Dec. 13, 1934, Franklin Roosevelt Papers, OF 788; S. Clay Williams to Walton Hamilton, Leon Henderson, Sidney Hillman, Leon Marshall, Blackwell Smith, Williams, and Whiteside, Dec. 15, 1934, with attached memorandum from Richberg to Chairman, National Industrial Recovery Board, Dec. 13, 1934, NRA Papers, Series 3, Box 3; Richberg to McIntyre, Jan. 4, 1935, with attached memorandum by McIntyre, Jan. 12, 1935, Franklin Roosevelt Papers, OF 788; Richberg to Roosevelt, Jan. 28, 1935, Franklin Roosevelt Papers, OF 375; Richberg to Roosevelt, Feb. 28, 1935, Franklin Roosevelt Papers, OF 6-U; Richberg to Roosevelt, March 8, 1935, Franklin Roosevelt Papers, OF 444; Richberg to Howe, April 23, 1935, Franklin Roosevelt Papers, OF 285; Raymond Clapper, notes, Feb. 10, 1939, Raymond Clapper Papers, Library of Congress, Box 18.
[18] Ickes, *Secret Diary*, 1:221.

reputation."[19] Somehow, Richberg's letter became public, much to his dismay, bringing Johnson into the dispute. He advised Richberg, "There is libel in your letter but none in my book."[20]

Given his exposed position in NEC and the stalemate in NRA, it was not surprising that Richberg should decide in the spring of 1935 that the recovery program was due for another shakeup. In a memorandum prepared for the president on March 4, he described the NRA as "losing effectiveness and becoming dangerous." If the administration was going "to meet legislative investigations and bring out a workable new Act" upon the expiration of the NIRA in June, some "consistent policy" would have to be decided upon. Richberg's principal recommendation for change was that "the President should have intimate contact with and control over the Board [NIRB] through *one person,* actively engaged in the administration of N.R.A. That person should *know* the President's policy and *carry it forward.* There should be no intervening committee." He would do away with the Industrial Emergency Committee, the division of the NEC which governed NRA policy.

Richberg judged his own relation to NRA (as head of the NEC and the Industrial Emergency Committee) as one of responsibility without authority: "In his present position Richberg has too much or too little responsibility. If he is relied upon to carry out the President's policy, he is too remote from the N.R.A. and too much occupied with N.E.C. to meet that obligation. If he is not expected to do this, he should be relieved of an apparent authority which takes away power from the N.R.A. Board." Since the president was the real head of the NEC, the solution to the failure of its coordinating function lay in appointing "a subordinate in close contact with him, relying not on 'prestige,' but on direct authority." Richberg

[19] Richberg to George Horace Lorimer, Dec. 14, 1934, Richberg Papers, L.C., Box 2.

[20] Hugh Johnson to Richberg, Dec. 21, 1934; Richberg to Johnson, Dec. 23, 1934; Johnson to Richberg, Jan. 7, 1935, formerly in the possession of Mrs. John H. Small III and recently deposited in Richberg Papers, L.C.; Washington *Post,* Dec. 24, 1934; New York *Herald Tribune,* Dec. 26, 1934. Richberg also sought sympathy at the White House; see Richberg to Early, Jan. 20, 1935; Early to Richberg, Jan. 31, 1935, Franklin Roosevelt Papers, OF 788.

decided that he was "not the type of man for the job that should be done. It calls for a high grade secretary or administrative assistant, and an adequate staff working directly for the President."[21]

Later in the month, Richberg brought more pressure to bear on the White House. He told Roosevelt that the NIRB "is functioning badly and will continue to discredit N.R.A. unless made stronger and more responsive to immediate necessities." Renewal of the enabling legislation was in a "dangerous" situation, and Richberg feared that either "a bad Bill or no Bill may result unless a definite program is adopted and vigorously pushed." What NRA needed was "a Chairman of the Board with recognized authority, able to carry out the President's policy and knowing what it is." This would insure "labor and industrial support." There was only one thing to do: appoint Richberg. He eased into this suggestion by reporting that "Hillman, the best informed, most level headed labor adviser, strongly urged today that I should be given and accept the active responsibility of heading N.R.A." Richberg concluded, "It is difficult to make a suggestion apparently for my own appointment. The fact is I am regarded generally as the actual head of N.R.A. I am simply suggesting a heavier burden of direct responsibility, but at the same time the delegation of sufficient authority to fulfill it."[22]

The frustrations of his NEC coordinating job and the continuing stalemate in NRA thus once again made Richberg feel compelled to come to the rescue. Clay Williams and Arthur Whiteside of the NIRB wanted to resign anyway. Furthermore, the National Industrial Recovery Act would come up for renewal on June 16, 1935, thus providing an opportunity to correct weaknesses in the law and to alter it to meet the objections of critics. A spreading defiance of the codes had brought a renewed sense of uncertainty to NRA. The time was thus opportune for Richberg to leave the NEC and move back into the NRA as acting chairman of the NIRB in the hope of setting things straight. Roosevelt approved Richberg's suggestions, and Frank Walker, a Montana lawyer who had preceded Richberg

[21] Richberg to Roosevelt, March 4, 1935, with attached memorandum, Richberg Papers, L.C., Box 2.

[22] Richberg to McIntyre, March 19, 1935, Franklin Roosevelt Papers, OF 466.

as director of the National Emergency Council, was brought back to his old job. Walker had a reputation for being able to calm ruffled nerves and for smoothing over difficult situations. Actually, the NEC was on its way to limbo.[23]

Though labor leaders like William Green of the American Federation of Labor and John L. Lewis of the United Mine Workers were not pleased with the prospect of Richberg heading up the NIRB, they agreed to the idea after receiving assurances that it would only be a temporary arrangement. Richberg wanted to resign from government in the next few months, once the future of NRA was settled. In addition, Philip Murray, vice president of the UMW, would be appointed to the NIRB under the reorganization, giving labor for the first time equal representation with industry on the Board.[24]

Despite his call for vigorous leadership, one of Richberg's first acts as temporary chairman was to issue a statement indicating that he planned only a holding action until the fate of NRA had been determined by Congress: "Pending the enactment of legislation it would be unwise to put into effect new major policies which should receive the sanction of the Congress." Nevertheless, he promised to honor "the wholehearted determination of the administration to carry forward the industrial recovery program upon the reasonable assumption that this will be approved by the Congress, and that the extension of the Act will be authorized." Despite the brave assertions of vigorous enforcement, it was clear that Richberg regarded the NRA as suspended in a hiatus until Congress acted.[25]

[23] Schlesinger, *The Age of Roosevelt*, 2:544–49; Hawley, *The New Deal*, 111–27; Richberg, *My Hero*, 185–88; Richberg to Whiteside, March 9, 1935, Richberg Papers, L.C., Box 2; Richberg to Roosevelt, March 25, 1935; Roosevelt to Richberg, March 25, 1935, Franklin Roosevelt Papers, OF 466; Rosenblatt to National Industrial Recovery Board, "Effect on Compliance of Uncertainty as to the Future of the National Recovery Administration," March 26, 1935, NRA Papers, Series 3, Box 3; teletype material, March 21, 1935, Richberg Papers, L.C., Box 45; Press Release, April 23, 1935, Franklin Roosevelt Papers, OF 788.

[24] Richberg, *My Hero*, 187–88; Schlesinger, *The Age of Roosevelt*, 2:164–65; Hawley, *The New Deal*, 119.

[25] Richberg, NRA Release No. 10625, March 22, 1935, NRA Papers, Series 223.

In the meantime, Richberg worked behind the scenes to win the president's support for strong NRA legislation. Beginning in late 1934, while still in the NEC, Richberg had begun to exert steady pressure on Roosevelt. He had helped prepare the NRA section of the State of the Union message, and had suggested that Roosevelt urge Congress "to extend Title I of the National Industrial Recovery Act for a period of at least two years, without substantial change." More experience was needed before finally passing permanent legislation, and another two years would provide this. All through the winter of 1934 and the spring of 1935, Richberg had worked on the program.[26] On February 20, Roosevelt sent a special message to Congress recommending extension of the NIRA for two years, further clarification and definition of policy and standards for administering the Act, inducements for the voluntary submission of codes by industry coupled with unquestioned authority to impose minimum labor and competitive standards if necessary, full protection for employee organization and collective bargaining, and application of the antitrust laws against monopolies and price fixing.[27] In an additional policy statement issued in May, the National Industrial Recovery Board recommended limiting NRA jurisdiction "to industries engaged in, or substantially affecting interstate commerce" in order "to prevent the N.R.A. from taking in too much territory and [to] strengthen its legal authority." Additionally, stronger enforcement powers were needed, "primarily through injunction or cease and desist orders," "provision for adequate protection of individual rights and small enterprises through opportunity for hearing and judicial review," and "public control of all compulsory processes."[28]

[26] Richberg to Roosevelt, Dec. 22, 1934, with attached draft message, Franklin Roosevelt Papers, President's Personal File 1820. Also see Smith to Richberg, Jan. 10, 1935, NRA Papers, Series 6, Box 13; Richberg to Roosevelt, Jan. 14, 1935; Richberg to McIntyre, Jan. 31, 1935, Franklin Roosevelt Papers, OF 788.

[27] Rosenman, ed., *The Public Papers and Addresses of Franklin D. Roosevelt with a Special Introduction and Explanatory Notes by President Roosevelt*, Vol. 4: *The Court Disapproves, 1935* (New York, 1938), 80–84. Also see Richberg to McIntyre, Feb. 15, 1935, with attached revised NRA message, Franklin Roosevelt Papers, PPF 1820.

[28] NRA Release No. 11297, May 16, 1935, Richberg Papers, L.C., Box 46.

In the face of mounting criticism of the NRA, Richberg worked to hold Roosevelt to a strong position. In mid-April, he warned that "if N.R.A. legislation is sufficiently devitalized to conform to the anti-monopoly ideas of Senators Borah and Nye, it will in my opinion be made so ineffective and unworkable that it would be worse than no law." Richberg served notice that "I could not honorably support such a bill," and wanted to be consulted "before any concessions are made to the defeatist position which some of your friends are sincerely urging because of their lack of information and experience." He feared such friends "failed to comprehend the minimum necessities of any legislation which is worth passing— or which can be legally upheld and enforced."[29]

Richberg continued his warnings through April. He was worried most by "the suggestion of a temporary extension of the present Act" for nine months or a year, and believed that "such a proposition would simply chloroform the N.R.A." Roosevelt could not back down on his recommendation for a two-year extension for several reasons: 1) "The present law needs to be strengthened to withstand legal attacks"; 2) "An adequate personnel cannot be obtained or maintained except for a two year effort to make the law effective"; 3) "Uncertainty over the continuance of the law in the last four months had weakened the support of industry and labor and demoralized compliance with the codes," a condition which "will grow steadily worse during another brief period of extension." Richberg saw the idea of a temporary extension as the "last-ditch effort" of NRA's opponents "to prevent the enactment of an improved law."[30] On May 1, he concluded, "My conviction is that the President would suffer less and the country benefit more by killing the

Also see Richberg's testimony to Congress on extending the NRA: U. S., Congress, Senate, 74th Cong., 1st sess., Committee on Finance, *Investigation of the National Recovery Administration*, Pursuant to S. Res. 79 (1935), I, 1–163; U. S., Congress, House, 74th Cong., 1st sess., Committee on Ways and Means, *Extension of the National Industrial Recovery Act* (1935), 10–183.

[29] Richberg to Roosevelt, April 13, 1935, Franklin Roosevelt Papers, OF 466.

[30] Richberg to Roosevelt, April 26, 1935, Franklin Roosevelt Papers, OF 466.

N.R.A. while it is still respectable than by having it linger on, feebly trying to do the impossible, until everyone will believe that it never was any good." Keeping the pressure on Roosevelt, he added, "I would not personally spend one week on such a futile effort," and neither would "every other man of any experience in the actual responsibilities of administration."[31]

Before the month of May was out, the problem of new legislation would be resolved by the Supreme Court ruling in the case of *United States* v. *A.L.A. Schechter Poultry Corp., et al.*, handed down on May 27. In fact, it was the knowledge that the Court was about to rule on the constitutionality of the NIRA, as well as the opposition of NRA's critics, that increased congressional reluctance to pass a new law quickly. It turned out that the fate of the NRA was determined by the Court and not by Congress.

The constitutionality of the NIRA had been a constant concern throughout the life of the administration; cases of code violations regularly presented themselves for litigation. From the beginning, General Johnson and Richberg had avoided rushing into a test of the law. They hoped to find a favorable case to present in the courts and desired to let the NRA prove itself in action, thereby building up a constituency which the Supreme Court might consider in evaluating the merits of the experiment. Richberg reasoned that the NRA was "acting under a broad mandate in a new field of administrative law . . . feeling our way and making mistakes which we would seek to correct as soon as discovered." He did not want "the constitutionality of the law itself [to] be subjected to attack on the basis of an administrative interpretation which would affect the judicial construction of the law." Time would develop administrative procedures that would bear out the validity of the law. Errors would be corrected. Perhaps new legislation would lessen the vulnerability of the NRA.[32]

But the failure of NRA to submit itself to the scrutiny of the Su-

[31] Richberg to McIntyre, n.d., and Richberg to Roosevelt, May 1, 1935, Franklin Roosevelt Papers, OF 466.

[32] Richberg, "The Truth about the Schechter Case," 1–2, Richberg Papers, L.C., Box 8. Also see Ickes, *Secret Diary*, 1:94, 101; Richberg, NRA Release No. 2067, Dec. 4, 1933, NRA Papers, Series 223; Richberg, *My Hero*, 190.

preme Court constituted an obstacle in gaining improved legislation. And the administration could not remain indefinitely unwill-
ing to have the constitutional issue settled. As a result, a test case
worked its way up to the Supreme Court by early 1935. This was
the Belcher case, involving violations of the Lumber and Timber
Products Code.[33]

The acting general counsel of NRA, Blackwell Smith, favored
"pushing for the Belcher case to the utmost of our ability."[34] He
feared that unless the case were "permitted to come on in due course
which would mean probably the last week in March," the NRA ran
the risk of an adverse decision being handed down in the Court's
fall term, possibly upsetting the NRA at a time when Congress would
not be in session and able to take corrective measures. The Belcher
case was not the best one that might be desired, but Smith felt the
issue had to be faced. He so advised the National Industrial Recovery Board on February 13, 1935, and on February 18, 1935, it in
turn recommended to the president that "no action be taken to prevent the Belcher case from being heard by the Supreme Court in
due course."[35]

Meanwhile, in March, Felix Frankfurter urged Roosevelt to
withhold action. He reported that Solicitor General Stanley Reed
of the Justice Department had informed him that "the N.R.A. people are anxious for a ruling from the Supreme Court even if adverse
in order to guide the new legislation." Frankfurter thought "that
was a suicidal policy from any point of view," and the solicitor general agreed. Though Reed thought the NRA position might be a reflection of Roosevelt's, Frankfurter assured him that "if he were
convinced, as he is, of the wisdom of dismissing the [Belcher] appeal he would have your support."[36]

[33] Schlesinger, *The Age of Roosevelt*, Vol. 3: *The Politics of Upheaval*,
1935–36 (Boston, 1960), 274–77; Richberg, "The Truth about the Schechter Case," 3–5; Richberg, *The Rainbow* (New York, 1936), 209–14.

[34] Smith to G. S. Arnold, Jan. 19, 1935, NRA Papers, Series 49, Box 567.

[35] Smith to National Industrial Recovery Board, Feb. 13, 1935; Marshall
to Roosevelt, Feb. 18, 1935, NRA Papers, Series 6, Box 14.

[36] Paula Tully to Felix Frankfurter, March 13, 1935, with attached
"Memorandum for the President from—F. F.," n.d., Felix Frankfurter Papers, Library of Congress, Box 34.

When Richberg took over as acting chairman of the National Industrial Recovery Board on March 21, one of his first decisions was to recommend carrying the Belcher case through to a conclusion. He did so with reluctance, believing that the lumber code provided a poor test case as it contained provisions on price fixing, production quotas, and other controls which were "of doubtful legality and questionable economic wisdom." The lumber code was one of the first to be approved, and perhaps for that reason contained provisions the NRA did not now wish to defend. Nonetheless, Richberg was afraid that "the dismissal of the appeal might put the Administration in the position of seeking to exercise illegal authority and to prevent a determination of the legality of its actions by the Supreme Court." Furthermore, all this might damage the enforcement of the codes and impair compliance even more. Hence, Richberg recommended proceeding and going through with the case.[37]

The final decision rested not with Richberg but with the Justice Department. Here the Frankfurter strategy temporarily held sway. On March 26, the Department announced that it would request a dismissal of its appeal because the "Code contains administrative provisions peculiar to itself with respect to the extension of discretionary powers to non-government agencies—a fact . . . which sets this Code in a class by itself." The NRA wanted to revise the code and eliminate this feature. Further, the lower court record provided an unsatisfactory foundation for considering the facts and evidence in the case.[38]

As Richberg had feared, the Belcher dismissal precipitated a highly unfavorable public reaction. Much of the press asserted that the NRA was afraid to go before the Court.[39] On April 3, Rich-

[37] Richberg, "The Truth about the Schechter Case," 5–6. Also see Richberg, The Rainbow, 215–17.

[38] Department of Justice, Press Release, March 25, 1935, NRA Papers, Series 49, Box 567; Schlesinger, The Age of Roosevelt, 3:276–77.

[39] Richberg, "The Truth about the Schechter Case," 6; Richberg, The Rainbow, 217; Schlesinger, The Age of Roosevelt, 3:277; Boston Transcript, March 26, 1935; New York Evening Sun, March 27, 1935; Baltimore Sun, March 27, 1935; Wall Street Journal, March 28, 1935; Indianapolis News, March 28, 1935; Philadelphia Inquirer, April 2, 1935;

berg wired Roosevelt, vacationing at sea on the Astor yacht *Nourmahal,* that public opinion on the dismissal had been adverse, making enforcement of the codes "generally impossible" and increasing the "hostility of Congress to new legislation." He urged that another case, recently sustaining the NRA in the New York Circuit Court of Appeals, be immediately expedited to the Court in order to offset the effects of the Belcher dismissal. He believed this would be "of extraordinary help in sustaining N.R.A. and advancing legislation." On April 4, Roosevelt suggested that Richberg consult with Attorney General Homer Cummings.[40]

Also on April 4, White House aide Thomas Corcoran, a Frankfurter protégé, relayed a message from Frankfurter to Roosevelt. Frankfurter confidentially had learned that Cummings, "under urging of Richberg to silence criticism on Belcher dismissal and pursuant to wire from you," planned to announce to the press that the Department of Justice would take immediate action to place a new test case before the Supreme Court. Frankfurter considered it "most impolitic and dangerous to yield to antagonistic press clamor," because the "fundamental situation" on the Court had not changed.[41] White House secretary Steve Early checked Frankfurter's views with Richberg and the Justice Department and found them both "in complete disagreement with Frankfurter's request that case be held in abeyance." Furthermore, they believed that "the importance and necessity of Supreme Court test is para-

---

Washington *Post,* April 3, 1935; Chicago *Journal of Commerce,* March 27, 1935; San Francisco *Chronicle,* April 6, 1935.

[40] Richberg to Roosevelt, April 3, 1935, Franklin Roosevelt Papers, OF 466; Roosevelt to Early, April 4, 1935, Franklin Roosevelt Papers, OF 200-M; Schlesinger, *The Age of Roosevelt,* 3:278. For a summary of NRA difficulties in enforcing the codes, see Rosenblatt, memoranda entitled "Effect on Compliance of Uncertainty as to the Future of the National Recovery Administration," April 8, 15, 22, 29, 1935, and Rosenblatt, memoranda entitled "Report on Compliance Conditions," May 6, 13, 1935, all in NRA Papers, Series 3, Box 3; A. G. McKnight to Richberg, March 27, 1935; A. G. McKnight to Richberg, March 30, 1935, NRA Papers, Series 49, Box 567; Richberg, NRA Release No. 10752, March 31, 1935, NRA Papers, Series 223.

[41] Thomas G. Corcoran to Roosevelt, April 4, 1935, Franklin Roosevelt Papers, OF 466.

mount and both believe case can be won." Roosevelt ordered a decision held up, but his message arrived in Washington too late.[42]

Accordingly, the Justice Department went ahead and issued a press release announcing that it would cooperate in expediting the case of the A.L.A. Schechter Poultry Corp., et al., to the Supreme Court. Richberg also put out a release backing up the action of the Justice Department.[43]

Frankfurter later found "sorry comfort" in observing "that the departure from the strategy that lay behind the side-tracking of the Belcher case has made the legislative situation regarding N.R.A. so much worse." Congress simply waited for the Court to decide the future of the NIRA. Everything now depended on what was soon dubbed the "sick chicken" case. Moreover, Frankfurter observed to Raymond Moley, "What makes the business so sad is that the President's absence from Washington should have been seized upon as an opportunity for embarrassing this situation by forcing an appeal."[44]

With the decision to rush the Schechter case to a conclusion, Homer Cummings appointed Richberg on April 22 to participate along with Solicitor General Stanley Reed in arguing the case before the Supreme Court. The attorney general, himself not in complete sympathy with NRA, wanted to share the responsibility. Richberg was only too happy to accept appointment. His paternal feeling toward NRA compelled him to become involved. In addition, he feared that Reed was not sufficiently knowledgeable about NRA to present a good case on his own.[45] Also Richberg suspected that

[42] Early to Roosevelt, April 4, 1935; Early to Roosevelt, April 5, 1935, Franklin Roosevelt Papers, OF 200-M-Misc.; Roosevelt to Attorney General, April 4, 1935, with copies to Early and Corcoran, and indication that Richberg and Stanley Reed also advised, Franklin Roosevelt Papers, OF 10; Schlesinger, *The Age of Roosevelt*, 3:278.

[43] Department of Justice, Press Release, April 4, 1935, NRA Papers, Series 49, Box 568; Richberg, NRA Release No. 10810, April 4, 1935, NRA Papers, Series 27.

[44] Frankfurter to Raymond Moley, May 2, 1935, Frankfurter Papers, Box 28.

[45] Homer Cummings to Richberg, April 22, 1935, NRA Papers, Series 3, Box 5; Richberg, *My Hero*, 193–95; Richberg, *The Rainbow*, 219–20; Schlesinger, *The Age of Roosevelt*, 3:279.

many officers in the Justice Department were unsympathetic to his cause, and in fact the NRA did encounter friction in working with the Department of Justice on the preparation of the case.[46]

Richberg immersed himself completely in readying his argument, scheduled for May 2–3 in the Supreme Court's old chambers in the Capitol Building. His task was largely one of mastering the arguments and legal research of the NRA staff and the Justice Department. Although he had a long record of legal and administrative experience in the NRA to draw upon, Richberg did not have the time, with his duties as chairman of the NIRB, to work up the legal aspects of the case personally. He had to rely on others for this. He was simply the star in a show with many people working behind the scenes to support him.

Richberg's argument before the Court emphasized the circumstances which had called the National Recovery Administration into being. The emergency created by the depression, nationwide in scope, required an exercise of power on a national scale. He relied heavily on a broad definition of the commerce power, one adequate to meet a national emergency, and urged the Court to evaluate the Poultry Code not as an isolated exercise of regulatory power, but as part of a broad attack on a nationwide problem. Furthermore, he argued that the need for cooperation among businessmen to stabilize the anarchy of an unbridled competitive system demanded a new understanding of the meaning of federal regulation. The country must move away from the purely negative approach of the antitrust laws to a more positive ideal as embodied in the NRA: "The power to regulate is not merely the power to prohibit wrongdoing; it must clearly also encompass a power to encourage and to organize cooperation in doing good." Richberg defended the competitive and labor standards laid down in the Act as sufficient guides for the president in carrying out the will of Congress. He admitted, however, that because of the variety of problems in different industries, the particulars of such standards had to be left to the develop-

[46] Thomas C. Billig to Smith and Scott, April 16, 1935; Scott to Smith, April 20, 1935; Philip E. Buck to Billig, R. J. Heilman, J. A. Fridinger, Frank Elmore, Jr., Allen Robinson, Stewart McDonald, Stein, April 28, 1935, all in NRA Papers, Series 49, Box 568.

ment of a law merchant among businessmen themselves. The codes of fair competition sought to do precisely this. The codes filled the gap left by Congress's inability to establish guidelines adaptable to every industry in the nation.

The Supreme Court disagreed with both Richberg's definition of the commerce power and his belief in the adequacy of the legislature's instructions to the executive for implementing public policy. It threw out the NRA in *United States* v. *A.L.A. Schechter Poultry Corp., et al.,* on May 27, 1935, as an illegal application of the federal power to regulate interstate commerce and as an unconstitutional delegation of the lawmaking power to the president.[47]

Although Richberg and others submitted plans for a new NRA with more carefully defined powers, Roosevelt decided to ask Congress to approve a temporary extension of only a skeleton agency rather than attempt to reconstitute a full-fledged program. The purpose of the temporary agency would be to liquidate the NRA, to analyze the information on industry and trade in NRA's possession, and to assist in implementing a proposed requirement that government contractors abide by certain minimum labor standards. Roosevelt's growing frustration with a series of adverse Supreme Court decisions against the New Deal, plus his increasing apprehension that government cooperation with the business community was an unreal expectation, undoubtedly contributed to his decision. Richberg's hopes for a modified but nevertheless large-scale NRA program were dashed.[48]

[47] Richberg, *The Rainbow,* 217–41; Richberg, *My Hero,* 189–96; Richberg, *Oral Argument of Hon. Donald R. Richberg on Behalf of the United States, United States* v. *A.L.A. Schechter Poultry Corp, et al.,* pamphlet in Richberg Papers, L.C., Box 47; 295 U. S. 495 (1935); Gregory Hankin to Billig, May 4, 1935, and "Outline of Schechter Opinion," n.d., both in NRA Papers, Series 49, Box 567. The quotation is from Richberg, *Oral Argument of Hon. Donald R. Richberg,* 6.

[48] [Richberg], "Memorandum to the President," May 31, 1935, with attached draft bill; Marshall to Richberg, May 31, 1935; Richberg to Roosevelt, June 13, 1935, Richberg Papers, L.C., Box 46; Frankfurter to Roosevelt, May 30, 1935, Frankfurter Papers, Box 34; Roosevelt to Attorney General and Solicitor General, June 8, 1935, Franklin Roosevelt Papers, OF 466; Press Release, June 4, 1935, OGR Papers, Series 76, Box 751; Rich-

With the end of an experiment that he dreamed would one day lead to a utopia of business-government cooperation and a rationally planned economy, Richberg submitted his formal resignation to the president on June 5. In a private note to Roosevelt on the same day, Richberg expressed his concern that "very little can be accomplished to save the great values of the N.R.A. under the limitations of the present program, as I understand it." If the president had decided to abandon the ideas behind the NRA, then Richberg's usefulness had ended: "I feel that I am a burden rather than an aid to the accomplishment of your apparent aims." Recognizing that he was "mentally fagged and physically depressed," and having lost Roosevelt's support for the kind of massive and permanent program he had in mind, Richberg retired to Rehoboth Beach, Delaware, for the summer, where he wrote a book about his NRA experiences.[49]

Just as Richberg's belief in his own impartiality had proved inaccurate when it came to labor-management relations, so too did his sense of his own indispensability. He could not possibly control the entire industrial recovery program, yet time after time he felt compelled to come to its rescue. The irony was that his deep commitment to the original principles of the National Industrial Recovery Act, which had been designed to offset the constrictive trends of the depression mainly through private initiative and private planning, prevented him from comprehending the full meaning of their gradual breakdown. The ideals of business-government cooperation simply had to be viable; Richberg could not tolerate the possibility that they might not be and saw no other alternatives. To Richberg's mind, a larger role for government was not the answer, for such a policy would have contradicted the most basic assumptions of industrial self-government underlying the experiment. The result was that his attempts to rescue the administration program consisted chiefly of relatively ineffective changes in imme-

---

berg, *My Hero*, 197–99; Hawley, *The New Deal*, 130–31; Schlesinger, *The Age of Roosevelt*, 3:287–90.

[49] Richberg to Roosevelt, June 5, 1935; Richberg to Roosevelt, June 5, 1935 (handwritten note), Franklin Roosevelt Papers, OF 466; Richberg, *My Hero*, 199–202.

diate tactics but not in basic principles or long-range strategy. Rich-berg believed in government-business cooperation as firmly when he left the administration as when he entered it, despite the evidence of the intervening two years that his faith was not completely justified. His own belief in the program as originally conceived contributed to the NRA's inability to break away from its mis-take of relying too heavily on the good will of private business for a solution to the depression. Despite numerous reforms and reor-ganizations, the assumptions underlying the industrial recovery pro-gram of 1935 were essentially the same as those of 1933.

In the end, Richberg's positive identification with the original plan he had helped to create, his personal loyalty to Roosevelt (who had given him assurances that he occupied a special place in the administration), and his own need for success and vindication impelled him toward the idea that he had a heavy responsibility for the success of the New Deal. And for the sake of his own psychic security, this was a responsibility he could not shirk.

CHAPTER IX

On the Sidelines

The story of Donald Richberg after 1935 is the story of a gradual alienation from the New Deal and Franklin Roosevelt, a strengthening of his identification with the businessman's approach to recovery, and a waning of political influence. Though he enjoyed something of a resurgence at the White House as an expert on constitutional reform and business-government relations in 1937–1938, Richberg was effectively disarmed of all political power by the time of the Second World War. Thenceforth, his political activities were confined to propaganda; he substituted preaching for action. And as Richberg drew farther and farther away from the exercise of power, his ideas about its use became more theoretical and less relevant to the realities around him. The old campaigner of 1912, 1924, and 1932 emerged as a conservative, invoking the values of his youth rather than coming to terms with the actualities of the welfare state. His intellectual problem was not that he changed, but that he failed to change. His personal problem was that he was no longer welcome among liberals, so that his business associates reinforced his identity with conservatism.

In the fall of 1935, after recovering from his NRA battles during the summer, Richberg decided to open up a law office of his own in Washington rather than return to Chicago. He had made many new friends in Washington during his days in government service and found the capital city an exciting place to be. Furthermore, the prospects of resuming a legal practice based on labor representation were slight after NRA so that there would be little attraction in going back to Chicago. He could not simply pick up where he had left off, for many of his former clients were no longer in sympathy with him.

Accordingly, Richberg opened up a law office, alone, on Jackson Place, a short distance from the White House. Despite his many personal contacts in Washington, the first months on his own were not very profitable, and Richberg gradually came to the conclusion that he would have to join a large firm if he expected to handle important cases. A solo operator could not expect to attract large clients who were likely to require a great deal of attention. Even if he could, Richberg did not relish the prospect of becoming dependent on a few substantial clients; this would hinder his feeling of independence even more than belonging to a large firm. Though he had never liked the idea of working in a large office, and had left his father's old firm in Chicago to practice alone in the 1920s partly for this reason, Richberg concluded that what he desired was simply not practical anymore.

In December of 1936, as he was reaching this conclusion, Joseph E. Davies invited Richberg to join his Washington firm as a senior partner. Though Richberg had no close personal acquaintance with Davies, his cousin Morgan Davies had been one of Richberg's partners before he left his father's firm in 1923. Joseph E. Davies was about to be appointed United States Ambassador to the USSR and wanted to bring in an older lawyer with an established reputation to head up the firm in his absence. He offered Richberg an attractive financial arrangement. With the prospect of financial security at last, plus his conclusion that it would be necessary to join a large firm in order to be a factor in Washington legal circles, Richberg accepted the invitation, becoming a partner in the firm of Davies, Richberg, Beebe, Busick, and Richardson.[1]

Richberg's return to private practice, alone in 1935 and then as a member of one of Washington's leading firms in 1936, did not mean the end of his activity in the Roosevelt administration. He was much too drawn to politics for that, and had too deep a need to relate his own work with the public welfare to lose interest in the New Deal. Though restricted to working on a volunteer basis

---

[1] Donald Richberg, *My Hero: The Indiscreet Memoirs of an Eventful but Unheroic Life* (New York, 1954), 201–203, 228–29.

behind the scenes, he took all precautions to keep his line to the White House in good repair. Before he joined Davies in late 1936, he did some speech writing for the presidential campaign and helped prepare the White House draft of the Democratic platform. He also wrote a campaign book entitled *Guilty! The Confession of Franklin D. Roosevelt, Written by a Friend.* It defended the New Deal against the charge that it was a socialist dictatorship designed to destroy free enterprise and pictured it as preserving and humanizing capitalism.[2]

Far more important than Richberg's campaign work in 1936 was his informal lobbying on behalf of continuing the ideals of the National Recovery Administration. Despite the experiences of the NRA, Richberg still believed that the way to permanent economic reform lay in cooperation between business and government and modification of the antitrust laws. He did not want to see Roosevelt launch an antibusiness or trustbusting campaign that would do irrevocable harm and destroy any possibility of cooperation for national economic planning. Raymond Moley spoke for a similar point of view.[3] Richberg believed that such a turn in the New Deal would be anachronistic and irrelevant to the two great realities of modern economic conditions: concentration and interdependence. He attributed the breakdown of the NRA mainly to difficulties in administration and execution of policy; its troubles must not be allowed to destroy faith in the principles on which it was founded. Richberg thus retained an idealized attitude toward what he regarded as the essentials of the NRA and failed to explain (except for administration reasons) why it had been so difficult to put them into effect in the real world of monopolies, labor strife, unfair competition, and managed markets. As a result of his uncritical attitude, Richberg did not modify his position and remained a spokesman for a business-government commonwealth of cooperation.

Richberg opposed the Louis Brandeis–Felix Frankfurter theory

---

[2] Ibid., 203–206; Donald Richberg to Stephen Early, Oct. 20, 1936, with attached "Memorandum concerning N.R.A.," Donald Richberg Papers, Library of Congress, Box 33; [Richberg], *Guilty! The Confession of Franklin D. Roosevelt, Written by a Friend* (Garden City, N. Y., 1936).

[3] Raymond Moley, *The First New Deal* (New York, 1966), 525–30.

that the ills of the depression could be attributed to economic concentration itself; a return to competition by breaking up large businesses into smaller units would compensate for the mismanagement of a few industrial czars who had tried to gain a stranglehold on the nation's economy. Richberg did not want to destroy a managed economy, but to control it for the benefit of workers and consumers as well as investors. To him, managing the economy offered the one hope that man could rationally control his destiny and spread prosperity; there was no logical necessity for trusting to the operation of the mystical laws of laissez faire which allegedly governed the free market.[4]

Richberg was very much concerned with keeping the president in contact with businessmen who he thought would be receptive to some sign from the White House that the end of NRA did not mean the beginning of trustbusting. As early as March 1936, Felix Frankfurter expressed concern to Solicitor General Stanley Reed over "the resurgence of Donald Richberg" and how it had "aroused alarm among some of our very best friends."[5] The president's own uncertainty about his future business policy kept the White House door open to spokesmen like Richberg as well as those of opposing views. The struggle between the antitrusters and the advocates of business-government planning was far from over.[6] Richberg kept himself in the forefront of those urging Roosevelt to stick to the ideals of NRA. He regularly bombarded the president with recommendations on policy and urged him not to sell the NRA short. During the 1936 campaign, he suggested that Roosevelt's spokesmen not "apologize for N.R.A." but "extol its temporary and permanent values."

Beyond campaign strategy, Richberg wanted the president to

[4] Richberg, The Rainbow (Garden City, N. Y., 1936), 224–84; Arthur M. Schlesinger, Jr., The Age of Roosevelt, Vol. 3: The Politics of Upheaval, 1935–1936 (Boston, 1960), 385–400.

[5] Felix Frankfurter to Stanley Reed, March 25, 1936, Felix Frankfurter Papers, Library of Congress, Box 32.

[6] See Ellis Wayne Hawley, The New Deal and the Problem of Monopoly: A Study in Economic Ambivalence (Princeton, N. J., 1966), 383–403, and Schlesinger, The Age of Roosevelt, 3:385–408, for a picture of the struggle over policy.

use the NRA experience as the foundation for a renewed program. As a first step, he proposed continuing the analysis of NRA records already underway and making "a comprehensive public report upon the N.R.A. as a whole." He was confident of the results of such a study and expected it to emphasize "the soundness of [the NRA] program, [and] the difficulties and the public service already accomplished and to be accomplished along the lines of the original N.R.A. program revised in the light of experience." All this would be a prelude to an "effort to draft or enact further legislation." But the important thing in the spring of 1936 was to start working on some kind of a plan to follow up NRA, "otherwise there will be much pulling and hauling and one or two very aggressive groups may take the lead in promoting a bad program which it will be hard to stop." Shortly thereafter, Roosevelt created a Committee of Industrial Analysis to complete the administration's evaluation of the NRA.[7]

At the same time, Richberg launched his personal campaign to bring Roosevelt together with friendly businessmen, and newspaperman Raymond Clapper noted in the spring of 1936 that "Richberg [has] been seeing Roosevelt [a] great deal secretly recently." Richberg's self-appointed mission was twofold: 1) to encourage the president to be patient and give businessmen another chance to work out a program, and 2) to make the business community realize that Roosevelt was going to be reelected in 1936 and that they must be prepared to work with him.[8]

Richberg feared that Roosevelt's patience was running out and that a crackdown on business was likely after the election. On the other side, too many businessmen distrusted the president; for this reason, Richberg had recommended to Roosevelt that the new

[7] Richberg to Franklin Roosevelt, Feb. 25, 1936, with attached "Memorandum as to the Future of the N.R.A. Program," Franklin D. Roosevelt Papers, Franklin D. Roosevelt Library, Official File 466-Misc.; Samuel I. Rosenman, ed., *The Public Papers and Addresses of Franklin D. Roosevelt with a Special Introduction and Explanatory Notes by President Roosevelt,* Vol. 5: *The People Approve, 1936* (New York, 1938), 152–58.

[8] Raymond Clapper, notes for March 23, 1936, Raymond Clapper Papers, Library of Congress, Box 210.

Committee of Industrial Analysis be (according to Clapper's testimony) "strictly a business men's proposition so they won't be scared off."[9] In the spring of 1936, he encouraged Roosevelt to include in his special Message to Congress on unemployment and relief an appeal to businessmen to meet with him and discuss ways of increasing employment. Richberg hoped that some "self-selected group of business managers" would voluntarily come forth and lay the foundation for a permanent organization to serve as a liaison between government and business in launching a new scheme for economic planning. Such a meeting between the president and friendly business leaders would create an atmosphere of cooperation.

Richberg urged the idea on Roosevelt as a practical way to utilize the NRA experience. Data in the government's possession could be made available to "business organizations seeking to improve the public service of private enterprise." For their part, industrialists would "undertake to bring about the expansion of the volume of employment and the volume of production." Richberg hoped that bringing businessmen together on this basis would "avoid even the appearances of the exercise of coercive influence by the national government to bring about such an organization." The feeling in industry that the NRA was an instrument of government regimentation had been one of the great obstacles to its success in Richberg's opinion. He saw the ultimate solution to the depression coming from the private sector; somehow the number of jobs had to be increased, for government relief and make-work programs could not continue indefinitely if capitalism was to survive. The needed mobilization of private resources, if it were to come about at all, or if it were not to be the result of a government dictatorship, would have to result from the voluntary cooperative efforts of the business community. Hopefully, the president could serve as the rallying point for such an effort.[10]

In his relief message of March 18, Roosevelt did not make the

[9] Ibid.

[10] Richberg to Roosevelt, March 6, 1936, with attached "Memorandum concerning Relief Message and Business Cooperation"; Richberg to Roosevelt, March 13, 1936, with attached "Memorandum for the President," Franklin Roosevelt Papers, President's Personal File 1820.

kind of explicit appeal for a White House business conference that Richberg had in mind, but he did urge the private sector to take the initiative in cooperative efforts to increase employment. The president offered the assistance of the federal government in such a project and implied that he would stand ready to listen to any suggestions coming from the business community.[11]

To Charles R. Hook, president of the American Rolling Mill Company and future head of the National Association of Manufacturers, Richberg urged that the business community not wait until after the November elections to respond to Roosevelt's gesture of goodwill. To postpone action in the futile hope of a Democratic defeat would only insure a continuing deterioration in relations between FDR and business. To avert an antibusiness program in 1937, industry should mobilize now.[12]

Although his efforts were unavailing in bringing about a concrete program right away, Richberg thought he saw signs of a softening attitude on both sides and continued to drum up support for his ideas. By autumn, he worked out a proposal for revising the antitrust laws as part of his plan of cooperation between businessmen and the federal government. In messages to the president and in addresses before groups of lawyers and businessmen, he recommended recasting the laws to acknowledge that "large business operations are a natural development" and that they should be controlled rather than destroyed. Cooperative arrangements within or among trades for expanding and stabilizing markets, production, and employment were desirable so long as they were "openly made with the resulting cooperation subject to public scrutiny." Most important, "The developing field of trade agreements should be supervised by an administrative agency charged with the duty of maintaining the laws against monopolistic and unfair trade practices, but authorized to sanction agreements clearly within the law or within any twilight zone, subject to the rights of public or pri-

[11] Rosenman, ed., *Public Papers and Addresses of Franklin D. Roosevelt*, 5:125–31; Clapper, notes for March 23, 1936, Clapper Papers, Box 210.

[12] Richberg to Charles R. Hook, April 10, 1936, and Richberg, "Memorandum on the Need for Immediate Non-Partisan Formulation of Constructive Policies," Richberg Papers, L.C., Box 38.

vate objectors to submit a complaint to the administrative commission for a decision, which like all commission orders would be subject to judicial review."

What Richberg wanted was "a clear legal distinction between mere size and actual monopolistic power, and also between the possession of power that may be abused and the actual abuse of power." The antitrust laws ought to establish more precise standards. Yet even by fair practices, competition often led to concentration. It was a natural development and should not be punished by law unless accomplished through illegitimate means, which could be legally defined and controlled. Richberg's recommendations thus reflected his persistent faith in the ideals of the NRA: the key to prosperity lay in industrial self-government and private initiative, supervised and assisted by a government agency designed to modify the antitrust laws in the public interest.[13]

Undeterred by the lack of concrete results in 1936, Richberg continued his personal campaign at the White House and in business circles throughout 1937. He regularly bombarded both camps with recommendations in letters, speeches, and private conversations. The essentials of his program remained unchanged, and he urged Roosevelt not to deviate from "the foundation principle of our political economy," which was "the self-regulation of commerce and the fixing of prices and wages by competition." The legitimate sphere of government action was in eliminating the excesses of competition, but not in fighting or taking over either management or labor. Richberg's goal was cooperation within and between management and labor, with the government's assistance, to stabilize the vagaries of the competitive system. He did not want government domination. Ideally, such matters as wages and hours "should be the product of collective bargaining," and not of fed-

[13] Richberg, "A Suggestion for Revision of the Anti-Trust Laws," *University of Pennsylvania Law Review* 85 (Nov. 1936), 11–15. Also see Richberg to Hook, Sept. 3, 1936, Richberg Papers, L.C., Box 38; Richberg to Early, Oct. 20, 1936, with attached "Memorandum concerning N.R.A.," Richberg Papers, L.C., Box 33; Richberg to Roosevelt, Nov. 16, 1936, with attached memorandum, "Civilizing Competition," Franklin Roosevelt Papers, PPF 2418.

eral decree. In other words, they should be settled privately.[14] Roosevelt always welcomed Richberg's suggestions, yet nothing concrete resulted from them. The president's reluctance about committing himself was undoubtedly the product of the continuing policy dispute in administration circles between the antitrusters and the government-business planners.

Richberg had his long-hoped-for chance to bring about a reconciliation between the business community and Roosevelt in the early part of 1938. He succeeded in arranging a meeting for January 11 between the president and a group of leading industrialists, including Ernest T. Weir of Weirton Steel, Lewis Brown of Johns-Manville, Colby Chester of the NAM, and Alfred P. Sloan of General Motors. Furthermore, it was followed a few days later by a similar gathering of business and labor leaders arranged by Adolf Berle and Rexford Tugwell.[15]

At the meeting set up by Richberg, the discussion centered on the relationship between production and purchasing power, a housing program, investment in capital goods, communication between business and government, and wages and hours legislation. Although the conferees were able to agree with Roosevelt's objectives, difficulties arose as to how to bring them about. The industry representatives favored a minimum of legislation, preferring to work

[14] Richberg to Marguerite LeHand, Dec. 29, 1937, with attached "D. R. Memo—1—Introductory Material," "D. R. Memo—2—Industrial Management and Labor," "D. R. Memo—3—Conclusion Material," Franklin Roosevelt Papers, PPF 1820. Also see Richberg to Roosevelt, Feb. 19, 1937, with attached memorandum; Richberg to Marvin McIntyre, July 28, 1937, Franklin Roosevelt Papers, OF 1961; Daniel Roper to Roosevelt, March 3, 1937, Franklin Roosevelt Papers, OF 3–Q; Roper to McIntyre, March 18, 1937, with attached memorandum, Roper to Roosevelt, March 18, 1937, Franklin Roosevelt Papers, OF 3; Roosevelt to Robert H. Jackson, Oct. 20, 1937, Franklin Roosevelt Papers, OF 358; Richberg to LeHand, Feb. 25, 1937, and Richberg to Roosevelt, Feb. 25, 1937, Richberg Papers, L.C., Box 2; Clapper, diary entry for Feb. 2 and May 29, 1937, Clapper Papers, Box 8; Richberg, "Future Federal Regulation of Business," *Vital Speeches of the Day* 3 (Feb. 1, 1937): 238–41; Richberg, "The Black-Connery Bill," *Vital Speeches of the Day* 3 (July 15, 1937): 585–87.

[15] Hawley, *The New Deal*, 396–403; Clapper, diary entries for Jan. 9, 12, and 14, 1938, Clapper Papers, Box 8.

through trade associations or other private means rather than a federal program. There was no opposition to the principle of collective bargaining, and Richberg told Raymond Clapper that the conferees agreed it was "here to stay." Senator Robert Wagner's National Labor Relations Act, passed in 1935 after the Supreme Court ruling against the NRA, was not discussed in explicit terms. The business representatives, however, definitely preferred handling labor relations by agreement and mediation rather than what Richberg described as the "process now being tried."

Richberg came away from the meeting optimistic. He thought there was a real chance that machinery for cooperative ventures might develop out of the conference, and was impressed by the apparent sincerity of both the president and the businessmen.[16] The next week, Roosevelt conferred with the Commerce Department's Business Advisory Council and representatives of the automobile industry in two separate meetings. Talk of renewed efforts at economic planning dominated all these sessions, yet the business community adhered to its belief that industry must have the decisive role in any cooperative efforts by government and business. Power must remain in its hands, not those of government officials.[17]

Hardly a week had passed before Richberg's high hopes were dashed. On January 14, Roosevelt struck out at holding companies during one of his news conferences. Richberg was deeply upset at this development, and told Clapper that the president's "loose talking" could undo his efforts to effect a business-government scheme of cooperation. According to Clapper, Richberg "forecast . . . that the days of democracy are numbered." Further, he believed that "within [the] next two weeks," the "destiny of [the] nation would be decided." If "this cooperative effort" failed, it would make each side more adamant than before, and end up with government domination of the economy and the possible end of free enterprise. Richberg feared "left wing advisers" were telling

[16] Clapper, diary entries for Jan. 12 and 14, 1938, Clapper Papers, Box 8.
[17] Hawley, *The New Deal*, 397. Also see Richberg to McIntyre, Jan. 25, 1938, Franklin Roosevelt Papers, PPF 8246; Richberg to McIntyre, Feb. 8, 1938, Richberg Papers, L.C., Box 2.

Roosevelt that business-government cooperation could not work. Clapper foresaw the possibility that what Roosevelt decided "in [the] next two weeks will determine whether Don will publicly break with him."[18]

Within the space of a few weeks, Richberg had plunged from extreme optimism to extreme pessimism. His tendency to overstate his views and to overreact to events seemed to be a function of his deep commitment to the principles of the business-government commonwealth. Having worked so hard for so long on promoting his program, he was unable to consider compromising it, and saw its fortunes in terms of all-or-nothing. After hearing about Roosevelt's January 14 press conference, Richberg seemed to Clapper a "crushed and disappointed man." At the end of the month, in an address to the Northeastern Lumbermen's Association, Richberg reiterated a statement which he took from Roosevelt's most recent State of the Union message: "No government can conscript cooperation." He sent a copy of his remarks to the president, remarks which predicted that "free enterprise and free government will survive, or, in the destruction of one, both will be destroyed."[19]

The worst blow was yet to come. In April, Richberg read a newspaper report quoting Roosevelt to the effect that he was in "substantial agreement" with the antimonopoly views of Senator William Borah of Idaho. Richberg immediately dispatched a note of disbelief to the president. He warned Roosevelt against the "school of 'trust busters' who extend a just hostility to monopolistic enterprises into an unwarranted and purely unreasoning hostility first, to all big business and second, to all efforts of business, whether big or little, to cooperate in promoting an orderly and fair competition to get rid of the hazards and insecurity resulting from a ruthless and anarchistic competition." It was unfair to assume that "cooperation is always a cloak for monopolistic conspiracy." He reminded Roosevelt, "The philosophy of the N.R.A. was wholly consistent with the New Deal," but doubted whether

[18] Clapper, diary entry for Jan. 14, 1938, Clapper Papers, Box 8.
[19] Ibid.; Richberg, "Government and Business," Address to Northeastern Lumbermen's Association, New York City, Jan. 26, 1938, copy in Franklin Roosevelt Papers, OF 1961.

the same could be said for the Borah position. Though the NRA had failed as an institution, Richberg was convinced that "in the last year or two, throughout the country . . . there has developed a much better understanding of the principles of the N.R.A. and widespread regret that they have not been carried forward." The economic recession of 1937–1938 demonstrated the need for a return to the ideals of the early New Deal.[20]

Despite Richberg's hopes that Roosevelt would reconsider his position, within a few days the president recommended that Congress authorize a massive investigation of monopoly and economic concentration, and the Temporary National Economic Committee (TNEC) came into being on June 16, 1938. Long befuddled as to which direction to take, Richberg's or Borah's, Roosevelt finally moved toward the latter, perhaps as much out of frustration as conviction. For the time being, the antitrusters had bested the advocates of business-government cooperation.[21]

By the spring of 1938, Richberg had thus fully defined the principal elements of his policy position. But the president decided to undertake a different approach to business and industry. Although Richberg maintained personal contact with Roosevelt for several more years, and consulted with him on personal and public matters, the two drifted farther and farther apart once the president had committed himself to the TNEC investigation. This was a difference over policy, and not the result of a personal clash. There was no dramatic break, but simply a deepening disagreement on economic questions.

Richberg's interest in the administration between 1935 and 1938 was not restricted solely to business-government relations. Roosevelt had a high regard for his views on constitutional questions and sought his counsel a number of times in 1936–1937. And because Roosevelt wanted his help on the Supreme Court problem, he was undoubtedly all the more willing to listen to Richberg's ideas on other matters—such as business policy—even though he eventually took a different tack.

[20] Richberg to Roosevelt, April 23, 1938, Franklin Roosevelt Papers, OF 277; Clapper, diary entry for May 19, 1938, Clapper Papers, Box 8.
[21] Hawley, *The New Deal*, 410–19.

Richberg was as disturbed as Roosevelt over the Supreme Court's record of striking down New Deal legislation. Of course, he had been most concerned with the Schechter decision, and once the Court acted, he turned immediately to developing new proposals in light of the decision. To Richberg, the Court's decision outlined not only the limits of government action but also its possibilities. He used the Schechter judgment as the foundation on which to build a new program—although Roosevelt eventually decided against continuing an NRA-like agency.[22]

Though the Court's decisions might point the way for shaping future legislation, Richberg nevertheless believed that its attitude was unnecessarily hostile to the New Deal. The problem was that there were no clear and absolute standards of judgment, so that lawyers and judges might disagree among themselves in construing the constitutionality of a law. Given this fact, the final decision usually rested on the judge's own political and social beliefs. Yet the nation should not be tyrannized by the personal political or economic views of a few men clothed in the robes of the judiciary, for the ultimate repository of constitutional authority in the American form of government was the people themselves. Only they could amend the Constitution. Only they, Richberg believed, could finally interpret it. Some way had to be found to make it feasible for the people to render an interpretation binding on the Court, lest it subvert the expressed desire of the majority by striking down the New Deal. Richberg dared not think what the consequences of such a situation might be. Perhaps the legislature could serve as the people's spokesman in authoritatively interpreting the Constitution.[23]

[22] [Richberg], "Memorandum to the President," May 31, 1935, Richberg Papers, L.C., Box 46; Richberg, The Rainbow, 224–41.

[23] Richberg, "Undermining the Constitution," Vital Speeches of the Day 2 (Jan. 13, 1936): 238–44; Richberg, "Should We Amend the Constitution?" Missouri Bar Journal 7 (March 1936): 45–46, 50–53; Richberg, "The Constitution and the New Deal," Annals of the American Academy of Political and Social Science 185 (May 1936): 56–64; Richberg to McIntyre, June 16, 1936, with attached memorandum, "Concerning the Constitution and the Supreme Court," Franklin Roosevelt Papers, President's Secretary's File; Richberg to Roosevelt, Nov. 16, 1936, with attached address

Although Richberg helped Roosevelt prepare the White House draft of a noncommittal plank on the judiciary for the 1936 Democratic platform, he had a well-developed program which he put forth to the president and anyone else who would listen. His method of attack was the same as his campaign on behalf of business-government planning. He sent salvos of messages and suggestions into the White House and propagandized his theories before numerous legal and business groups. Richberg was a regular on the luncheon and banquet circuit and spoke all over the country.[24]

Richberg's idea was to remove certain constitutional questions from the appellate jurisdiction of the Supreme Court. He based his proposal on Article I, Section 8, of the Constitution, which bestowed on Congress the authority "to make all laws which shall be necessary and proper for carrying into execution" its specifically enumerated powers. To Richberg, the solution seemed inevitable: "Where the Congress has been granted an *express* power, such as the power to regulate commerce . . . then under the Constitution it is solely a question of legislative judgment, *not subject to judicial review,* as to what extent and character of regulation is 'necessary and proper.' " The Supreme Court could not substitute its judgment for that of Congress in determining the scope or appropriateness of legislation under the powers explicitly granted to the legislature in the Constitution. Congress should declare the review of these discretionary powers off-limits to the courts. Exercises of implied powers not specifically granted by the Constitution would remain subject to review. The legislature would thus emerge as the authoritative spokesman of the people's will.

Furthermore, to assure that judges would respect the preroga-

---

by Richberg, "The Function of the Supreme Court under the Constitution," Oct. 12, 1936, Franklin Roosevelt Papers, PPF 2418.

[24] For a picture of Richberg's informal lobbying on behalf of constitutional reform, see n. 23. On preparing the 1936 platform, see Richberg, "Memorandum for Judge Rosenman," May 23, 1949, with attached copy of Richberg to McIntyre, June 16, 1936, and "Memorandum for President—in re Constitutional Issues," Richberg Papers, L.C., Box 33; Richberg, *My Hero,* 203–205.

tives of the legislature, Richberg suggested redefining the federal judiciary's lifetime tenure "during good behavior." The Constitution protected the tenure of federal justices, but Richberg believed it was possible for Congress to define the meaning of good behavior so as "to penalize any refusal to perform, or any violation of, their official duties, as defined by Congress." If a judge violated the definition of appellate jurisdiction as established by Congress, he would be subject to removal. Surely the judges themselves could not define good behavior. Some outside authority must have the power to do so, and that authority was Congress.

Richberg also suggested that Congress delimit the jurisdiction of the lower courts to require that all constitutional issues be referred to the Supreme Court for immediate adjudication. He thereby hoped to avoid what he regarded as the all-too-common spectacle of conflicting opinions on the same question handed down by local courts around the country.[25]

Finally, Richberg also toyed with another way of curbing the Supreme Court. He thought it might be possible to permit Congress to reenact legislation declared unconstitutional by the Supreme Court once a general election had intervened. Presumably the disputed legislation would be an issue in the campaign, and therefore the newly elected representatives and senators would be able to give an accurate expression of the people's will. They could give the people's interpretation of the Constitution as applied to the law in question. If such an expression of the ultimate authority of the people could thus be given, it ought to be binding on the Supreme Court.

Richberg believed that most of his proposals could be implemented without resorting to a constitutional amendment. In fact, he considered an amendment inappropriate, for there was nothing basically wrong with the Constitution itself, but only with the meaning assigned to it by certain judges. The solution lay not in amend-

[25] Richberg to Roosevelt, Nov. 16, 1936, with attached memorandum, "The Constitutional Issue," Nov. 16, 1936, "Outline Draft of a Bill to Amend the Judicial Code," and "The Function of the Supreme Court under the Constitution," address by Richberg, Oct. 12, 1936, all in Franklin Roosevelt Papers, PPF 2418.

ing it to meet a temporary disagreement over its meaning, but in
providing a way for the final authority—the people and not the
Court—to offer its interpretation.[26]

Though Roosevelt maintained a keen interest in all proposals
for court reform, Richberg's suggestions did not come to fruition
in official policy. In late December 1936 he sent the president another idea which was less elaborate than his earlier suggestions.
He proposed that federal judges reaching the age of seventy years
should be retired from active service at the discretion of the president. The retired judge would remain an official member of his
court and continue to receive full compensation, but he would
serve in an inactive capacity and would not be counted in the number of judges fixed by law for making up a court. In the event of a
disqualification or some other indisposition of one of the active
members of the court, he could be recalled for temporary duty.
Richberg was convinced that such a proposal for introducing
younger blood into the federal court system was constitutional, for
the judge retained both his lifetime tenure and his regular compensation, as required by the Constitution. But Attorney General
Homer Cummings disagreed, and Roosevelt consequently shelved
the idea early in January 1937.[27]

Richberg heard no more from the White House about court
reform until later in January, when he was called in at the last
minute to help prepare the final documents in Roosevelt's court-
packing plan. By then, the main outlines of policy had been determined, and Richberg assisted only in the task of formulating them
in palatable language. Roosevelt had decided to seek authority to
reform the entire federal court system and to make an additional
appointment to the judiciary for every member over seventy years
of age who had served ten years or more and did not resign within
six months of his seventieth birthday. He would not be allowed to
add more than six justices to the Supreme Court in this manner.

[26] Richberg, "Should We Amend the Constitution?" 45–46, 50–53; Richberg, "The Constitution and the New Deal," 56–64.

[27] Richberg, "Memorandum of Judge Rosenman," May 23, 1949, with
copy of Richberg to Roosevelt, Dec. 28, 1936, and draft statutory amendment, Richberg Papers, L.C., Box 33; Richberg, My Hero, 220–21.

Along with Cummings, Solicitor General Stanley Reed, and Samuel Rosenman, one of Roosevelt's intimate advisers while governor of New York, Richberg worked on an outline of the program to be issued by the attorney general, the draft bill for implementing the plan, and the president's Message to Congress.[28]

Although Richberg was not in complete agreement with the chosen method of attacking the Supreme Court problem, he recognized that a policy decision had been determined and did not argue for a different approach. Richberg gave Roosevelt his loyalty throughout the Court fight. Only when the plan encountered intractable opposition and became bogged down in Congress did Richberg come forth with a different idea. In June, he proposed returning to his suggestion of December 1936 for active and inactive membership on federal courts. Since the Supreme Court had recently rendered a series of decisions favorable to the New Deal, the real battle had been won, and the Court had been forced to update its interpretation of the Constitution. Roosevelt thus could afford to compromise on his original plan. Richberg thought of his earlier idea as a way out of the president's dilemma, but Roosevelt was not receptive.[29]

With the breakdown of the court-packing plan in 1937 and Roosevelt's rejection of his proposals for reviving a program of business-government cooperation, Richberg moved away from the inner circle of the president's advisers. Occasionally, he consulted with Roosevelt on matters of public policy, as in 1939–1940 when he represented American oil companies contesting the expropriation of their properties in Mexico, and later when he suggested proposals for administrative reorganization to cope with the demands of wartime mobilization after Pearl Harbor in 1941.[30] But

[28] Richberg, *My Hero,* 221–22; Rosenman, *Working with Roosevelt* (New York, 1952), 144–58.

[29] Richberg, *My Hero,* 221–26; Robert E. Sherwood, *Roosevelt and Hopkins: An Intimate History* (New York, 1950), 89–90; Richberg, "Memorandum for Judge Rosenman," May 23, 1949, with copy of Richberg to Homer Cummings, June 24, 1937, and "Outline of a Bill," Richberg Papers, L.C., Box 33.

[30] On Mexico, see Richberg to LeHand, Jan. 30, 1940; Richberg to Edwin M. Watson, June 24, 1940, Richberg Papers, L.C., Box 2; Richberg, *My*

his influence at the White House rapidly diminished after 1938. Of course, this process had been going on since 1935, but was symbolized by Roosevelt's avowal of an antitrust program in 1938.

Although personally friendly, Roosevelt and Richberg drew farther and farther apart. For a while after the court fight in 1937, Richberg had hopes that the president might appoint him to a vacancy on the Supreme Court, and Roosevelt did give him serious consideration. But their growing estrangement on policy matters precluded this. And certainly Richberg's reputation as a "traitor" to organized labor would mean a knock-down fight in the Senate over his nomination, something the president would not wish to invite. Richberg himself had doubts about whether he really wanted such a position; it would mean a drastic cut in income once again and furthermore would require him to cut back his activities as a presidential adviser and informal spokesman for business-government cooperation. As on so many questions, Richberg's position was ambiguous. He wanted the honor of being offered appointment, yet he wanted to do other things as well. But the problem never arose.[31]

The result of Richberg's gradual alienation from the New Deal was that he had no place to turn except the private practice of law. Already well established in one of Washington's leading and most prosperous firms, after 1938 he devoted his energies more and more to representing business clients. Though he occasionally represented labor clients after his NRA days, these few links to the union movement were finally all severed by the early 1940s.[32] Richberg was no longer welcome in the liberal camp, so he turned to the conservative camp for support. And there he was destined to find it.

Hero, 248–68; E. David Cronon, *Joseph Daniels in Mexico* (Madison, Wis., 1960), 236–49. On wartime reorganization, see Richberg to Watson, Dec. 11, 1941, with attached "Memorandum for the President"; Roosevelt to Richberg, Dec. 12, 1941; Richberg to McIntyre, Jan. 9, 1942, Franklin Roosevelt Papers, OF 1961.

[31] Richberg to McIntyre, June 9, 1937, Richberg Papers, L.C., Box 33; McIntyre to Department of Justice, June 14, 1937, Franklin Roosevelt Papers, OF 1961; Clapper, diary entries for Aug. 14, 1937, and Jan. 9, 1938, Clapper Papers, Box 8; Richberg, *My Hero*, 226–27.

[32] Richberg, *My Hero*, 276.

CHAPTER X

Reaping the Whirlwind

Once he had lost his place among Franklin Roosevelt's close advisers, Donald Richberg divided his attention between the practice of law and propaganda work designed to influence the administration from the outside. In the latter regard, he was convinced that Roosevelt had to be brought back to the principles which had guided the early days of the New Deal. But Richberg's publicity work was symbolic of his decline in political stature. Unable to control power himself, or after 1938 even to have an intimate influence over those who did, he was forced to turn to the platform as the only available outlet for his ideas about public affairs. In terms of effectiveness, of course, this was the least viable way of influencing the administration, yet Richberg had no other choice. He would have preferred to remain among the president's confidants, but differences over policy gradually had forced him out. Nonetheless, Richberg's habit of giving advice had been cultivated for too long simply to be set aside, so he relied on propaganda as a means of perpetuating whatever influence he had left. He would not stand by silently and be ignored while the administration pursued what he regarded as wrongheaded policies.

At least Richberg was well on his way to attaining the kind of financial security which had eluded him during his days of government service. His position as a senior partner in one of Washington's leading law firms assured that. Over the next two decades, he served as counsel or director of such corporations as the United Light and Power System, American Natural Gas Company, Standard Oil of California, American Light and Traction Company, Continental Gas and Electric Corporation, A. P. Giannini's Transamerica Corporation, the Scripps-Howard Newspaper Alliance, and a number of railroad managements. From 1938 until 1941, he represented Standard Oil of California, Standard Oil of New Jersey, Sinclair, and Dutch Shell in their attempts to recover control of oil reserves which they had developed in Mexico but which had been expropriated by the government of President Lázaro Cárdenas. Though hardly involving the bulk of his energies, Richberg continued to engage in some labor litigation on behalf of the railway employee organizations (still the most conservative sector of the labor movement) until 1943, when he and his union clients belatedly decided that they could no longer work together.[1]

Not surprisingly, Richberg's work in corporation law had consequences for his thinking about industrial relations. It reinforced his previous commitment against government paternalism in any form. But given the direction which liberals in government were taking, it also meant that Richberg would never come to terms with the trend toward big government which was inherent in the growing demand for more and more social welfare legislation. President Harry Truman's proposed Fair Deal program exemplified the heavy reliance on government which Richberg abhorred. The result was that the ideological immobility which had become apparent in Richberg during the New Deal became even more sharply defined. In the context of the 1940s and 1950s, Richberg's ideas about labor relations were out of touch with contemporary trends, so that he appeared to be parroting the clichés of the most conservative elements in the business community. Yet Richberg believed that he was keeping faith with principles which had always

[1] Donald Richberg, *My Hero: The Indiscreet Memoirs of an Eventful but Unheroic Life* (New York, 1954), 228–29, 248–68, 276, 323–26; Richberg, *Labor Union Monopoly: A Clear and Present Danger* (Chicago, 1957), viii–ix; E. David Cronon, *Josephus Daniels in Mexico* (Madison, Wis., 1960), 236–49; Washington *Post*, Jan. 17, 1939; Richberg, "Certificate of Necessity" [Feb. 25, 1946], Donald Richberg Papers, Library of Congress, Box 57; Richberg, Address to Thirty-Fourth Convention, Brotherhood of Locomotive Firemen and Enginemen, Denver, Colo., July 23, 1941, Richberg Papers, L.C., Box 22.

offered the only hope for genuine stability in industrial relations.

In the 1920s, Richberg's objective had been to redefine industrial relations in terms of what he believed was the single most important reality of the modern economy: the interdependence of producers. Labor contributors and capital contributors had a mutual self-interest in the success of what was a common undertaking; neither could carry on without the other. From this basic premise Richberg evolved his particular approach to labor relations. Granted the complementary nature of labor and capital interests, industrial peace would come about provided each was able to protect those interests. The problem in the 1920s had been to make it possible for labor to uphold its role in the program by guaranteeing its right to organize into unions and by requiring businessmen to engage in collective bargaining with their workers. Business was adequately organized already, and in fact dominated the labor-capital relationship. The result was that the interests of investors were placed before those of employees, creating constant labor unrest. Until organized, the individual worker was ineffective in dealing on a basis of equality with his employer, so that unionization and collective bargaining became the prerequisites to industrial peace.

A vital feature of Richberg's scheme had been its emphasis on private bargaining and agreement by the parties themselves. His proposals for new labor legislation did not mean the domination of the federal government in industrial relations. Public control would have taken decision-making power away from those who contributed their own talent or wealth to the success of an enterprise and placed it in the hands of a political directorate, perhaps leading to a form of socialism. Such a solution to labor's problems, in Richberg's thinking, would destroy the very object which he was seeking on behalf of the railway employee organizations—namely, the right to have a say in their own destiny. The purpose of his legislative and court battles of the 1920s was simply to make labor's legal privileges equal to those of capital. This would make it possible—in the face of overwhelming employer dominance—for organized labor to look after its own interests. In other words, Richberg's purpose was to expand the rights of certain private organizations and not to turn to government paternalism as the answer. Although Richberg talked much of planning and control in the 1920s and 1930s, he meant planning and control by the private sector, not the public. Anything else would compromise the essential characteristics of the free enterprise system—something which neither he nor his clients wished to do.

By the 1940s and 1950s, Richberg's ideas coincided not with those of organized labor but more with those of the business community. To many union leaders, the federal government and the Democratic party seemed to provide surer protection than a balance of interests between capital and labor. Furthermore, the great labor strikes of the late 1930s and of the period of readjustment after World War II seemed to belie the feasibility of a voluntary system for preserving industrial peace without a powerful government policeman to contain labor strife and require settlements. Even Richberg came to believe that in strikes involving the public interest compulsory arbitration would be necessary, though he saw this as a last resort and retained his faith that genuine cooperative efforts would yield agreements. In addition, the whole depression and wartime experience had accustomed Americans to a vastly expanded role for government in the economy. The welfare state liberal preferred to rely on the federal government as the guarantor of the public good, and not on a delicate, self-sustaining balance of interests among labor, capital, and consumers. In fact, this shift in emphasis from private to public domination marked one of the differences between the old liberalism and the new. But Richberg remained wedded to what was essentially his original ideal, an ideal less and less identified with the liberal viewpoint in the postwar world.

It was precisely the emphasis of the new liberalism on government initiative and public control that alarmed Richberg most after the war. His vision of liberalism had never encompassed state socialism, but he feared that such a trend was emerging. The danger was clear in labor relations. In former times, Richberg believed, access to political power had been the special weapon of business; it invoked the government's duty to preserve law and order and to protect property as a way of breaking strikes and imposing settlements by force. But the labor union was no longer as helpless as it had been in the 1920s. Richberg felt that it had become involved in a conspiracy to use its loyalty to the Democratic party for obtaining special-interest legislation which would enable it to dominate the labor-capital relationship. Such was the apparent purpose of Senator Robert Wagner's National Labor Relations Act of 1935. Richberg believed that the Wagner Act granted labor an increase in rights without a corresponding increase in responsibilities and had denied employers equal protection under the law. It enumerated unfair employer practices, but did not define unfair employee practices. It failed to regulate the internal organization of unions, while endowing them with an exclusive right to represent all workers in plants where the closed shop was permitted. It prohibited employer-dominated unions, but did not explicitly prevent the use of coercion or intimidation by employee organizations against workers who refused to join a union. It did not require labor to bargain in good faith, while penalizing management for failing to do so.

In Richberg's view, collective bargaining had become "collective coercion" by organized labor. He insisted that the best way to preserve the greatest amount of liberty for all parties was through self-restraint and self-discipline, not intimidation or coercion, for this would obviate the need for the compulsory discipline of government. Such liberty could only be realized through a mutual balancing of interests, a balance that Richberg believed had been epitomized in the Railway Labor Act of 1926 with its reciprocal obligations for both labor and capital in the railroading industry. But beginning in the Roosevelt administration, it seemed that the unions—not management—insisted on upsetting this balance. Richberg felt that the true libertarian must therefore move against the pretensions of organized labor as he had once moved against those of big business.[2]

[2] Richberg to David B. Robertson and Bert M. Jewell, Feb. 25, 1949, Richberg Papers, L.C., Box 2; Richberg, Address to Thirty-Fourth Convention, B. of L.F. and E., July 23, 1941; Richberg Papers, L.C., Box 22; "Should We Adopt the Proposed New Federal Industrial Relations Act?" *American Forum of the Air* 7 (July 17, 1945); Richberg, "Where Is Organized Labor Going?" Address to Rotary Club, Washington, D. C., Feb. 27, 1946; Richberg, "Essentials of a Government Labor Policy," Address

Even before the 1930s were out, Richberg was proposing various plans for revising the Wagner Act. Besides voicing his criticisms in speeches and articles, Richberg formulated specific recommendations which he provided for the use of certain businessmen who were urging the secretary of commerce to support amendments to the law. Among the beneficiaries of Richberg's handiwork were Henry I. Harriman of the United States Chamber of Commerce, John D. Biggers of Libby-Owens-Ford Glass Company, and William L. Bett of SKF Industries.[3] By far his most concerted effort, however, came toward the end of the Second World War. Public agitation over the danger of labor strikes during the war and postwar periods and Richberg's own apprehension of what he soon would be calling "labor union monopoly" induced him to join in the movement that eventually led to the passage of the Taft-Hartley Act in 1947. Richberg was the principal author of plans for a comprehensive revision of the Wagner Act which were embodied in a new Federal Industrial Relations Act. Democratic Senator Carl A. Hatch of New Mexico and Republican Senators Harold H. Burton of Ohio and Joseph H. Ball of Minnesota introduced the measure into Congress on June 20, 1945.

The Ball-Burton-Hatch bill was the product of a self-appointed drafting committee formed in Philadelphia on February 4, 1944. The original impetus behind the project had come from a small group of lawyers, businessmen, and public officials who came together in late 1942 and early 1943 and who were motivated by a common concern for developing more precise legal procedures for the orderly settlement of labor disputes. Instrumental in bringing

---

to Thirteenth Annual Midwest Conference on Industrial Relations, University of Chicago, Oct. 18, 1946, all in Richberg Papers, L.C., Box 23; Richberg, "Significant Developments in Labor Law, 1941–1946," *George Washington Law Review* 14 (June 1946): 537–63; Richberg, *My Hero*, 320–21, 346–60; Richberg, *Labor Union Monopoly*.

[3] Richberg, *My Hero*, 299–300; Washington *News*, Oct. 29, 1938; Henry I. Harriman to John D. Biggers, April 25, 1939, with attached memorandum, "Suggested Amendments to the National Labor Relations Act of 1935"; Biggers to William L. Bett, May 19, 1939, Richberg Papers, L.C., Box 43.

coherence to these initial discussions was William Draper Lewis, director of the American Law Institute and Richberg's old comrade-in-arms from the days of the Progressive National Service of 1913–1914. The eventual outcome was the organization of a bipartisan voluntary group known as the Committee to Promote Industrial Peace.

By the time the Ball-Burton-Hatch bill was introduced in Congress, the membership of the committee included Richberg as chairman, Lewis, George W. Alger, Harold Evans, Samuel S. Fels, Lawrence Hunt, Leon C. Marshall, Charles B. Rugg, George B. Sjoselius, Kirk Smith, Arthur D. Whiteside, and Jerome J. Rothschild. Fels, the Philadelphia businessman and philanthropist, agreed to fund the expenses of the committee, which came to less than $5,000. The members served without compensation and decided from the beginning that no official representatives of employer or labor organizations would be allowed to join. The announced objective was to create a committee of disinterested and bipartisan citizens who would produce a comprehensive labor relations bill designed to protect the public welfare above all other interests. Of course, the background or current business and legal connections of most of the committee's members meant that they were hardly noncommittal about labor questions, but no members were admitted for the specific purpose of serving as spokesmen for capital or labor-interest groups. The committee proceeded by having Richberg prepare the initial drafts of legislation; then the rest of the members reviewed the proposals and suggested changes. Ultimately, the committee draft was presented for final revision to the three senators who eventually sponsored it in Congress. In the later stages of the work, the services of Frederic P. Lee, former legislative counsel of the United States Senate, were engaged to perfect the technical legal requirements of the draft bill.[4]

---

[4] Richberg, "The Proposed Federal Industrial Relations Act," *Political Science Quarterly* 61 (June 1946): 189–94; Committee to Promote Industrial Peace and Carl A. Hatch, Harold H. Burton, and Joseph H. Ball, *Federal Industrial Relations Act: Revised Draft*, June 1945, 3–5, copy in Richberg Papers, L.C., Box 44; Richberg, *My Hero*, 299; Richberg to Howard W. Smith, March 6, 1947, Richberg Papers, L.C., Box 43.

The resulting legislation clearly reflected Richberg's balance-of-interests concept of industrial relations. As in the Railway Labor Act of 1926, the bill imposed a legal duty on employers and employees alike to exert every reasonable effort to settle disputes by negotiation and agreement and to avoid changing existing conditions of work (such as by strikes or lockouts) while procedures for settlement were being carried out. A system of mediation and voluntary arbitration was set up, with provision for compulsory arbitration in disputes which, on the basis of a finding of fact by the Federal Labor Relations Board (to replace the National Labor Relations Board), threatened to cut off services essential to the public welfare. Awards under compulsory arbitration, however, normally would be in effect for one year and at most two years. The provisions of the Wagner Act relating to unfair labor practices were redefined and expanded to cover unfair practices by either management or labor, instead of by the former only. In instances where labor agreements provided that membership in a union would be required as a condition of employment, the Act subjected employee organizations to standards relating to the representativeness of their leadership, approval of agreements by vote of union members, and equal membership rights for all employees. The powers of the government to seek injunctive relief as a means of enforcing the bill were expanded. Specially appointed bipartisan adjustment boards and an Unfair Labor Practices Tribunal were provided for handling grievances over the enforcement of contracts or over the labor practices of either management or unions. Only controversies which threatened to affect interstate commerce were covered by the bill, and certain categories of workers were normally excluded altogether: state and federal employees, workers in establishments employing less than twenty persons, agricultural laborers, domestic servants, workers employed by labor organizations, and those covered by the Railway Labor Act.[5]

Richberg worked hard to arouse interest in the proposed legislation, debating and speaking at every opportunity. He hoped to capi-

[5] Richberg, "The Proposed Federal Industrial Relations Act," 194–204; Committee to Promote Industrial Peace and Hatch, Burton, Ball, *Federal Industrial Relations Act*, 6–71.

talize on the antilabor feeling that had led to the Smith-Connally War Labor Disputes Act of 1943. But in the absence of great labor conflicts in the spring and summer of 1945 and the domination of other political issues centering on the cessation of hostilities in Europe and Asia, the campaign for the Ball-Burton-Hatch bill slackened. Furthermore, Senator Burton resigned from Congress in September 1945 to accept an appointment to the Supreme Court, thus removing one of the principal sponsors of the particular measure which Richberg was promoting. The ultimate significance of the Ball-Burton-Hatch bill was to be symbolic, as it signified a trend toward more restrictive labor legislation which would culminate in the next two years. Many people in and out of Congress shared Richberg's fears, so that a movement for new labor legislation was likely to develop with or without the prodding of the Committee to Promote Industrial Peace. But it took several labor crises in steel, automobiles, coal, and railroading in the late 1945 and early 1946 to activate the latent congressional demand for action against the alleged power of labor unions. In January 1946 the House Rules Committee substituted a bill similar to the Ball-Burton-Hatch proposal, framed by Republican Representative Francis Case of South Dakota, for a more mild measure backed by the Truman administration. Along with many other people, Richberg had a minor role in helping to formulate the Case bill, and he lobbied at the White House in a futile effort to head off a presidential veto. Ultimately, the Taft-Hartley Act of 1947, passed by a Republican Congress over President Truman's veto, accomplished many of the goals Richberg had worked for, though personally he had no direct hand in the actual drafting of the bill, but only offered suggestions to interested congressmen.[6]

For Richberg, the Taft-Hartley Act was a step in the right direc-

[6] Richberg, *My Hero*, 299–301; Richberg to Harry S Truman, May 31, 1946, with "Memorandum Concerning Revised Case Bill," Richberg Papers, L.C., Box 33; Richberg to Smith, March 6, 1947; Smith to Richberg, March 12, 1947; Richberg to Smith, April 1, 1947; Smith to Richberg, April 3, 1947; Richberg to Walker Stone, April 23, 1947, Richberg Papers, L.C., Box 43; Gerald D. Reilly, "The Legislative History of the Taft-Hartley Act," *George Washington Law Review* 29 (Dec. 1960): 289–90.

tion, but he continued to agitate for further revision of the nation's labor laws. He volunteered specific recommendations to one of the Act's sponsors, Senator Robert A. Taft of Ohio, looking toward the refinement of both the substantive and administrative features of the law.[7] For the most part, however, Richberg worked through propaganda. In 1957, he published *Labor Union Monopoly,* one of his most successful polemics; it summarized his analysis of post-New Deal trends in industrial relations. Copies of this short treatise were distributed by Edward A. Rumely's Committee for Constitutional Government, and purchases were made by the National Association of Manufacturers and by many of the nation's foremost corporations (including, among many others, Daystrom Instrument, Dow Chemical, General Electric, B. F. Goodrich, Guaranty Trust of New York, Minneapolis-Honeywell, Socony Mobil, Standard Oil of California, Sun Oil, and Stewart Warner Corporation).[8] Besides producing a voluminous number of articles for publication and speaking on the banquet circuit as often as he was able, in 1948 Richberg defended Arizona's right-to-work law, forbidding the closed shop, in the United States Supreme Court, and won his case in a majority opinion written by Justice Hugo Black.[9]

On balance, however, Richberg devoted by far the greatest amount of his time to propaganda work rather than new legislation or legal advocacy insofar as his personal campaign for reforming labor relations was concerned. This became especially true as retirement age approached. The later years of life freed Richberg for what he described in his second autobiographical effort, *My Hero,* published in 1954, as a "personal crusade for liberty." In 1947, he and his wife moved to Charlottesville, Virginia. Richberg did not

[7] Richberg to Robert A. Taft, Feb. 3, 1949, with attached memorandum, "In re Revision of Taft-Hartley Act, January 14, 1949," Richberg Papers, L.C., Box 2.

[8] Richberg, *Labor Union Monopoly;* Edward A. Rumely to Richberg, Oct. 17, 1958, Richberg Papers, L.C., Box 4; Memorandum, "A few of the purchasers of . . . Labor Union Monopoly . . . ," Richberg Papers, L.C., Box 16.

[9] Richberg, *My Hero,* 331–32; *American Federation of Labor, Arizona State Federation of Labor, et al.,* v. *American Sash & Door Company, et al.,* 335 U. S. 538 (1949).

stop practicing law, but rather went into semiretirement. He maintained his partnership in Davies, Richberg, Beebe, Busick, and Richardson (which became Davies, Richberg, Tydings, Beebe, and Landa in 1951), and remained active as a director of the American Natural Gas Company. He continued to argue cases, including four successful suits before the Supreme Court. In 1947, he was elected to the Board of Trustees of American University in Washington, D. C. In 1953, he joined a Task Force of the Commission on Organization of the Executive Branch of the Government, under former President Herbert Hoover as chairman. He regularly served on a committee to direct the annual conferences of the University of Virginia's Institute of Public Affairs. And from 1949 to 1953, Richberg undertook an entirely new experience for him; he became a visiting lecturer in constitutional law at the University of Virginia Law School. His first seminar took as its theme "The theory and principles of local self-government as originally developed in the federal constitution and as affected by modern pressures for social legislation."[10]

During his years of residency in the South, Richberg's concern with states' rights and local government became nearly as compelling as his alarm over developments in organized labor. Of course, such a concern was a logical outgrowth of his longstanding fear of government paternalism in labor relations—whether on behalf of management or the unions. If private individuals and organizations should have as much control over their own affairs as was consistent with the public welfare, then the same was true of local as opposed to national government. This position induced Richberg to write and argue against federal civil rights bills proposed by both the Truman and Eisenhower administrations, and led him to the active defense of attempts in Virginia to circumvent the Supreme Court's 1954 school desegregation decision. Two years

[10] Richberg, *My Hero*, 317–45; Ben Moreell to Richberg, Nov. 6, 1953, Richberg Papers, L.C., Box 3; Commission on Organization of the Executive Branch of the Government, Herbert Hoover, Chairman, Citation, May 31, 1955, Richberg Papers, L.C., Box 51; Richberg to George Creel, May 12, 1952, George Creel Papers, Library of Congress, Box 4; [Richberg], "Outline of Projects" and "Outline of Seminar," Richberg Papers, L.C., Box 33.

after the Court's ruling, Richberg co-authored a bill "to prevent white and colored children from being compelled to attend mixed schools contrary to the wishes of such children and their parents." It was sponsored in the Virginia General Assembly by State Senator Edward O. McCue.[11]

Although Richberg doubted that all men were equal culturally and socially, and sometimes utilized outmoded anthropological theories in support of his contentions, the heart of his argument was more concerned with the nature of the federal union than with racial questions per se. For the most part, Richberg restricted himself to debating the rights of local versus central government in matters such as schooling which were essentially the responsibility of the individual community. He argued that the freedom of the individual person included the right to associate or not to associate with whomever he chose and that this personal right had a counterpart in the rights of local versus national government. Even in the case of publicly financed schools, the weight of the majority state and local opinion—as against national opinion—should have been controlling in Richberg's view.[12] Taking his position to its logical

[11] [Richberg], Draft of a Bill [1956]; Richberg, Memorandum, "A Legal Commentary on Senator McCue's Segregation Bill" [1956]; Richberg, "Memorandum for Senator McCue" [1956], Richberg Papers, L.C., Box 49; Roanoke, Va., Times, July 26, 1956; Richberg, "—Nor Can Government," American Affairs 10 (Jan. 1948): Supplement; Richberg to Richard B. Russell, July 16, 1957; Richberg, "Comment on Civil Rights Bill," July 16, 1957, Richberg Papers, L.C., Box 33.

[12] Richberg to Editor [John H. Colburn, Richmond Times-Dispatch], Sept. 7, 1951, Richberg Papers, L.C., Box 3; Richberg, "Aspects of the Race Problem," unidentified newspaper clipping, Aug. 8, 1958, Richberg Papers, L.C., Box 49; Richberg to E. J. Oglesby, July 16, 1956, printed letter, Richberg Papers, L.C., Box 4; Richberg, Letter to Editor, Richmond Times-Dispatch, Dec. 7, 1958. Although Richberg's arguments emphasized constitutional questions, his views on the relations of the races were explicit: "By aeons of achievement Caucasoids, and Mongoloids, have proved themselves superior to Negroids in all parts of the world. To maintain a superior culture a people must take pride in it and protect it from deterioration. It is a scientific fact that the breeding of a superior and an inferior degenerates the superior. Scientifically sound laws against miscegenation (as in Virginia) demonstrate one reason for requiring certain racial segregations, particularly

conclusion, he worked to prevent his old college fraternity, Phi Gamma Delta, from capitulating to outside pressure for lifting restrictions against the admission of Negroes.[13] In matters of racial segregation as well as in labor relations, Richberg's argument turned on the threat of federal interference, and the implications that government dictation from the center would have for individual liberty.

The threat of "creeping socialism" and federal paternalism seemed all the more ominous to Richberg as time went on. He believed that the trend had been obscured by the candidacies of many Republican officeseekers, who seemed to capitulate to the allegedly socializing programs of the Democrats, so that Americans could not really perceive what was happening to them. Eventually, Richberg concluded that the tide could be stemmed only by a drastic reorganization of the country's political party system. The objective of such a shakeup would be to place the supporters of states' rights in one party and the proponents of the welfare state in another. Once the implications of what the socializers and the conservatives represented were clearly separated and identified, Americans could make their choice. The obscurantism created by some Republican party platforms would be ended, and with it would end the threat that the socializing forces in America would win by default. As the 1952 presidential election approached, Richberg felt that the time had come for the antisocialists to make their stand.[14]

Such was the purpose of the Committee to Explore Political Realignment, which was founded by about a hundred like-minded citizens, including Richberg, in September 1951. The new committee was the brainchild of Republican Senator Karl Mundt of South Dakota, a longtime proponent of party realignment. The Mundt program contemplated converting the informal alliance of

---

segregation in schools for impressionable children." Richberg to Editor [Colburn], Sept. 7, 1951, Richberg Papers, L.C., Box 3.

[13] Richberg to Edward H. DeHart, Jan. 11, 1950; Richberg to Cecil J. Wilkinson, March 1, 1950; [Richberg], "Notes on Committee Report" [1950 Ekklesia of Phi Gamma Delta], Richberg Papers, L.C., Box 55.

[14] Chicago *Tribune*, Feb. 25, 1949; Richberg to A. Willis Robertson, Sept. 18, 1951, Richberg Papers, L.C., Box 3; Richberg, *My Hero*, 320–23.

conservative Republicans and Southern Democrats that had operated in Congress against New Deal–Fair Deal legislation since 1937 into a majority force among the nation's voters. Mundt hoped that the work of the committee might stem "the encroachment of socialism and the all-inclusive centralized super-state" through a restructuring of the party system which would give voters a clear choice of political alternatives. Richberg joined the executive committee of the new organization, along with former Republican Senator from New Jersey Albert W. Hawkes, former American Farm Bureau Federation president Edward A. O'Neal, former Democratic senator from Nebraska Edward R. Burke, former Carleton College president Donald J. Cowling, former Democratic governor of New Jersey and secretary of the navy Charles Edison, former Republican governor of Maine Horace A. Hildreth, and commentator Felix Morley. The only purpose of the group was to investigate the possibility of realigning conservatives and liberals strictly into two separate parties with no intermingling. From the beginning, the formation of a third party was ruled out; the most optimistic hope of the committee was that the Republicans might someday—perhaps in 1956—become the vehicle of the country's antisocialist forces. In fact, the executive committee resolved to discontinue its operations once the work of investigation had been completed; Mundt expected the committee would remain active from three to six months.

As anticipated, the Mundt group finished its work by the end of the year, and the executive committee voted to dissolve effective December 31, 1951. In a final report made public in mid-December, the committee announced its conclusion that further organizing action would be inappropriate for the time being. It had decided that a genuine restructuring of the party system would have to "spring from the grass roots and cannot properly or effectively be imposed from the top." Operating on this premise, the committee concluded that "the case for political realignment should therefore be explored, emphasized and expedited primarily by local leadership." It was hoped that public opinion would rally to the Mundt program after the 1952 presidential nominating conventions had taken place, for at that time, the committee reasoned, the need for party realignment would become more apparent than ever.[15]

The Committee to Explore Political Realignment made little if any impact on politics in 1952. Such an outcome was symbolic of the political impotence to which Richberg and other old liberals like him had arrived by the 1950s. Except for this exercise in futility, he had no significant part in the presidential election, though he served on two campaign committees—the Virginia Democrats for Eisenhower and the Citizens for Eisenhower-Nixon. But such had been Richberg's situation in presidential campaigns ever since 1940; at most he could claim the role of the elder—but definitely inactive—statesman. In 1952 he carried on a heavy correspondence with friends of similar persuasion who were likewise on the sidelines, such as George Creel and Felix Morley. That year his preference for a Democratic presidential nominee was Senator Richard Russell of Georgia. But because he thought it unlikely that the Democrats would turn away from what he regarded as a social welfare candidate, Richberg pinned his hopes on the Republican party instead. Although he initially favored Taft, he ultimately supported Eisenhower as an acceptable compromise with his ideal.[16]

Once he had drifted away from the New Deal, Richberg was simply no longer a factor in the political equation. His later years were spent primarily in writing and broadcasting propaganda. Most of his efforts were directed to audiences who were already con-

[15] New York *Times*, Sept. 18, 1951; Washington *Daily News*, Sept. 18, 1951; Karl E. Mundt to Richberg, Sept. 21, 1951, Richberg Papers, L.C., Box 3; "Outline of *The Case for Political Realignment*," n.d.; Memorandum by Edward R. Burke, Donald J. Cowling, Charles Edison, Albert W. Hawkes, Horace A. Hildreth, Felix Morley, Edward A. O'Neal, and Richberg, Nov. 1951; Executive Committee, Committee to Explore Political Realignment, Agenda and Minutes, Sept. 22, Oct. 1, Oct. 26, Nov. 30, 1951; Committee to Explore Political Realignment, *Summary of Findings and Conclusions*, Dec. 10, 1951, all in Richberg Papers, L.C., Box 42.

[16] Walter Williams to Richberg, Oct. 31, 1952; E. J. Oglesby to Richberg, Nov. 7, 1952; Felix Morley to Creel, April 4, 1952; Morley to Creel, April 14, 1952; Creel to Richberg, April 19, 1952; Richberg to Taft, Oct. 12, 1951; Richberg Papers, L.C., Box 3; Richberg to Creel, March 1, 1952; Richberg to Creel, April 5, 1952; Richberg to Creel, May 12, 1952; Richberg to Creel, Sept. 10, 1952, Creel Papers, Box 4.

vinced of what he was saying, so that even as a publicist his impact was of doubtful consequence. Typical of his efforts was an interpretive study of the American past entitled *Only the Brave Are Free*. Co-authored with Albert Britt, an old friend and past president of Knox College in Galesburg, Illinois, and professor of history at Scripps College in Claremont, California, it emphasized the incompatibility of the welfare state and individual liberty. After the manuscript was rejected by Rinehart; Simon and Schuster; McGraw Hill; Knopf; Henry Holt; Longmans Green; Houghton Mifflin; and Harper, it was finally published by Caxton Printers of Caldwell, Idaho.[17]

Local activities occupied much of Richberg's time. In 1954 the Freedoms Foundation at Valley Forge awarded him the George Washington Honor Medal for one of his articles, "The Rights and Wrongs of Labor," and in 1955 the Daughters of the American Revolution presented him with an Award of Merit. For a time in 1955, Richberg wrote a series of guest editorials for the Richmond *News Leader*, edited by James J. Kilpatrick. And in 1957 he was elected an honorary life member of the Charlottesville-Albemarle Defenders of State Sovereignty and Individual Liberties, a group organized following the Supreme Court's 1954 desegregation ruling. Though occasionally plagued by heart trouble, Richberg remained active to the very end of his life. He died November 27, 1960.[18]

Although Richberg had identified wholeheartedly with the Progressives in the early part of the century, his later apparently conservative political position turned out to be not entirely inconsistent. It simply revealed the tremendous metamorphosis that

[17] Richberg and Albert Britt, *Only the Brave Are Free: A Condensed Review of the Growth of Self-Government in America* (Caldwell, Idaho, 1958); [Britt] to Jean Parker Waterbury, Oct. 15, 1954, Richberg Papers, L.C., Box 3.

[18] Freedoms Foundation of Valley Forge, Certificate of Award, Feb. 22, 1954, Richberg Papers, L.C., Box 51; Charlottesville, Va., *Daily Progress*, Nov. 4, 1955; James J. Kilpatrick to Richberg, June 24, 1955; Richberg to Kilpatrick, June 29, 1955; Kilpatrick to Richberg, June 30, 1955; Kilpatrick to Richberg, Jan. 2, 1956, Richberg Papers, L.C., Box 4; Charlottesville *Daily Progress*, Sept. 7, 1957.

liberalism had undergone through the twentieth century. As a Progressive in 1912, Richberg could hardly have foreseen and identified with the welfare state ideals of the middle of the twentieth century. He could not anticipate what such ideals would mean in terms of the growth of government power over the individual person. His liberalism had more in common with the nineteenth century than with the welfare state. Even as a labor lawyer in the 1920s, when his reputation as a liberal was strongest, he saw himself as fighting for the right of labor to do things for itself—freeing it from the coercion of management, which had denied the worker his right of association and liberty of contract. Richberg was battling for ancient constitutional rights, and usually sought support for his efforts by arguing that his proposals were not a departure from past legal principles, but only a new codification of them. In the National Recovery Administration, Richberg once again conceived his task as that of assisting in a process of self-government, not federal regulation. The main thrust of the experiment lay in the private rather than the public sector. Believing that the long-term solution to the depression would have to come from private business, rather than government spending and welfare programs, he remained an advocate of the business-government commonwealth of cooperation for the rest of his life.

Until the advent of the New Deal, Richberg's idea of liberalism seemed to coincide with that of many progressives and labor leaders. But once the Roosevelt administration, impelled by the necessities of the depression, gave the country a fleeting glimpse of the welfare state, liberalism came more and more to be identified with big government and federal programs. Welfare seemed to be replacing the old ideals of competition and individual achievement. Such a development contradicted what Richberg believed had been the real goals of his progressive and New Deal career. Intead of liberating people from the impediments that prevented them from controlling their own destiny, the government was taking over the very thing that made a man free, i.e., his ability to run his own life without being dependent on others.

Throughout, the personal factor affected Richberg's career. Like most men, he needed personal recognition and wanted to feel that what he did was consistent with the public interest. The roots of his reform career could be traced to his self-conscious and sometimes compulsive desire to devote his energies to public rather than private service. Such was the underlying rationale for his work as a Progressive, as a labor lawyer, as a New Dealer, and as a propagandist against "labor union monopoly." But his need for personal recognition also meant that the approval—and hence influence—of his associates counted for much. Perhaps Richberg's happiest days were as a Progressive and labor lawyer, when he enjoyed the confidence of his liberal and labor friends. Untroubled by conflicting loyalties, as was to have been the situation during the New Deal, Richberg could envision a happy coincidence between his work and the public welfare. The problem of dissonance between his views and those of the younger generation of liberals was not so easily resolved at a later time, but the need to do so was as apparent in Richberg as ever.

It was the New Deal experience that made Richberg's position as an old-fashioned liberal very clear. As such it marked the turning point in his relations with organized labor. And after the demise of the National Recovery Administration, his ideological immobility made him persist in advocating programs that President Roosevelt no longer found desirable or politically acceptable. As his identification with business grew more pronounced, Richberg became more of a liability to the administration, so that by 1938, when the president decided on a trustbusting campaign, Richberg found himself outside the sphere of Roosevelt's intimate advisers. Deserted by those who possessed real political power, and supported principally by the business community, Richberg became more theoretical and less effective in his political activities. Unable to exercise power directly, he turned to sermonizing in the hope of influencing government indirectly. But this was the mark of political impotence, not political power. It meant the effective end of Donald Richberg's influence on public policy.

Bibliographical Note

What follows is by no means an exhaustive review of all the source materials of value to this study. The footnotes for each chapter indicate the items of direct relevance to particular passages. A number of secondary works contain references to Donald Richberg, but very few provide more than a fleeting glimpse of the man and his work. Consequently, heaviest reliance has been placed upon several collections of manuscripts located in the Library of Congress and the National Archives in Washington, D. C.; the Franklin D. Roosevelt Library in Hyde Park, N. Y.; the University of Chicago Library and the Chicago Historical Society; the State Historical Society of Wisconsin in Madison; the Federal Records Center in Suitland, Md.; the Oral History Research Office of Columbia University in New York City; and the Social Welfare History Archives of the University of Minnesota in Minneapolis.

The following were the manuscript collections most valuable to the completion of this study: Donald Richberg Papers, Harold Ickes Papers, Felix Frankfurter Papers, George Norris Papers, and Raymond Clapper Papers, all at the Library of Congress; Donald Richberg Papers, Chicago Historical Society; Franklin D. Roosevelt Papers, Franklin D. Roosevelt Library; National Recovery Administration Papers, Record Group 9, National Archives; Raymond Robins Papers and Charles McCarthy Papers, State Historical Society of Wisconsin; Charles E. Merriam Papers, University of Chicago; and Papers of the Office of Government Reports, Record Group 44, Federal Records Center, Suitland.

A number of other collections proved useful in addition to the above: Theodore Roosevelt Papers, George Creel Papers, Joseph E. Davies Papers, Charles Evans Hughes Papers, Progressive National Committee (1936) Papers, American Federation of Labor Papers (Samuel Gompers and William Green Letterbooks), all at the Library of Congress; American Federation of Labor Papers and Donald Richberg Papers (speech and article material), State Historical Society of Wisconsin; Samuel I. Rosenman Papers, Frances Perkins Papers, Leon Henderson Papers, Lowell Mellett Papers, Harry Hopkins Papers, Louis McHenry Howe Papers, and the Diaries of Henry Morgenthau, Jr., all at the Franklin D. Roosevelt Library; Julius Rosenwald Papers and University of Chicago President's Papers (1889–1925), University of Chicago Library; Survey Associates Papers, Social Welfare History Archives of the University of Minnesota.

The Oral History Research Office at Columbia University had twenty-eight oral history memoirs that contained references to Donald Richberg. Several of these proved to be of little value, but others yielded significant information. Especially important were the reminiscences of Thomas I. Emerson, Rexford Tugwell, Boris Shishkin, Charles Fahy, John P. Frey, William W. Cumberland, William H. Davis, Gardner Jackson, Lindsay Rogers, Chester T. Lane, and James M. Landis.

Unfortunately, the National Recovery Administration Papers contain very little material by or about General Hugh Johnson, the first administrator. His files were apparently removed when he retired from the NRA in the fall of 1934. A considerable part of these materials have since been lost, although a historian is currently at work on a biography of Johnson and has had access to the remainder. The papers were not available to me. The Papers of Raymond Moley will soon be ready for research at the Hoover Institution on War, Revolution, and Peace in Stanford, California, but were not accessible at the time of writing. Mr. Moley, however, granted me an interview, as did Richberg's widow, Mrs. John H. Small III of Charlottesville, Virginia, and his former associate, John S. Lord of Chicago. David E. Lilienthal and Samuel I. Rosenman corresponded with me concerning certain aspects of Richberg's career. In addition, Mrs. Small loaned me several hundred manuscript items, and permitted most of this material, except certain documents relating to the Richberg family and ancestry, to be added to the Richberg Papers at the Library of Congress. Mr. Lord, head of the Chicago law firm of Lord, Bissell, and Brook, also opened to me his office files of correspondence with Richberg.

The most useful printed primary and secondary works and periodical materials have been indicated in the footnotes. The Richberg Papers in the Library of Congress contain virtually a complete file of all Richberg's speeches and writings, published and unpublished. In addition, the clippings files of the National Recovery Administration Papers provided voluminous newspaper material for the 1930s. The New York *Times*, Chicago *Tribune*, and *Literary Digest* were systematically reviewed also. Published diaries, autobiographies, and government documents abound for the New Deal years, but exist in much less generous quantities for the other phases of Richberg's career.

Few secondary works give more than passing mention to Donald Richberg. Authors usually introduce him at the particular point where he has a bearing on the subject under examination, and then promptly lead him offstage. Arthur M. Schlesinger, Jr., in *The Age of Roosevelt*, Vol. 1: *The Crisis of the Old Order, 1919–1933*, Vol. 2: *The Coming of the New Deal*, Vol. 3: *The Politics of Upheaval, 1935–1936* (Boston, 1957–1960), provides the best glimpse of Richberg in a comprehensive history, and takes measure of his personal foibles as well as his achievements and intellectual life. Another study is Christopher Lasch, "Donald Richberg and the Idea of a National Interest" (M.A. thesis [Columbia University, 1955]). Perhaps the most valuable of numerous secondary accounts for this study have been the following: Irving Bernstein, *The Lean Years: A History of the American Worker, 1920–1933* (Boston, 1960), and *The New Deal Collective Bargaining Policy* (Berkeley, Calif., 1950); Robert H. Zieger, *Republicans and Labor, 1919–1929* (Lexington, Ky., 1969); Sidney Fine, *The Automobile under the Blue Eagle: Labor, Management, and the Automobile Manufacturing Code* (Ann Arbor, Mich., 1963); Otis L. Graham, Jr., *An Encore for Reform: The Old Progressives and the New*

Deal (New York, 1967); Ellis Wayne Hawley, *The New Deal and the Problem of Monopoly: A Study in Economic Ambivalence* (Princeton, N. J., 1966); and J. Joseph Huthmacher, *Senator Robert F. Wagner and the Rise of Urban Liberalism* (New York, 1968). There are, of course, literally hundreds of other secondary accounts of relevance to this subject, but in the final analysis, the story of Donald Richberg emerges most clearly from manuscript collections, government documents, periodical literature, and newspapers.

Index

Design by James Wageman

*This book has been set in Rudolf Ruzicka's
Fairfield with Eric Gill's Perpetua
used for display.*

*Composed, printed & bound
by Kingsport Press*